GLOBAL SYMPOSIUM

&

Gretchen Carlson

#BeFierce

BE
FIERCE

BE
FIERCE

STOP HARASSMENT AND
TAKE YOUR POWER BACK

GRETCHEN CARLSON

CENTER
STREET®

NEW YORK   NASHVILLE

Center Street
Hachette Book Group
1290 Avenue of the Americas, New York, NY 10104
centerstreet.com
twitter.com/centerstreet

First Edition: September 2017

Center Street is a division of Hachette Book Group, Inc. The Center Street name and logo are trademarks of Hachette Book Group, Inc.

The publisher is not responsible for websites (or their content) that are not owned by the publisher.

The Hachette Speakers Bureau provides a wide range of authors for speaking events. To find out more, go to www.HachetteSpeakersBureau.com or call (866) 376-6591.

Print book interior design by Timothy Shaner, NightandDayDesign.biz

ISBNs: 978-1-4789-9217-2 (hardcover), 978-1-4789-9215-8 (ebook)

Printed in the United States of America

LSC-C

10 9 8 7 6 5 4 3 2 1

To my children, Kaia and Christian,

and to the thousands of women

whose voices have never been heard.

AUTHOR'S NOTE

This book contains information obtained from many women—some very well known, others just private citizens trying to live their lives and do their jobs. Many women contacted me to share their stories, and I interviewed countless women concerning their experiences in the workplace. I have included information obtained from many of these conversations. To preserve the privacy and anonymity of the persons involved, I have often changed the names and certain other information (such as occupations, job titles, or the locations where the alleged harassment occurred) that could be used to identify specific individuals.

As is often the case when relating events of the past, the information recounted herein is based largely on the recollections of the interviewees. The recounting of these stories, often in the women's own words, serves to show just how pervasive sexual harassment has been (and continues to be), and to underscore the enormous toll it is taking on American businesses and workers.

This book is intended to provide general information and inspiration to its readers. Neither the author nor the publisher is rendering legal or other professional advice. If you believe that your rights have been or are being violated, you should consult with an employment attorney, because laws vary depending on where you live or work.

CONTENTS

Introduction:
Are You Done Taking Sh*t? 1

1: Speaking the Unspeakable 13

2: You Can't Break a Badass 37

3: Don't Rob My Dream! 55

4: You Have the Right 77

5: "Asking for It" 105

6: Forced into Silence 123

7: Men Who Defend 133

8: Enough Already! 155

9: Our Children Are Watching 173

10: Be Fierce 193

Join Me 207

Selected Resources 209

Reading List 215

Notes 217

Acknowledgments 230

BE
FIERCE

Are You Done Taking Sh*t?

Go back to Minnesota & Shut the Hell Up!!

Gretchen needs to let it go. She brought it on herself!

So what if someone said a couple things to you?
Grow up, move on and stop whining.

Gretchen, your show sucked! You are a dumb old never-has-been!

Hope nobody hires you, Skank!

Gold digger MILF!

I wouldn't stand with you or next to a disgraceful person like you!!
I hope people will walk away & let you suffer, Bitch!!

Welcome to my daily Twitter feed. Imagine having to swallow this kind of hate with your morning coffee! After many years on TV, I wasn't a stranger to mean tweets. I used to laugh at them, even read them out loud on the air. But now the meanness was like being stabbed with a dagger, and it seemed to have no purpose except to hurt me. It didn't surprise me that one of these peoples' favorite weapons was to attack my age or looks: "Minimally talented, over the hill," crowed one critic. "Old and washed up," another. Many tweets were typical of what other women who've experienced harassment say they hear all the time: "You're too ugly to be sexually harassed . . . you *wish* you looked that good!" "Desperate old cow."

Hmm . . . so only hot young babes get sexually harassed? Only fame-seeking, money-grubbing old hags complain? In the convoluted logic of the Twitterverse, my experience couldn't be valid because I wasn't young enough or pretty enough. And even if I were, my experience couldn't be valid because I opened my mouth and spoke up for myself, making me a bitch. I resisted the impulse to reply to the male tweeters: "Does your mother, wife, or sister know you're talking trash to a woman on social media?" I didn't know *what* I would say to the female tweeters—there were plenty of those too.

One morning, as I was hunched over my iPad scrolling through a fresh batch of vitriol, I glanced up and saw my thirteen-year-old daughter, Kaia, watching me.

"Mom, you have a funny look on your face," she said. "What are you reading?"

"It's nothing, honey." I smiled, but Kaia's radar was finely attuned to my moods. She was, unfortunately, very aware of what was going on in her mom's life. She knew that it *wasn't* nothing.

Our children really see us. They hear us. And when I took on this fight, I had my children and their future foremost in my mind.

Many people have heard about the sexual harassment case I filed against my former boss. That lawsuit was settled, and there are things I can't discuss about it. That's the nature of a settlement. But when it was all over, I decided I wasn't ready to shut up and sit down.

Labor Day 2016 became a marker in my life—not just the first day of school for my kids, but a change in the way I'd done things for the last twenty-five years.

Every year on the day after Labor Day, my husband, Casey, and I have made sure that one or both of us drives the kids to school and drops them off. (They're now at ages where they don't want us to come in!) This tradition has also involved Casey and me then driving into the city together to go to work. But 2016 was, of course, different for me. As we made our way into the city, I was actually going in to get a haircut. For the first time in a long time, I wasn't going to work to report the news.

Instead—on this day—I *was* the news.

We got into the city an hour before my appointment, so Casey dropped me off and went on his way. With an hour to kill, I walked into a nearby nail salon to get a pedicure. There I was, all by myself in the salon.

During that hour, the news about me started trickling out; first one report, and then dozens and dozens more. I began to read about myself on Twitter and Facebook and Instagram as if I were having an out-of-body experience. I sat there with tears streaming down my face. The nice lady helping me out was probably wondering what the heck was wrong with me. But she didn't ask, and I didn't tell.

My life had become surreal. But then—as if nothing was happening—I still needed to get my hair cut. Once in the salon, the young woman sitting next to me at the hair washing basin—a total stranger—looked at me and simply said two words, "Thank you." I felt more tears welling up again. My eyes burned. It wasn't like I was sad. I'm not sure I can even describe the emotion. I just knew my life would never be the same. At that moment I knew the issue of sexual harassment was bigger than just my story. So I decided I would write a new, powerful, *real* story, for me and for so many others.

My decision to take on the issue of harassment didn't happen instantly. It took me a while to get my head straight. At first, encounters with friends and colleagues were painful and awkward. People didn't know what to say to me. I didn't hear from some people I'd expected to hear from. On the other hand, I received supportive letters and emails from people I hadn't heard from in decades.

Those were difficult days as I tried to regain a sense of equilibrium and purpose. I have always been a forward-looking person. When I was a child, participating in violin competitions, my beloved grandfather always told me that I needed failure in order to really appreciate success. He wanted me to see that the best of life wasn't found only in winning, but also in picking yourself back up and thriving after times of disappointment. So, when my job at Fox ended, I immediately began thinking about what I could do next.

I didn't have to wait long for an answer. Something amazing started to happen: the floodgates opened. Thousands of emails, texts, calls, and social media comments poured in, as women shared their stories, their pain, and their hopes. The messages were intimate, the stories heartbreaking. Time and again, women wrote about how they had been holding it all in, but now felt they could talk to me.

Late into the night, I sat at my computer and immersed myself in the lives of women I had never met, but now felt I knew more intimately than my neighbors. Some of my own misconceptions were shattered. It's easy to assume that sexual harassment flourishes in certain industries. There is the "Mad Men" culture of advertising. There is the sometimes female-unfriendly culture of sports. There are industries, such as fashion, modeling, and beauty pageants, where some degree of objectification is commonplace.

But my mailbox showed a more pervasive reality. These women belonged to virtually every profession and walk of life: police officers, teachers, oil rig operators, musicians, Wall Street bankers, saleswomen, sports executives, army officers, journalists, accountants, engineers, waitresses, TV broadcasters, soldiers, tech workers, lawyers, secretaries, and corporate executives.

The truth is much more startling and complex than I had realized. You can be sexually harassed if you're pretty or not pretty, if you're strong or not strong, if you're in advertising or trucking, or are a college student. This book isn't just about women in the workplace being harassed and standing up to power. It's about our teenagers too, who go off to college full of hopes and dreams and far too often have them stripped away in one unexpected act of harassment or violence. It's so important to set the right mind-set early on in our young girls (and boys), to prepare them and let them know they have a voice, and, most important, to teach them how to use it. From young to middle age, girls to boys, women to men—we all need to learn how to be fierce.

Remember this: Harassment isn't something you ask for. You don't have to smile or "bring it on." You don't have to say a word. You can be dressed in a short skirt or army fatigues or hospital scrubs. And in spite of the lingering doubt and guilt that most women feel, it's not about something *you* did. It's about what somebody else did to you.

Years and even decades after the fact, many of the women who reached out to me were still shell-shocked and disbelieving. Such as Carmen, a flight attendant supervisor whose boss often sat in meetings detailing the porn he'd watched the night before while drawing penises on his notepad. When Carmen finally got up the nerve to complain to human resources, she was called "crazy" and fired. In spite of her sterling record, she was never able to find work in the industry again. No one stood up for her. "It was like whiplash," she said. "One minute I was happily employed in a career I loved. The next minute, I was out."

Silence is the most powerful weapon of the harasser. When women are not allowed or enabled to give voice to their experiences, they disappear. "When I was fired, I stopped existing," one woman told me. "Life went on at my company as if I'd never been there."

I heard variations of this story many times, and I've seen how haunted these women are, how often they play back the events in their minds and wonder if they did something wrong or could have acted differently. Even a young enlisted woman soldier who was raped in her trailer by two men who broke in at night remembers her only thought being, "Am I going to get in trouble?"

Their experiences are shocking—they're worse than anything you can imagine. But the words also resonate. Like the mean tweets on my phone every day, they have the power to wound, destroy, and silence women. Whoever said, "words can never hurt you" didn't hear *these* words: the broker whose coworkers called her such vulgar names I can't print them here; the popular executive who became an "agitator" when she reported a colleague to Human Resources; the woman whose harasser defended himself by saying, "You think I'd hit *that*?"; the young girl whose nickname was "Bat Shit"—for "bat shit crazy."

Ugly stuff.

Repeatedly in my conversations with women, they used the term "old boys' club" to describe their work environments. It's a notion

I thought was retired long ago. But no: There's the old boys' club in banking, the old boys' club in movie production, the old boys' club in retail, the old boys' club in hospital administration. It exists in Congress, in the military, in scientific research, in the restaurant industry, and in law enforcement—the references are across the board. I started to wait for it when I conducted interviews—the moment when the term "old boys' club" would show up. It happened almost every time.

We all know that it's a "man's world" in certain work environments, but the culture exists even in industries that are traditionally geared to women and families, such as retail, nursing, and food services. A 2016 study published in the *Harvard Business Review* noted the insidious nature of a male-dominated work culture, saying, "Some men use the subjugation of women as a way to relate to other men and prove their masculinity, while reinforcing women's lower status. At the same time, women who want to be part of the high-status group may play along with sexual harassment because they do not want to be further alienated from the high-status group (men). Women may even start to adopt the same behaviors as men to fit in and be 'one of the guys.' This creates an irony that women may be ignoring or downplaying sexual harassment to gain access to the 'boys' club' while men are using sexual harassment to keep women out."

This analysis reveals the circular trap in which women often find themselves when they try to thrive in male-dominated environments. Changing the culture of harassment is not a simple choice between being strong and being weak, or getting along versus standing up for yourself. Time and again, I have been blown away by the courage many women express in demanding to be heard and fighting for respect in their workplaces. Against unbelievable odds—shame, retaliation, even lost jobs and careers—women are refusing to take it anymore. They are on the front lines of a long war, and there's no way to sugarcoat it.

As any lawyer or adviser who deals with these issues will tell you, the personal and professional cost is often very high. I've heard stories about women being fired for complaining, being pushed out when they rejected their boss's advances, and being sidelined for not playing along with coarse and inappropriate behaviors. And most of them have had to walk away from their careers. The attorney Lisa Bloom, who has represented women for over thirty years, put it to me bluntly: "Of all the women I know who have publicly complained, not one is working in her chosen career today." Think about it: that is a terrifying reality. "Unfortunately, there's a stigma to complaining," Bloom said. "These women are labeled as troublemakers. It sticks."

After my experience with harassment, as the weeks went on, I learned that every woman has a story. At least, I never met one who didn't. My own story, which was widely covered in the media, opened up a conversation in homes and workplaces across America. People came up to me in restaurants and airport lounges, plopped right down and started talking. My own friends and colleagues told me things they'd never revealed before. Some opened up to their husbands for the first time about past experiences.

A friend who had been married for twenty years described walking the dogs with her husband one evening, and blurting out the story of how she'd been grabbed and almost raped by a boss early in her career. Her husband was stunned. "Why did you never tell me about this before?" he asked. "I had no idea." She told him that she'd considered it a blot on her character, and didn't want him to know about it.

Another friend confessed that she had "forgotten" or blocked out an experience that had happened decades earlier, when she was just starting her career in sales. Her manager had backed her up against a wall in a conference room one day and kissed her. She'd pushed him off and walked away. She never even considered reporting it. "I thought it went with the territory," she said. In fact, she was proud of herself for handling the incident so coolly and unemotionally.

After I left Fox, I was interviewed by ABC's Amy Robach for a one-hour *20/20* special. Accustomed to being the one asking the questions, I turned the tables and asked Amy if *she* had ever experienced sexual harassment. She was visibly jarred; the emotion of a memory flashed across her face. "Yes, I have," she admitted. The look she gave me suggested that she had never talked about it before. Hers and other women's stories are now demanding to be told.

Statistics support anecdotal evidence about the low rate of reporting, even today. According to the US Equal Employment Opportunity Commission (EEOC), 70 percent of women who experience sexual harassment at their jobs don't report it for fear it will cause negative repercussions, both personally and professionally. The most recent data from the Bureau of Justice Statistics estimated that there are more than 43,000 workplace rapes and sexual assaults a year. But women's advocates say that this number vastly underreports such crimes, because many victims are afraid to speak up or are discouraged from coming forward.

You cannot experience sexual harassment without suffering psychological wounds. This isn't just my opinion. I know, because I too have experienced and suffered from it. Multiple research studies have shown serious effects that include depression, PTSD, sleep disorders, and in the worst cases, suicide attempts. The hardest hit are young women, whose confidence and self-esteem are especially fragile. One study showed that for a teenage girl, a single incident of sexual harassment could have repercussions well into her thirties.

It's not just the harassment itself that has psychological consequences. The stress of keeping such a bitter secret is tremendous. Like the friend I described earlier, many women I've spoken with never even told their husbands. After I appeared on *20/20*, a woman wrote me, saying, "I was in the US Air Force from 1977 to 1984. I was drugged and raped by three military police officers. This has plagued my life. I am now a 100 percent disabled veteran with PTSD. It has been so hard. I can't forget what happened." So, nearly forty years after the incident, this woman was still suffering from an assault that ruined her life.

A daytime TV star was fired after persistent harassment halted her career at the age of thirty-five. She still feels the shock twenty years later. "I became reclusive. I never got my speed back," she told me. "I was no longer the smart, bubbly person people saw on TV. I was damaged."

Still another woman spoke of grieving for her lost youth—the seven years she spent during her twenties taking a sexual harassment case to court. "All my friends were getting married, planning lives," she told me. "I was in court. Normal life was taken from me."

Sexual harassment is traumatic. This is confirmed by studies measuring the psychological effects of harassment, whether it is verbal or physical. A 2014 study from the University of Mary Washington found what it called "insidious trauma"—small traumas happening every day—summarizing, "Women become caught in a Catch-22; if they speak out about how they are treated, they are likely to be labeled 'overly sensitive,' and if they say nothing, they have to live with these experiences without the chance of social support or vindication. The ambiguous and subtle nature of sexual objectification, particularly the experience of body evaluation, can make this experience of discrimination difficult to acknowledge, discuss, and cope with."

In my home office, I began to print out the stories of women who contacted me. Soon they formed piles on my desk. I didn't know what I would do with them, or what I could do *for* them, but the voices filled my mind and my dreams. They took me out of my own problems, and set me squarely at the center of a cultural battle. One day, surrounded by the evidence of a crisis that cried out to be addressed, I decided to do something. It was a familiar feeling. My life has always worked in mysterious ways, and it has gone in different directions from what I thought I was going to do. Now, it seemed, I was about to dive into something new once again. I decided to start a movement—a preposterously bold idea. But if not me, who would pick up this cause? Who would speak up for these women and give them a voice?

I began to reach out to the women who wrote to me. They were pretty surprised to hear from me directly, never having expected their emails or Facebook posts to be read or responded to. That had always been their experience—a complete absence of response, and the overwhelming sense that no one cared. When they wrote to me, they were dropping their stories into a deep wishing well, with no expectation that they would ever be received.

On the phone and in person, their testimony was long, painful, and often tearful. It was very emotional for me too, because I was still going through my own struggles. I forced myself to take breaks, walk my dog, close my eyes, and breathe. I needed to be sharp and focused—to really listen. I've been interviewing wounded, traumatized people for twenty-five years, but I've never felt the way I did when speaking with these women. Theirs were preventable tragedies, deliberately perpetrated in our culture. I couldn't stand the thought that a new generation of girls, including my daughter, might have to face similar indignities.

But I also heard evidence of plenty of grit, and I was proud of their courage and determination. I began to see that together, we could do something about it and create a meaningful fight for women's rights in our time. I had made a personal choice that I wasn't going to take it anymore—but that wasn't the end of the story.

Being bold exacts a price of its own, as evidenced by those nasty tweets. After I left Fox and launched my public movement, I learned that shame is a powerful force. There's no logic to it, no fairness, and no explanation. The standard notions of right and wrong don't apply. Here's the way it works: You are shamed . . . therefore you are *ashamed*.

The shame extends beyond harassment to assault and rape, and is experienced even by women who are powerful. It wasn't until 2017 that Jane Fonda finally summoned the courage to talk about her experience. In an interview with *The Edit* magazine, she said, "To show you the extent to which a patriarchy takes a toll on females; I've been raped, I've been sexually abused as a child, and I've been fired because I wouldn't sleep with my boss, and I always thought it was my fault; that I didn't do or say the right thing." That's Jane Fonda! The last person you'd think would be full of shame. I'm sure it cost her a lot emotionally to finally speak out at the age of seventy-nine.

Beth, who was an executive in a large health services company, admitted to me that she could never bring herself to lodge a complaint over sexual harassment, although she experienced it from both bosses and coworkers. It felt shameful to her. Only when she learned that she was being paid $25,000 less a year than her male peers did she speak up. It felt safer to her to complain about money. "I was too scared to be labeled when the discrimination was sexual in nature," she confessed. "I am now sorry for that. If I (and others) had the courage back in the 1990s, maybe it wouldn't be happening to other women today."

But now there's a loud rumbling in the culture—a sense that it's time to stand up and turn the floodlights on the injustice women often suffer by being objectified, made to feel like victims, forced to settle for less, and expected to tolerate being ignored, unheard, and marginalized. Together, we can end the harassment, if we decide we're not going to take it anymore.

This book is a rallying cry for all women who want to take control of their lives and own their personal power. It's a warning that we will not be underestimated, intimidated, or held back. We will not be silenced by the ways of the establishment or power. We will tell the truth. We will be fierce.

ONE

Speaking the Unspeakable

was living moment by moment in the days immediately after my story broke, not knowing exactly what might happen next. I was all by myself those first few days, as my husband and children were in California. I had planned to go with them, but now I couldn't. It was good that my kids were away. I didn't want them to see the reporters parking their cars outside our house, or hear the phone ringing at all hours of the night. I sat there alone, enduring it. I cried and prayed and thought. I did a lot of thinking. I wondered what would happen to me next. This was the hardest thing I had ever done. And it was still Wednesday. I was sleepless for the first forty-eight hours.

I'd promised Casey I would somehow get to San Francisco that Friday to accompany him to a wedding. So, exhausted, I packed a bag and made my way to Newark Airport. For the record, I'm an incredibly organized person, but on this day, I was out of sorts. When I got to the airport, my confirmation number didn't work, which was odd. I started to panic when the United Airlines representative told me that I'd somehow purchased a ticket for the wrong day, and I wasn't booked on the flight. And, oh, by the way, every flight to San Francisco was sold out that day. But I *had* to get there.

I was desperate. I quickly looked on my phone for a flight on any other airline going to California. I bought a new ticket on my phone and raced to another terminal, which meant getting a cab. Once in the cab, I realized I had inadvertently purchased a ticket for a flight that was leaving much later in the day. Ugh. Now I needed to get on the phone with a real person to try to get on an earlier flight, but the representative told me it was completely sold out. I asked—begged—if there was any way to get a seat. She put me on hold for what seemed like an eternity, and by the time she came back, I was actually at the front desk, gasping for breath. Just as I approached, she came back on and said, "I got you on the flight." Relief!

As I made my way through the security line, the TSA agent, seeing me in a sweat, asked how my day had been going. "I've had better days," I said. He looked down at my license and then at my face, and then back down again, and kindly replied, "Oh, Ms. Carlson, I totally understand. Have a better week ahead!"

But the most emotional moment came when I got to the gate. When the flight attendant called for my row to board, I handed her my ticket and waited for her to scan it. She paused and looked up at me with tears in her eyes, took my hand, and said, "For all of us women— thank you." My eyes burned as I felt my own tears welling up. They still do today when I think of her. I said, "Thank you so much for saying that," to which she responded, "No, thank *you*!"

I have had similar encounters on other flights since that day. Complete strangers have felt a connection and have had the compassion and decency to say kind words to me. To all of you out there, I want you to know that your words changed my world, lifted my spirits, and contributed to this book.

I thought I was alone, but I was not. During my darkest days, an army of people—everyday people—was marching with me, giving me the power and courage to wake up each morning and approach my new life with optimism and hope.

It was the same way when I started my career in television. It was the early 1990s, when women were storming the workplace. I felt empowered and eager to rise on my merits. I had been raised in an era in which I was told nothing could hold me back. I had read plenty of stories from earlier decades, when women had to fight every day to achieve even a modicum of respect. My idols were women like Barbara Walters, who had paved the way for me. It didn't enter my mind that my gender was an obstacle. I was determined to be bold and make my mark.

Early in my career, working for the CBS affiliate in Cleveland, I was part of a grand experiment—two female coanchors sharing the news desk. We thought this was a tremendously important step, a great idea. When the ratings eventually proved otherwise and I was fired, it was devastating. But I eventually found another job, and then another. I always believed that I would be able to grow in my career and make it to the national scene because I worked harder than anyone else and never quit. I often gave talks to young women who aspired to do what I was doing. "Nothing can hold you back," I told them confidently. "The key is working twice as hard and twice as smart as everyone else." I believed I was living proof of the dictate, which I had heard since I was a child, thanks to my mom telling me so; that I could do anything if I was willing to put in the effort. I wasn't naive. I knew discrimination and sexual harassment went on, but I thought I was tough enough not to let it get in the way of my career.

I was a product of my times, a little sister of the women who made names for themselves in broadcast journalism—women like Diane Sawyer, Jane Pauley, Katie Couric, Connie Chung, Oprah Winfrey, and Christiane Amanpour. I was part of the next generation of female broadcasters, continuing to carry the torch. In my first job in broadcast journalism, I covered the Virginia general assembly, and it was common for the men there to call me "honey" or "sweetie." Every single time, I replied, "My name is Gretchen." Eventually, they got it—mostly. I made opportunities for myself, with the help of good bosses and coworkers. And in spite of my later experiences, I have never lost faith in this basic promise of opportunity. But now I understand not just how far we have come, but also *how far we still have to go*.

Researching the history of the fight against discrimination and harassment in the workplace, I was surprised to find that until the 1970s, the term "sexual harassment" didn't even exist, or was a trivial

concern. The general thinking was twofold: first, that if sexual harassment existed, it was a personal matter, not the responsibility of a company, but a dispute between two (or more) individuals. Second, many
people believed that a complaint of harassment was evidence that a
woman couldn't cut it in a tough man's world—and that maybe they
weren't *meant* to cut it. There was an inclination to blame women for
bringing on unwelcome attention by the way they acted or how they
dressed. It was expected that women who had problems with their
coworkers or bosses, including sexual harassment and other discrimi-
natory behaviors, should just quit.

At the time, women didn't think they had the right or the recourse
to complain, so the silence grew. The first real case of sexual harassment in the United States was brought in 1974. Paulette Barnes was
an African American payroll clerk at the US Environmental Protection Agency. Soon after she began working at the agency, Barnes's boss
started hassling her to have sex with him. He told her it would be good
for her career if she did. Even after she firmly told him she preferred to
keep their relationship professional, he kept after her. He retaliated by
making her work life miserable, and eventually fired her.

Barnes brought her case to court, asserting that her boss's actions
were a form of workplace discrimination based on her sex that was
forbidden under Title VII. But the court disagreed, ruling that what
happened to her did not qualify as discrimination, but was merely the
actions of an individual who felt rejected by her.

Three years later, an appeals court overturned the ruling, stating:

But for her womanhood . . . her participation in sexual activity would never have been solicited. To say, then, that she was
victimized in her employment simply because she declined
the invitation is to ignore the asserted fact that she was invited
only because she was a woman subordinate to the inviter in
the hierarchy of agency personnel.

The court established that Barnes's claim fell under Title VII of the Civil Rights Act of 1964, which offered protection for women. Section 703(a) of Title VII states that it is "an unlawful employment practice" for an employer to discriminate in hiring, firing, or in applying the conditions of employment because of "race, color, religion, sex, or national origin."

Barnes ultimately won her case, and was paid $18,000 in back pay. But the idea that sexual harassment was a form of discrimination against women was still a matter of debate.

"Sexual harassment" first made it into the language in 1975, when activists at Cornell University formed a group to support another woman who had finally quit her job following her boss's severe sexual violations, which went unaddressed by her employer, the university. The group hosted events that garnered so much public attention that *Time* magazine wrote a piece using the new term "sexual harassment."

In truth, most companies just wished the whole issue would remain under wraps. As Catharine MacKinnon wrote in her groundbreaking 1979 book, *Sexual Harassment of Working Women*, sexual harassment of women "is sufficiently pervasive in American society as to be nearly invisible." She also noted that sexual harassment was "literally unspeakable" in society, and thus difficult to identify and address.

In January and April 1981, the US Senate Committee on Labor and Human Resources, chaired by Orrin Hatch, convened to wrestle with the problems of gender discrimination, including sexual harassment. In his opening statement, Hatch said, "It is anathema to everything we stand for as a nation that some women are subjected to various forms of sexual harassment in order to obtain, keep, or advance in their jobs. Surely this is a practice which is abhorrent to all but the offenders, but this committee will not be afraid to address it." (Having made this statement, it is ironic that Hatch would go on to attack Anita Hill at the Clarence Thomas hearings a decade later.)

One loud voice of dissent belonged to Phyllis Schlafly, a crusader for keeping women in the home. "Non-criminal sexual harassment on the job is not a problem for the virtuous woman except in the rarest of cases. When a woman walks across the room, she speaks with a universal body language that most men intuitively understand. Men hardly ever ask sexual favors of women from whom the certain answer is 'no.'" In Schlafly's opinion, "the most cruel and damaging sexual harassment taking place today is the harassment by feminists and their federal government allies against the role of motherhood and the role of the dependent wife." These were old-fashioned views in 1981—in fact, there was a loud outcry at the hearing when she spoke— yet Schlafly would continue to promote them until her death in 2016, at the age of ninety-two.

As the legal landscape shifted to make room for protections against sexual harassment, the criteria itself had to change to more accurately reflect women's experiences. For example, the usual measure for evaluating sexual harassment was the "reasonable person" standard. That is, would a reasonable person view the behavior as offensive or harassing? But in 1991, the US Court of Appeals for the Ninth Circuit ruled in *Ellison v. Brady* that the "reasonable person" standard had a male bias in these cases. Men might not consider certain behaviors—jokes, compliments, and so forth—to be harassing, whereas women might feel uncomfortable and threatened. So, the court adopted a "reasonable *woman*" standard, and this was adopted by the EEOC.

Some of those early pioneers experienced a level of overt harassment that at first glance seems impossible to imagine today. Madeline, a TV broadcaster who started her career in the 1980s, recalled for me the first time she asked her boss, a man in his forties, for a raise. She says he blatantly asked her for a sexual favor. Wow, I thought. How awful. I shuddered to think how she felt as a twenty-five-year-old being in such an incredibly stressful and impossible situation. "I was embarrassed," she replied. "But I thought that kind of thing was normal."

And it *was* normal for her. For a time, she says she worked with a man who was unbelievably crude and abusive. "The experience was hell on earth," she recalled. The end, Madeline says, finally came when he got angry with her one day, and slapped her across the face.

"What did you just do to me?" she cried in shock.

"It's no big deal," he said dismissively.

She recalls that she complained to her boss but the result wasn't a good one for her: she was removed from the broadcast. "He prospered, but I struggled to get my groove back after that," she said. When I heard Madeline's story, I was so angry that she was the one who had to leave. Why do women have to leave, while men accused of harassment often get to stay? I was about to find out this was more often the norm than not.

"It was a lonely time for me," Madeline said. But somehow she never gave up and is still working in her profession today. Let me say that again: Madeline is working in her profession today! It's so important for me to share her victorious story with you because her win is one we can all celebrate and learn from. She was beaten down and treated like dirt, but Madeline kept going. Her win is a testament to never giving up, even in the darkest hours, and from that, we too can dig deep to find the same inner strength.

Sexual harassment is one piece of a much larger issue related to all efforts to disempower women, especially in the workplace. In my conversations with dozens of women, I've seen instances of direct sexual harassment that are often part of a larger scenario of discrimination and disempowerment. Thus, the woman who is sexually harassed might also be blocked from promotion or sidelined in other ways.

The imperatives are not just personal and moral, but are pocketbook issues as well. A recent study from the consulting firm McKinsey found that advancing women's equality could add $12 trillion to global growth, meaning $500 billion in economic growth in America alone. That should get the attention of companies focusing on the bottom line!

In January 2015, the EEOC created its Select Commission on the Study of Harassment in the Workplace in an effort to find ways of preventing harassment. The sixteen-member commission included people with backgrounds in employment law, employer and employee advocacy, and organized labor. The commission's report, published a year later, found that workplace harassment is unfortunately not on the decline but *on the rise*, with little chance of improving under the current efforts to address it, which are overly focused on avoiding legal liability and less geared toward eradicating harassment. The idea that sexual harassment in the workplace is getting worse is a shocking and outrageous reality—and certainly a wakeup call about our workplace culture. It also underscores the necessity for this book and for a more open discussion about why sexual harassment occurs and what we're going to do to fix it.

Repeatedly while talking to women, I had the eerie sensation that I was riding a time machine back to another era. But it also occurred to me that the issue of empowerment is not just about grievances. It's also about being fulfilled, happy, and confident. It's about doing work you love, and not being afraid or chastened. It's about standing up for yourself and not second-guessing or being obsessed with other people's opinions. It's about going to work every day without the fear that being a woman is going to get in the way of doing your job.

I have found that sexual harassment is an equal-opportunity plight. Women can experience it even when they are in executive or high-profile positions. But there's no question that women who are most vulnerable suffer the greater number of incidents. For example, a 2016 survey conducted by Hart Research Associates found that *40 percent* of women working in nonmanagerial positions in the fast-food industry have experienced sexual harassment at work, including sexual jokes or teasing, touching, or kissing, or comments about sexual orientation. The women surveyed reported increased stress, anxiety, depression, loss of appetite, and difficulty sleeping as a result of this harassment. Sadly, 42 percent of them said they felt they had to accept the harassment if they wanted to keep their jobs. I think it's fair to say that women working nonmanagerial jobs in fast food establishments probably can't afford to lose their jobs, and accepting harassment is a matter of protecting their livelihoods. Few have the resources or clout to fight their circumstances, so I believe it is incumbent on all of us to fight on their behalf.

"CAN'T YOU JUST GET ALONG?"

Many women have told me about "that guy"—the jerk in the office who hassles women—and it's much worse if he's in a position of power. He would no doubt claim that he means no harm, that he's just being friendly, that his actions are actually a form of flattery and appreciation of the women he targets. This, he would argue, is the *opposite* of a hostile workplace; it's a *friendly* workplace.

Women have an especially hard time fending off these kinds of advances. Consider this scenario: A man comes up to you while you're at your desk and rubs your shoulders while mentioning he likes the dress you're wearing. What do you do? You might fear that "Don't touch me" sounds hostile. Or that jumping out of your chair seems like an overreaction. It might feel as if saying politely, "I'd prefer if you didn't . . ." sounds squeamish.

In this way, many women get trapped in a kind of compliance with sexual harassment. Not wanting to seem rude or unnecessarily "touchy," they cringe and say nothing. And the woman who does eventually complain gets a predictable response: "I thought you liked it."

One woman told me about a poll that was conducted in her department, rating women from one to ten based on how "hot" they were. "It was humiliating, but none of the women dared say anything. They didn't want to seem humorless."

A lot of men are confused when what they regard as flattering words or friendly goofing around are not appreciated as such. We have to be clear about what constitutes crossing the line. At the same time, women want to be equal partners in our work environments. We want the freedom to make friends and develop collegial relationships with both men and women. We want to be able to laugh and tell stories, express our personalities and be *human*. A "strictly by the book" mentality is a poor solution—kind of like locking yourself in your house so you won't get hit by a car. Women are forced to grapple with the complexity of social dynamics and fit in comfortably while maintaining their rights and dignity.

This can get especially tricky in environments where there is a macho culture. One woman described to me how stressful it was to work in her small tech company, where she was the only woman on her team. The men around her blew off steam with a constant barrage of vulgarities, sometimes directed at her, but mostly just as the background to her days. "It was distracting and disgusting," she told me. "I couldn't concentrate. It was like having a jackhammer pounding in the room for twelve hours a day. It would drive anyone nuts." She mostly let it go because it was the way she got along in the culture.

No woman wants to be known as the office nag—the one who's always calling out people in conversations for being inappropriate. So how do you know when to speak up and what to say? There are a thousand stitches in the tapestry of doubt. How do you know you're being sexually harassed? That might seem like a silly question; of course you'd know. But one of the reasons many women struggle so much with reporting it is that they aren't always sure if it's going on.

Is it sexual harassment if a coworker has a pornographic photo displayed in plain view?

Is it sexual harassment if people tell off-color jokes?

Is it sexual harassment if people talk about their sexual conquests at meetings?

Is it sexual harassment if people compliment you on your physical attributes: "Great rack," and so forth?

Is it sexual harassment if you get wolf whistles when you walk into a room?

Is it sexual harassment if someone pats you on the butt?

Is it sexual harassment if a coworker or boss pesters you to date him?

Is it sexual harassment if people make lewd suggestions about your sex life?

Is it sexual harassment if a coworker stares at you throughout the day in a suggestive manner?

Is it sexual harassment if people make sexual innuendos in meetings?

Is it sexual harassment if an executive has a sexual affair with a woman and promotes her over the other women in the company?

All of these can be classified as sexual harassment if they create a climate of discomfort. The law recognizes two kinds of sexual harassment: (1) quid pro quo behavior—performing sexual favors in exchange for keeping or doing well in your job, and (2) a hostile work environment: the creation of an abusive environment that affects the ability of an employee to do his or her work because of gender.

The EEOC defines sexual harassment in this way:

> Unwelcome sexual advances, requests for sexual favors, and other verbal or physical conduct of a sexual nature when:
> - Submission to such conduct is made either explicitly or implicitly a term or condition of an individual's employment, or
> - Submission to or rejection of such conduct by an individual is used as a basis for employment decisions affecting such individual, or
> - Such conduct has the purpose or effect of unreasonably interfering with an individual's work performance or creating an intimidating, hostile, or offensive working environment.

This definition is only one kind of harassment, though. Remember, abuse based on gender, whether it is intended to harm the victim or not, is sexual harassment, and it does not have to be sexual. It just has to be gender based.

The bottom line: you have the right to not be subject to *unwelcome* sexual behaviors in the workplace—whether they seem minor or severe. But I must caution you that even though the law is clear, the legal process is far from it. You might have the law on your side, but getting there is complicated, difficult, and often expensive. Before you even file an EEOC claim, you must pursue a complaint within your company and be able to show that the company was unresponsive. Only then can you go to the EEOC. There, the result can be frustrating and ultimately disappointing. Except in very rare circumstances, the EEOC will not take on your case. It may conduct a minor investigation and instead declare that you have a "right to sue." After that, it's up to you to decide whether to initiate a civil suit or, if your company requires it, enter into arbitration. This process can take years.

ABUSE OF POWER

Powerful harassers can seem to hold all the cards, even when women themselves have power within a company. A former executive in a large architectural firm who resigned after being harassed for a long time told me, "A man in a position of power can make or break a career." She told me her boss threatened her that if she spoke out, he would be forced to make a move—and it wouldn't be pleasant. When she complained, her boss made good on his promise and subjected her to a nightmare of retaliation, including hacking her computer. When she complained to HR, she says her boss countered with an accusation that she was stealing from the company—effectively diverting the discussion from his own misdeeds. "How could I fight that?" she asked.

The typical harasser has advantages at his disposal, as opposed to the typical victim. It starts with the HR department. No matter how solid the harassment policies, HR is a function of the company, staffed by executives who have the company's interests at heart.

For fifteen years, Paula looked forward to going to work every day because her workplace was the great outdoors. As a park ranger in a beautiful southern state, Paula loved her job, and she got used to people saying, "Wow, I've never met a female park ranger before." Comments like that made her so happy. She felt she was really doing something to help people experience and appreciate the environment. "It wasn't just a career," she said. "It was my life." She was one of few women at her level, but that didn't bother her. She was tough, and she thought she could handle anything that came her way. She ignored what she deemed to be casual harassment, such as the time she says one of her coworkers put a sex toy in an envelope with work papers, or the supervisor who suggested she couldn't handle things the male officers handled. She even ignored the fact that in meetings she felt as if her suggestions were downplayed, while men who made the same suggestions were praised for them. How many of us have felt that? I know I have!

At a conference out of town, Paula claims that one of her fellow rangers, a married man, got drunk and followed her down the hall as she was going to her room. She says he pushed her against a wall and started kissing her and telling her he loved her. Paula was scared. "I worried I wouldn't be able to get back to my room," she said. She says she finally pulled herself away from him and fled down the hall, slamming the door.

Paula's first reaction was to say nothing. She didn't want to be *that* woman everyone was talking about. But a week later at her annual evaluation, she broke down and told her supervisor. She begged him not to tell people about it, and the situation was quietly disposed of. She realized how grave the consequences would be for her only a year later, when she applied for a supervisory position. She told me that her boss denied her the promotion because she'd "had an affair" with a married man. She was horrified. She hadn't had an affair—she'd been assaulted.

It was the breaking point for Paula, who had tolerated various forms of harassment and discrimination for years. She hired a lawyer and sued. Then she says things really deteriorated. "Launching a lawsuit has been like being stuck in a trap that I can't get out of," she said. "My boss told my coworkers, 'I have a special place in hell for anyone who testifies against me.'"

Paula continues to work, and in spite of her agony, she sees a positive side. "This is the way things change," she said. "I can tell my children I was a part of that change."

When I heard this story, I thought, We need more Paulas! We need more women who will choose to stay and fight for themselves, and not think their only option is to quit and leave behind the work they love. Even though I can certainly sympathize with those who decide to leave, or who have no other choice because they are fired or forced out, the truth is that when you leave, it perpetuates the idea that harassers are untouchable—they can get away with it.

It's not that the choice isn't agonizing. Sometimes it seems to be a matter of your job or your dignity: pick one. I dare any man faced with this choice not to come out swinging. "I've made a deal with the devil," a young female paramedic wrote me. "I get to keep the job I've dreamed of since I was a little girl, and in exchange I ignore the constant taunts and tricks—used condoms in my locker, lewd graffiti—about me!—in the bathroom. I've accepted this is just the way it's going to be for me."

How many women have made this deal? It's easy to sit on the outside and claim that they should have exposed their harassers. But those righteous critics don't have a clue what that decision really means. They have no idea what it feels like to try and summon up the courage to make the biggest decision in your life for something you've worked so hard for. In so many of these cases, the women have been in their careers for decades. And they face a terrible choice where they feel incredibly alone. You may start pulling away from your colleagues. You may wonder if anyone really supports you. You will probably hear people accusing you of being aloof and unsocial, when in reality you're just coming to work, putting your head down, and trying to do your best job. You ask yourself every day, How can I behave normally when I don't trust anybody? It's like walking down the hallway with a knife in your back, blood dripping down, scared to look behind you, wondering what might be next, knowing it probably won't be good. And yet people find it so easy to casually judge who you are without knowing any of the facts.

What also makes the issue so tough to handle is that harassers rarely act alone. They need people to cover for them, and because they often control compensation, careers, and so forth, enlisting enablers is not hard for them to do. In my mind, enablers are as blameworthy as the harassers themselves.

Susan, who spent twenty-five years in law enforcement with a sheriff's office in the Midwest, had always dreamed of being a police officer. She admitted, "I became a cop because I wanted to prove to my family that I wasn't weak." Like Paula, she says she encountered plenty of bad behavior—guys spouting vulgarities, patting her behind, trying to kiss her. She figured things would get better as she proved herself and advanced up the ranks, but she says it didn't happen. To her surprise, when she tried to lobby for improvements on behalf of the women at her station, she claims it was her female colleagues who didn't always appreciate her efforts. Rather than being grateful and supportive, she says they became angry at her for making waves and calling attention to them. Talk about a no-win situation.

After that, Susan says, she began to experience a shift in the way she was treated by the administration. There was an effort to demoralize her. "You 'grieve' something, you have a black mark against you," she said. "You're not a member of the team anymore."

If Susan suspected the department didn't have her back, that suspicion was confirmed for her by the danger she says she was put in every day. One of her jobs was to transport inmates to court in a van. Typically, this was a two-person job, handling ten to twelve prisoners. But Susan says her supervisor reassigned her partner and she was forced to do it alone. "There I was, 120 pounds, sitting in a vehicle with all these prisoners, wondering what I'd do if something went wrong, if one of them tried to make a run for it," she said. "Every day I woke up with a terrible feeling—What was going to happen today? Everyone was looking for me to make a mistake." She kept telling herself just to hold on for another five years until she turned fifty and could retire. She says she didn't even consider staying on until age fifty-five, even though it meant an extra $1,000 a month. "By the time I retired, I was poison," she said. "There was no party. There wasn't even a card."

Today I'd like to give Susan a party and a card. She kept fighting as long as she could, and has paved the way for other female police officers to thrive. They may not know Susan, but they should thank her.

"WHAT TOOK YOU SO LONG?"

When a woman comes forward after months or years of harassment, the chorus of criticism is loud: "What took you so long?" people ask suspiciously. These armchair critics have a very simplistic view of what any self-respecting woman should do if she is harassed: March right into HR. File a complaint with the EEOC. Hire a lawyer. Immediately seek justice. And if she doesn't, she isn't deemed credible. But these reactions fail to consider the very real and valid reasons many women fail to report harassment the moment it happens. Here are just a few:

> She is traumatized.
> The power differential is great.
> The company culture is intimidating.
> She has observed the abuser getting away with it before.
> She doesn't have hard proof.
> She doesn't have the resources for a legal fight.
> She wants to keep her job.

Thinking about why women don't come forward, I was reminded of a thirty-part series on domestic violence that I did earlier in my career when I was at a local television station in Dallas. To my knowledge, a series of this magnitude had never been done before on local news, and boy, did I learn a lot. I started the project struggling with the same question so many others do: Why don't women just leave their abusive spouses? I figured, I'm a strong woman; I certainly would if I found myself in that kind of situation. But I found out that there are many reasons why women don't leave. First and most important, they fear for their lives. But they also fear that they won't be believed, that they will end up being ostracized and maybe even lose custody of their kids. Domestic violence is a different issue from sexual harassment, but can you see a theme here? Whether or not women decide to come forward, they're the ones who suffer the blowback.

Even high-profile women, who might seem to have their own power base in a company, can be reluctant to complain. It took Karla Amezola years to come forward. By any measure, Karla was a star in Spanish-language television. Born in San Diego and raised in Tijuana by her mother and grandmother, Karla fell in love with journalism when she served an internship at Telemundo. Her talent and ambition led to a job anchoring the five o'clock and eleven o'clock evening news broadcasts on Estrella TV, the Spanish-language network. But she says that soon after she started, she began to receive inappropriate notices from the vice president of news, Andrés Angulo. According to news reports and Karla's legal complaint, Angulo often made sexually provocative comments around the newsroom and in meetings. This was so commonplace, she told me, that "our ears got used to his language, which included obscene references to body parts."

One day, Karla recalls, Angulo called her into his office. "I was looking at your picture on Facebook," he said. "You are so sexy. The picture makes me feel like you are looking at me with that sexy look. Where did you take it?"

He was referring to a photo she'd posted of just her face.

"In Hawaii, with my boyfriend," she replied, trying to deflect his attention.

But Angulo would not be deflected. Karla recounted that he later sent a Facebook message that stated, "Your profile picture that is looking at me with that smile almost diabolically. I like it. And I like you. You have to be more obedient and tame. But I like you."

Early on, Karla says, he told her that he was untouchable in the company, and his behavior indicated that he really believed it. He often spoke of having sex with her coworkers, and said to her, "None of them I like as much as you, and I would f——k you as I f——d one of them last week." Or he would say, "I want you to go to my house today, I want to do to you what I do to others." Or he would say, "I'm dying to f——k you."

Karla was young, only in her late twenties, and told me she thought she could handle Angulo by keeping her head down, and by proving her worth to the network. But by late 2015, Karla told Angulo that he had to stop or she was prepared to report him to HR. Soon after, another employee actually did report Angulo for sexual harassment, and Karla was interviewed as a witness. She told me it was then she decided to tell HR everything that had been going on.

But telling her truth came with consequences. Karla says Angulo began a campaign of retaliation against her; telling coworkers that she was a bad reporter and irresponsible, even though she had earned Emmy nominations and had won the Golden Mike Award for her reporting. Only when Karla hired an attorney and filed a lawsuit in June 2016 did she finally see an investigation being opened. But to what end? Soon after, Angulo informed her that she would no longer be anchoring the five o'clock broadcast and eight months after filing the lawsuit, Karla was fired.

Angulo was asked to resign the same day and has made no statements about the case. In the meantime, the network has not directly addressed Karla's claims, or acknowledged or denied them, except to state, "Univision Communications, Inc. (UCI) has long maintained a strict policy prohibiting sexual harassment in any form. We encourage all UCI employees to immediately report such incidents without fear of reprisal. UCI is committed to fostering a workplace culture that is free of unlawful harassment."

As of this writing, the case is still in court to determine if Karla will be forced to arbitrate (as her contract states) or will be able to have her day in front of a jury. The court will also decide whether or not Karla's secret weapon—tape recordings of her encounters with Angulo—will be admissible. Note to anyone living in California: one-party consent recordings are illegal, but Karla's lawyer is trying to make a claim of extenuating circumstances.

When her story hit the media, Karla said, "I wanted to disappear. I didn't want people to know." But then she started receiving messages from women at other stations and in other occupations, who wrote, "This happened to me." Like me, she has become an unexpected standard-bearer for women who demand to be heard.

Karla is confident that she will return to journalism and the work she loves, but in the meantime she is supporting herself by driving for car services. She says she's doing what she has to do, holding her head up high with no shame. Often her female passengers tell her their own stories, and this award-winning reporter is writing them down, preparing for a time when she can tell them to the world.

LET'S TALK ABOUT HR

If the worst happens to you, you might find yourself heading to HR, but the department may not be as benevolent as it seems. One manager, whose job was in jeopardy the moment after reporting harassment, told me frankly, "Its role within the company is to be the guardian of the culture. But in my case, HR failed its leadership mandate. How can I tell people to trust HR?"

"HR is the KGB. They're not your friend," noted Nancy Erika Smith, a prominent civil rights lawyer who has been representing women in sexual harassment cases since the 1980s, and is one of my lawyers. "The first mistake many women make is to think of HR as their friend. A lot of people go to HR thinking, 'They'll help me when they hear what's happening.' It's like going to police internal affairs to say, 'This cop abused me.' They're going to take care of their own. If you want to keep your job in HR, you'd better protect the people with the power, the people who make money."

Smith's words are a wake-up call for those who have learned to think of HR as a benevolent and nurturing face of their company, kind of like the mom and dad of the workplace. Indeed, the concept of "human resources," as a modern reimagining of the old personnel department, was first developed in the early 1980s. The new title was intended to present the image of companies as caring and people focused. That is, HR is the home not just of paychecks and time sheets, but also the beating heart of a company, where people and their well-being are valued.

Employees are regularly told that if they have any grievances, HR is there to listen. But workers are perhaps lulled into an unrealistic view about exactly what HR can or will do for them.

The first thing to understand is that HR's primary role is to serve the business. Most companies want their employees to be happy, fulfilled, and successful, but in the day-to-day operations, especially in large corporations, tough choices get made that aren't necessarily good for the people doing the work. Sometimes what may be good for an individual employee—such as flextime or a generous pension plan—is not seen as advancing the company's bottom line. I think that most of us understand these realities.

However, the role of HR becomes murkier when there is a dispute, especially if it involves a complaint against a high-ranking executive. Susan Fowler, an engineer at Uber, certainly found this to be the case. As a new employee with the company, she says that she experienced aggressive sexual harassment from her manager, who sent her a series of messages over the company chat line. He bluntly said that he was in an open relationship with his girlfriend, and was looking for women to have sex with. She took screen shots of the messages and brought them to HR.

"Uber was a pretty good-sized company at that time, and I had pretty standard expectations of how they would handle situations like this," she wrote in a blog post describing her experience. But that's not what happened. Instead, she wrote, "I was told by both HR and upper management that even though this was clearly sexual harassment and he was propositioning me, it was this man's first offense, and that they wouldn't feel comfortable giving him anything other than a warning and a stern talking-to." They explained that the man was a high performer for the company, and it was probably just an innocent mistake.

But in the coming months, as Fowler began to talk to other women in the company, she says that she learned that some of them had experienced the same thing she did, and had also filed reports with HR. So, the excuse that it was the manager's first offense seemed implausible. A few of the women decided to challenge the assertion by scheduling meetings with HR. But she says the HR representative still blatantly told Fowler that hers was the only complaint.

There were many quick developments in the Uber story once Fowler's piece circulated on the Internet. Uber realized the company had a big problem and seemingly took aggressive steps to address it, even hiring the former attorney general Eric Holder to lead an investigation. Travis Kalanick, Uber's cofounder and CEO, also issued a public apology. But Holder's report, delivered on June 13, 2017, was a scalding indictment of the culture at Uber under Kalanick's leadership. The report came with a list of recommendations, aimed squarely at drastic changes that would be a "reformulation" of Uber's cultural values. Changes in employee practices would include greater transparency in performance reviews and criteria for promotions, limiting alcohol consumption at work events and during work hours, a prohibition on romantic relationships between managers and employees, and strengthening employment policies against harassment and discrimination. In unanimously accepting the report, Uber's board also called for a change in leadership and asked Kalanick to take a leave of absence, which he announced he was doing that same day. That wasn't enough for some of Uber's key investors, though. Within a week, Kalanick was forced to resign, although at this writing he maintains a position on the board.

Fowler set in motion a dramatic change that was a call to arms for women in tech to no longer put up with mistreatment. As one example, in June 2017, more than two dozen women in Silicon Valley startups found the courage to tell the *New York Times* about their experiences of persistent sexual harassment in the industry. The Uber story is also a warning to men in this profession—many of whom are young and whom we might think should know better—that the time is now. Women are speaking with loud voices. But let's not forget that it's a long process, requiring constant vigilance. In a bitter irony, while publicly announcing the Uber investigation findings, one board member made a blatantly sexist remark and was forced to resign on the spot.

Nancy Erika Smith also says that HR departments may set traps for the woman who complains. "The woman may not want to say everything, or be as direct, because she's afraid, so they lead her on: 'What you're saying is you're not really getting along with him.' It's like going to a deposition without having a lawyer with you. You get sucked into admitting things in certain formulations that later hurt you in that case." In a large agency that Smith has sued many times, she says the HR director instituted a new rule that employees are not allowed to file a complaint with HR until they've come and spoken to her first. "What's the reason?" Smith asked. "Intimidation. To get you to say things that will later put you in a bad light."

Fran's story is a good example of this underhanded behavior. When Fran began working in the marketing department of a large sporting goods company, she says that her new boss boasted that his department was a close-knit group. He joked that Fran would have to earn her way in as one of the "guys." Fran found the rowdy boys-will-be-boys atmosphere unsettling, especially the frequent jokes and comments about her body.

She didn't want to start complaining right away in a new job, but she finally did say to her boss, "Can you ask the guys to lay off on the sex references? It's not very professional."

He didn't take her seriously, and warned her, "Being professional in this industry means learning to accept a certain amount of that kind of talk." Then he gave her a hard look. "I hope you're going to be a good fit here," he said. "I know it's not everyone's style. But the last woman who worked in our group got along great."

This was such a loaded conversation that Fran's head was spinning. She decided she needed help and guidance, so she made an appointment with HR. She came to the meeting prepared with notes and specific examples of the behavior she found objectionable, including a record of how her boss had responded to her complaint.

The HR representative heard her out, then suggested, "Why don't we get your boss in here and settle this now."

Fran was horrified. She was just there for advice, not to make a complaint.

"Have you had these problems getting along with coworkers before?" she was asked.

"I usually get along pretty well with people."

"Maybe you're overly sensitive," the rep suggested.

The back and forth went on like this for some time. Fran felt confused by the exchange. All she'd wanted was advice, but the tone of the meeting felt more ominous. It seemed as if the HR employee was trying to subtly place the onus on her to explain her reaction, instead of focusing on the harassment. And after their meeting, it soon became clear to her that her boss had been told about her complaint. In fact, it seemed like everyone knew. There was no more teasing; there was nothing at all. Her coworkers were barely civil to her. Her boss was openly critical of her work. She tolerated it for a month, and then quit.

In spite of the risks involved in bringing complaints to HR, under established workplace law, employees making sexual harassment claims are required to have made an effort to inform the company (usually through HR) that the harassment is going on. The court has ruled that an employee's fear of retaliation is not sufficient reason to avoid reporting the harassment. In theory, it makes sense that a company should be given the opportunity to address a situation in the workplace before it becomes a lawsuit. But as a practical matter, it doesn't always work that way. The law's presumption is that companies always operate in good faith when addressing employees' complaints. It also places the burden on the complainant, even in a traumatized state, to go by the book in handling the problem.

So what can an employee do? I'm not a lawyer, but it makes good sense to me that the best way to stand up for yourself is to be clear-eyed about how the power dynamic works in your company. If there is a prescribed process for filing complaints, follow it to the letter. If you don't want to make a complaint, but need guidance, seek it elsewhere—don't go to HR. Don't get bogged down in thinking about fair versus unfair, or what is right. You can find many more specific guidelines in chapter 4, but begin with the knowledge that this is a chess game. You can't win if you don't know the rules.

I'd like to make a few more important points. Since my story broke and I've spoken about HR publicly, I've heard from many people who've had difficult experiences with HR. But I've also heard from HR managers who wanted me to know they are working hard to do the right thing. Some of them tweeted about it, like this one: "Dear Gretchen Carlson, HR isn't the enemy . . . we want to help."

Another HR director told me, "I believe that the way to have productive employees is to have an atmosphere of trust—to be honest and have integrity." He took his mission seriously, "to treat every employee with respect." I believe that many HR managers feel the same responsibility, but even those with the best intentions can be hampered by the company they work for. Remember, in some cases, HR employees can be called on to investigate the *very people who are paying their salaries*. That's a huge problem.

Obviously, the culture and tone of a corporation is set from the top. And that is what sometimes needs changing. Maybe that change is as simple as having more women at the top and throughout an organization. The HR director of one international company told me something profound: "Eighty percent of our workforce is women, and therefore we don't have a lot of sexual harassment claims." Wow. Of course! When more women are put in decision-making roles and are therefore part of setting the tone of the corporation, it makes sense there would be less sexual harassment. In those cases, *women* are the ones determining what's acceptable and what's not.

My lesson: too many of us as women have been put in horrible situations in which we feel a lot like David in the Bible story about David-versus-Goliath. The underdog with little power. If you happen to find yourself in that kind of fight right now in your company, remember: *you are not alone*. Believe in yourself even though you may have never gone into a battle like this one before. Keep pressing ahead with your head held high and confidence brimming, because while David undoubtedly never believed he could take down the giant standing before him, that's exactly what he did, and all it took was just one stone in a slingshot.

TWO

You Can't Break a Badass

A friend once joked, "People who don't know you very well don't know you're really a badass underneath it all." "Badass" might seem like a strange label for me. After all, one of my colleagues used to disparagingly call me "Little Bo Peep." But I've always had that toughness, even when it didn't show. Now I'm channeling my badass side, to make sure change happens. And I've been gratified to meet so many other women who have joined the club. I like this quote from the writer Anne Lamott: "Anger is good, a bad attitude is excellent, and the medicinal powers of shouting and complaining cannot be overestimated."

As I was gearing up for my fight, I relied on badass music to motivate me. I listened to songs that would evoke strong emotions and keep me going. Over the past year, I sure needed it. The two favorites I kept coming back to were "I Will Survive" by Gloria Gaynor, and "Survivor" by Destiny's Child. They did for me what music has always done in my life: ignite a fighting spirit within me to never, ever give up. In fact, I had these songs playing when I did the photo shoot for the cover of this book. (I've never liked photo shoots, so it's always good to have extra inspiration.) So now I want to urge you to find your own ways of preparing for the fight. You don't want to be a bystander in your own life. Find what makes your badass mentality come to the surface and be present. Find what it is that makes you feel invincible and in control. For me, hearing those words every single day encouraged me to continue with the fight and let me know I wasn't alone. It fueled me to keep pressing forward against all odds.

In retrospect, I've come to see that being a badass—a person who stands up for herself—starts young, which is why I want to model this attitude for my kids. We live in a bully culture, as every teenager is well aware. It's difficult for parents to get the message across to their daughters that they should be strong and have self-esteem, when what they hear in the school hallways can send a different message entirely.

BOLD LITTLE GIRLS

When I was six, I was fearless. As I think about myself then, the memory tugs at me in a special way—a way that says *that* was the real me. I didn't know the meaning of shame. I had a ferocity about achieving my goals, a confidence that I could walk into any situation and charm the crowd. I was a natural performer, a little dynamo. The memory of this pure self-confidence still makes me smile.

I was born in Anoka, Minnesota, the kind of small town where everyone knows your name. This was the place they mean when they talk about the heartland—a warm community with church suppers, ice skating in the winter, boating and swimming in the summer, big feasts on the holidays, and lots of love. If I was unafraid, it was because I had such a strong support system. I was adored by my parents and grandparents, and they let me know it every day. My maternal grandfather, who was a Lutheran minister, had a nickname for me: he called me "Sparkles."

I still remember one of the first times I stood up for myself. I was in kindergarten, and I was so excited about going to school. I was very proud of myself because I had learned to read. But on the first day, when our teacher divided the class into readers and nonreaders (yep, they used to do that!), she put me in the group with those who couldn't read. I was indignant, frustrated, and upset. I kept going up to her desk, and saying, "But I know how to read!" I can still remember running home from school, slamming the back door, crying, and shouting to my mom, "But, Mom—I know how to read! I know how to read!"

I've thought of that story many times in my adult life—specifically about how one event can set the course for the rest of your life. What if I hadn't fought back? How might that have affected my academic career, my self-esteem and self-confidence, moving forward? But also it's been my stalwart example of perseverance that I always harken back to. Whenever I've been told I can't do something, somewhere inside me that little girl is still shouting, "Yes I can!"

That tenacity served me well as an accomplished musician. At six years old, I begged my parents to let me play a musical instrument. My choice was the piano, but when the teacher told me my fingers may be too small, I had to find a different instrument. The violin came to me almost by accident, but when I held it in my hands, it was love at first touch.

Once I started playing, I was unstoppable. I adored it, and was thrilled to find out I could do it. I had a gift—I could sight-read music—and I got good at it very quickly. I wasn't shy about showing the world what I could do. After three months of practice, I felt confident enough to play at the Christmas concert at our church. When I bravely approached the choir director with this request, she was surprised. "Didn't you just start playing?" she asked. Yes, I told her, but I *knew* I could do it. And I did.

I went on to become a serious violinist, and was competing on an advanced level by the time I was thirteen. (Joshua Bell, now a world-famous violinist, was one of my competitors then—we tied in our first competition against one another.) I also played for Pinchas Zukerman and Isaac Stern—twice. I threw myself into it 110 percent, practicing three to four hours a day, studying with the world-famous teacher Dorothy DeLay at the Juilliard School of music in New York and spending summers at the prestigious Aspen Music Festival. It became a central aspect of who I was and still am—going after a goal and pouring myself into it, confident I could achieve anything I set my mind to. I wasn't a sweet, shy little princess. I was a bold, plump, forceful tomboy with a devilish sense of humor, and the ability to perfectly execute a Brahms or Paganini violin concerto at the same time.

My mother was my original role model—although, I have to say, the first time she heard me refer to myself as a "badass," she probably cringed. "Honey, do you really have to use that word?" she asked. I laughed, because she was unaware that she was pretty much a badass too. Karen Carlson was—and is—a force of nature. Strong, outgoing, unshakable, she was the center of her children's world. Growing up, I relied on her guidance, and was inspired by her "never give up" attitude.

Just to show how impressive my mother is: at the age of sixty-eight, after my dad retired from his car dealership, she decided to take over and run it. She's now seventy-six, still working in a job she loves and is good at. When General Motors shuttered dealerships—privately held companies that had been in families for decades (in our case, almost one hundred years)—my mother took the fight public. That's my mom. The dealership was forced to try and stay afloat for more than a year without receiving any new car inventory from GM. It had to make it by selling only used cars and relying on income from the service and body shops. But my mom never gave up. She rallied nearly every politician in the state of Minnesota to help her in her cause—and her tenacity finally paid off. She got Main Motor back, and it is still open for business today. As she said, "I never worked so hard to get back something I already owned."

Even so, my mom wasn't always so keen on my sharing stories with her about inequality in the workplace. But her position changed when she was suddenly back at work. Now I was the one who listened to her complaints!

Another important role model for me was my Minnesota violin teacher, Mary West. She taught me so much more than just the notes. Most of all, she let me shine. In my music world, girls and boys were treated equally. The only question was how well you could play. In this gender-neutral environment, I was driven to reach the top, and I never thought for a moment that I couldn't. You can imagine my shock when I entered the *real* world and discovered this thing called discrimination against women. I never saw bullying or disrespect in my musical cocoon.

I thrived in that world. But another aspect of my drive and hard work wasn't so healthy. I was obsessed with being perfect. I hated coming in second place. I set my bar very high, and when I didn't measure up—even when it was through no fault of my own—I was consumed by disappointment in myself. I would lay awake at night going over everything in my head, and the worrying didn't help much. I was overly self-critical, and never entirely satisfied with my performance.

I still struggle with perfectionist tendencies today. In fact, I call myself a recovering perfectionist. And though I've developed a thick skin after twenty-five years as a television journalist and a former Miss America, a part of me does still worry. When I feel as if I've displeased someone, or not measured up to their expectations (no matter how outlandish), my stomach still churns. You know what I'm talking about, right?

This "pleasing syndrome" commonly develops in young girls, and often follows them into adulthood. The expectations and rewards come from compliance, not resistance. It's one reason women remain silent about harassment, trying to work around it rather than confronting it. There's still so much emphasis in our culture on women and girls being quiet that it effectively drowns out their voices.

And sometimes the message is confusing. When I first started working, women were told to wear suits and be more like men. Then a decade later, we were told to embrace our feminine side. We were told to excel, but then to pull back. So, what were we supposed to do? At one point in my career, I was even instructed to not "pop," and not look too smart, so I wouldn't take attention away from anyone else. It's that kind of diminishment that can eat away at you. I'd never heard of a man being told not to "pop."

Women do not want to be unpleasant or strident—even when circumstances call for a strong reaction. They're more likely to make excuses for the men who harass them. "I didn't want to ruin his career," one woman told me, describing her reluctance to report her supervisor. He had grabbed her in a hotel elevator when they were on a business trip, but she was worried about *him*. "It was just an off night," she said. "He'd been drinking." She let it go. And when it happened again, she began to face a terrible realization: it doesn't go away because you ignore it. Abusers are encouraged by silence. They're emboldened by acquiescence. What would it mean if we all stopped being so damn nice?

Long ago, I made a conscious decision that I was going to tamp down my tendency toward perfectionism and pleasing, especially in front of my daughter. I wanted to show her that it was possible to excel without being consumed by fear and nerves.

I'm most proud of the times I've stepped way out of my comfort zone and stood up for myself—such as the time I walked off the set of a morning show when my cohost made a denigrating comment about women.

I got a lot of pushback for my actions. Some people said I was *angry*, which is a slur when used to describe women. (They love to call women angry when we're not!) I wasn't angry, and I replied that I was kidding. But that's not really true. Looking back, I think my body was telling me to leave before my mind caught up with it. It's interesting that on that day I had more positive responses from women than I ever had before. Trust me: women got it.

Still, I didn't always get a chance to show my feisty "Sparkles" side. That was OK; I was a journalist. Even when reporters achieve a certain amount of celebrity, they have to be careful not to make themselves the story. But I was always conscious of the way I had to fight for respect. And today, I can call myself a proud badass.

When I speak to women now who've also been sexually harassed or bullied or subjugated in any way, I often see myself in them. I am most struck by what powerhouses they were in their careers until they got sidelined by some random jerk. "People called me a piranha—that was my nickname," said a Wall Street trader who lost her job after she complained of harassment. "I was strong, but they took the wind out of my sails." In conversations, these women struggle to explain to me how good they were at their jobs, how professional, how tough. They want someone to know that about them. They feel diminished by the experience, weakened in the eyes of their peers, and the world. I try to assure them that what happened to them isn't an indication of strength or weakness. I've felt those self-doubts myself. But the end-game is to rise up stronger, and together, we can.

ANITA, COME BACK

When I was asked to leave my last job, it had been many years since I'd thought about Anita Hill. If I was appalled watching her being subjected to such terrible treatment by the Senate in the full view of the nation, I later comforted myself with the belief that her experience had been something of a wake-up call for America. I guess I should have known better. The culture that allowed for Anita's harassment in the first place was deeply embedded in every institution—and in the minds and hearts of too many people—for it to simply disappear. Today, more than twenty-five years after Anita sat in that chamber and was roundly belittled, we are still in the thick of it.

In 1991, at the time of Clarence Thomas's Supreme Court confirmation hearing, I was new to my first job in TV in Richmond, Virginia. Anita Hill's live testimony was one of the first stories I covered. I remember being glued to the small TV set on my office desk as she described in painful detail the sexual harassment she'd experienced while working for Thomas at the US Department of Education and then, ironically, at the EEOC.

Now, in the context of what I know today, I can see the familiar threads of a sexual harasser's behavior—the impulse to deny and blame the victim; the physical and emotional toll it took on Anita; and most of all, the tremendous courage it took to step forward. But back then, I just listened with my heart in my throat.

In her quiet, detailed testimony to the committee, Anita acknowledged that she'd had a good relationship with Thomas, and that he was something of a mentor to her. But early on in Anita's employment under Thomas at the Department of Education, he'd asked her to go out with him socially. She declined, saying she thought that a social relationship with the person supervising her was a bad idea. She figured Thomas would see it the same way. "However, to my regret," she told the Senate committee, "in the following few weeks, he continued to ask me out on several occasions. He pressed me to justify my reasons for saying no to him."

Things deteriorated further when, Anita said, Thomas frequently used their work meetings to discuss sex, including describing scenes he'd seen in pornographic films. When he was promoted to chairman of the EEOC, she said she thought carefully about whether to go with him. Ultimately, based on his recent better behavior and her strong desire to work in the civil rights arena, she decided it was safe to make the move.

She joined Thomas at the EEOC, and for the first few months there was nothing amiss. However, during the fall and winter of 1982, his sexually suggestive behavior resumed, culminating in the Coke can incident, which received wide coverage after Anita described it: "Thomas was drinking a Coke in his office. He got up from the table at which we were working, went over to his desk to get the Coke, looked at the can and asked, 'Who has put pubic hair on my Coke?'" This story particularly enraged her detractors. Senator Orrin Hatch even accused her of plagiarizing a scene from *The Exorcist.*

"Telling the world is the most difficult experience of my life," she told the senators in her restrained, quiet voice. "I may have used poor judgment early on in my relationship with this issue. I was aware, however, that telling at any point in my career could adversely affect my future career. And I did not want early on to burn all the bridges to the EEOC."

I was captivated by the Senate hearings, and can still recall my first reaction, which was to think that she was telling the truth. I wasn't exactly surprised to see that some people (especially the all-male Senate committee) didn't believe her. But I was stunned at the public shaming that Hill received. It spoke volumes about what happens when you dare to speak the truth to those in power.

Senator John Danforth openly mused that Anita must be suffering from a condition called "erotomania," in which a person is deluded in believing another person is in love with her. Other senators slammed her for not doing something about Thomas when she was working for him. The media picked up the narrative, with the conservative writer David Brock referring to Anita as "a little bit nutty and a little bit slutty," a slur on her character that was completely unfounded. (A decade later, in his book *Blinded by the Right*, Brock confessed that he had deliberately set out to destroy Hill's character.)

Thomas, who declared that Anita's testimony was part of a "high-tech lynching," was easily confirmed four days after she testified. That was a disappointment to Hill's supporters, but her treatment in the Senate had an entirely opposite result: it activated a passionate women's activism.

Thanks to Anita Hill, for a brief moment, the awareness that women were sexually harassed in the workplace got a public hearing—and many women were outraged by the way she was callously dismissed and shamed during the process. It's no accident that the 1992 election was called "the year of the woman," as many women decided to run for public office.

Coincidentally, just as that news was breaking, I was experiencing my own first encounter with workplace harassment. It was chilling, and completely unexpected. I was in a car with a cameraman I didn't know well, miles from the station, when suddenly he started talking about how much he'd enjoyed touching my breasts when he put the microphone under my blouse. He continued his graphic monologue the entire way. Alone with him, still far away from Richmond, I felt sheer terror. I was shaking like never before. It's amazing how your body reacts when in your mind you think you have everything under control. As we drove, I pressed myself against the passenger door and prayed I wouldn't have to jump out of a moving car and roll like I'd seen in movies. I wondered how much it might hurt. There were no cell phones back then; I was completely alone with him in rural Virginia, and I was panicked.

When we got back to the station, I put my head down and vowed to tell no one, but I was still trembling so badly my fingers were bouncing off the computer keys as I tried to file my story. Even all these years later, I can still see exactly where I was sitting at my desk with what seemed like the weight of the world on my shoulders, all the while hoping no one would notice me—or my shaking fingers. After all, this was my brand-new career. What I remember most is how much I *didn't* want to tell anyone, and how fearful I was of any possible repercussions to me. Like so many of the women I've spoken to, this is the first thing that comes to mind when you find yourself in one of these situations. You don't want to be blamed, and you're scared to death that it will be traced back to you. With Anita Hill's experience echoing in my mind, I wanted to avoid a similar fate.

But my boss, noticing my ashen face and trembling hands, pulled me into his office and demanded to know what had happened. I didn't want to, but feeling sick to my stomach and taking a great leap of faith, I told him. My boss was a good guy. He didn't expose me, and the cameraman was eventually let go for other reasons.

Women never forget that feeling of being helpless to stop a sexually charged incident that they did not invite. What is so upsetting is that more than twenty-five years later, I'm not sure things have really changed that much. Many of us have fooled ourselves into thinking the climate has improved, as more women enter the workforce and rise to positions of influence. I now know that it's the *silence* around sexual harassment (often reinforced by forced arbitration procedures, which I will discuss more in chapter 6) that feeds that false impression.

UNFRIENDLY FIRE IN THE MILITARY

In a nation where patriotism is revered, why does it seem that we turn a blind eye to the sexual harassment and assault that happens daily to women who choose to serve their country in the military? These are our daughters, sisters, mothers, and wives; they embark on their careers with the same idealism and ambition that anyone feels. I think that most people would admiringly call them badasses, but too often they are also victims of both sexual harassment and assault. Let's be clear that sexual harassment is a different matter than assault and rape. But I'll tell you one thing they have in common: women who report being harassed and women who report being raped can be equally not believed. And in both cases, the abuse can often be more about power than about sex. *It's about a powerful person doing something to someone who has less power.* That's why it has especially touched me to hear from so many women in the military.

THE CRISIS OF MILITARY ASSAULT

It's been more than twenty-five years since the Tailhook scandal rocked the nation. Tailhook is an association of current and retired navy and marine pilots. In 1991, at the annual Tailhook Symposium in Las Vegas, dozens of women were sexually harassed and assaulted by drunk pilots on a rampage. It came to light only in 1992, when Lt. Paula Coughlin reported that she had been sexually assaulted. Coughlin, a helicopter pilot and admiral's aide, related a terrifying incident that occurred in a hallway of the Las Vegas Hilton. On her way to her room she encountered a large gathering of very drunk pilots, who formed a gauntlet, touching her, ripping her clothes, and trying to drag her to the ground. She thought she was going to be gang-raped. Coughlin finally made it to her room, shaken and distraught. It would later come out that other women were also forced to walk the gauntlet over a three-day period.

When Coughlin reported the incident to her boss, Rear Admiral John Snyder, he told her, "That's what you get when you go to a hotel party with a bunch of drunk aviators." But Coughlin persisted, and in mid-1992 her report became public, shocking the nation and bringing swift outrage from the George H. W. Bush administration. The Defense Department conducted a full investigation, unraveling a tradition of sexually assaultive practices that were commonplace.

Most people probably figure that Tailhook was part of the "bad old days." But the culture that made Tailhook commonplace still exists in today's military. Paula Coughlin is currently on the board of directors of Protect Our Defenders, an organization whose mission is to end the epidemic of rape and sexual harassment in the military. And assault in the military remains an urgent issue.

Missouri senator Claire McCaskill and New York senator Kirsten Gillibrand are working diligently to change that. In 2015, McCaskill successfully sponsored a bill that increased protections for military sexual assault victims. Senator McCaskill, who was a career prosecutor before entering politics, told me, "When I started working on this, seven or eight years ago, I realized the military is where the civilian criminal justice system was back in the eighties, when back in my state, it was still legal to rape your wife. There was not the rape shield law. You could make inquiries in court about someone's sexual history and how many partners they've had, and what kind of birth control they use. They weren't even holding onto the rape kit evidence for longer than six months within the military. There was this horrible situation, so we began, and we have changed wholesale, the power the commanders have. We've turned the old system on its head."

The sweeping reforms enacted into law through the efforts of McCaskill and Gillibrand include:

- Establishing a Special Victims' Counsel, which has no parallel in the United States, even in the civilian justice system. Every victim who reports an assault gets assigned his/her own independent lawyer to protect their rights and fight for their interests.
- Eliminating the "good soldier" defense, which held that if a soldier accused of rape had an otherwise sterling *military* record, the case was automatically weighted in his favor, under the unbelievable assumption that a good soldier could not have done a bad thing.
- Requiring a minimum sentence of dishonorable discharge for anyone convicted of sexual assault.
- Giving more deference to women reporting sexual assault— eliminating the statute of limitations for reporting, and allowing

them to challenge their discharge when it occurs in the context of sexual assault.

These are important developments, but Senator Gillibrand argues that they don't go far enough. Since commanders, not prosecutors, decide the validity of sexual assault claims, Gillibrand believes this can—and does—lead to abuse of power and retaliation. When I interviewed her, Senator Gillibrand was bullish on this point. "My concern is that we don't have a criminal justice system in the military that is worthy of the sacrifice that men and women actually make," she said. "To have a climate where last year there were twenty thousand estimated incidents of unwanted sexual contact, sexual assault, and rape in the military is unconscionable. And only two in ten report it."

She added that among those who do report, 62 percent describe suffering retaliation. "They have reported retaliation either administratively or peer to peer. More than half of these retaliations are coming from within the chain of command. So, we really have to get the decision point out of the chain of command and give it to somebody who is actually trained. A real lawyer, a real prosecutor, who doesn't necessarily know the victim or the accused, and can make an unbiased judgment based on the facts and evidence alone." Although Gillibrand introduced legislation in 2015 and 2016, with some Republican support, to date it has not passed.

Speaking with female military veterans, I began to understand the gravity of the crisis. Sandra, who was medically discharged from the air force, was only nineteen when she joined the military. Here is her story.

One evening, Sandra and a female friend were relaxing and drinking beers, and joking with a few of the guys at a bar on the base. Sandra says that one of them tried to kiss her, but she wiggled out of his grasp and went back to her trailer. Late that night she woke to find two men in her room, touching her sexually. One of them was the guy from the bar. Struggling to wake up, she tried to push them off and kept telling them to stop. But she didn't scream. "A girl on my base had reported being raped," she said, "and everyone hated her because they said she made the squadron look bad. I thought I was going to get in trouble."

After a friend took her to the hospital, Sandra's commander told her she must file a complaint. He treated her rape claim seriously, but also recommended that she not seek a judicial remedy against the men. He didn't think she could win, because "you didn't scream and act like a normal rape victim." Sandra says her attackers were merely punished with a reduction in rank and pay, but never prosecuted for the sexual assault.

Sandra was haunted by the conclusion that her failure to scream made her less credible. When she came out of the military, she tried counseling and antidepressants, but it was difficult to get care. There was no "rape" box to check off on the veteran medical claim. But Sandra is not completely powerless. "I'm raising my boys differently— that's how change happens," she said.

Still, assault and rape remain at crisis levels in the military. In 2014, the Department of Defense Sexual Assault Prevention and Response Office enlisted the RAND Corporation (RAND being an acronym for research and development) to assess the rates of sexual assault, harassment, and gender discrimination in the military. The study surveyed more than a half a million service members, finding that a whopping 20,300 active-duty members (1 percent of men and nearly 5 percent of women) had been sexually assaulted in just the year prior to the survey. And an estimated 116,600 members (22 percent of women and 7 percent of men) had been sexually harassed in the same period. That's unacceptable.

And both male and female veterans who suffer sexual assault in the military are at higher risk for homelessness and suicide. According to Lyndsay Ayer, who studies military suicide for RAND, rape is one of the most common issues female veterans talk about when calling suicide crisis lines, and the inadequate way they believe the military handles it. When women in crisis are sidelined, ignored or blamed, the experience becomes a new form of trauma.

THE DRIP, DRIP, DRIP OF MISOGYNY

While rape in the military is a horrific issue, female service members also report facing persistent misogyny in their daily lives. The daily drip, drip, drip of harassment is like torture. When I spoke with Elizabeth, I was reminded of myself. Like me, she was raised in a warm, loving family and with the belief she could do anything. She never had an inkling that being a woman would set her back. In fact, she remembers her puzzlement when she went to college and heard so many people talking about women's rights issues. She didn't understand it, because she'd never experienced it. Beautiful, fit, and strong, with a sharp mind and outgoing personality, she seemed set on a path of success. Elizabeth was a badass.

After 9/11, she was inspired to join the army, and started active duty after graduation, but says she immediately found that her looks and gender took precedence over her skills and commitment. ("Now I knew what those women in college were talking about!" she said.)

During her active-duty career, Elizabeth says her safety was first jeopardized at a two-month military training exercise with her lieutenant peers. Late one weekend evening, Elizabeth was shocked to discover that one of them had broken into her barracks room. This is what she told me: "As I opened my door, I noticed only one person in the room, and he was lying on my bed. Who in the world was he? A little frightened, I tried to poke my head into the room just enough to try to discover his identity. I soon recognized him as a member of my platoon. Feeling slightly less frightened, I walked straight up to my bedside, and forcefully asked, 'What are you doing in here?' He said, 'I'm just lying down, come lay next to me.' I immediately shouted, '*Get out of my room!*' He refused. I continued to shout the same demand. And, after many failed attempts, I finally leaned down to yell straight in his ear: 'GET THE F——K OUT OF MY ROOM!' He finally relented and left, grumbling, 'Fine . . . *geez.*'"

That was the first instance of threatening behavior and harassment. After that experience, Elizabeth says she was subjected to significant bullying every day, rude comments and sexual teasing by her peers, leaders and even subordinates. "You should use that body for kinky sex and one-night stands," one soldier told her.

The harassment escalated, with several soldiers constantly urging her to go to strip clubs. One evening she was working on her computer and was called into another room, where she found four men sitting in front of an upright pole with dollar bills in their mouths. "Dance for us," they cried, waving the money at her. When she initially raised concerns to superior officers, she says one major responded, "What—only a dollar? She's at least worth five or ten."

Elizabeth was crushed by these experiences, and it was especially galling to have her complaint dismissed so casually. *She* was the men's superior officer, and according to article 89 of the Uniform Code of Military Justice, "any person subject to this chapter who behaves with disrespect toward his superior commissioned officer shall be punished as a court-martial may direct." Clearly, she thought to herself, article 89 didn't apply to women officers.

"I came into the military with so much drive," she said, "and suddenly a significant goal was to protect myself from being assaulted." Serving in the military, Elizabeth felt as if she was fighting three wars: the first was the real war, the second to protect herself, and the third to gain respect.

In the years since she left the military, Elizabeth has never stopped striving and believing in herself. Rather than being embittered by her experience, she has reached out to other female veterans. "We were never treated as part of the team while serving, or as veterans," she said. Together, they give each other the support they never received from the military. Together, they can do better for one another.

Elizabeth's impulse to come together in a support community was a way to take back her power. The support of other women can make all the difference. I've spent most of my life in competitive environments where winning meant standing out. It was true in violin competitions. It was true in the Miss America pageant. It's been true in television broadcasting. Not that I didn't have a support system of family, friends, and colleagues—but I was used to being evaluated for what I alone did.

Today, I have a dramatically different experience and perspective. The goal of ending sexual harassment requires a level of collaboration I've never encountered before. It's like a chain of inspiration. If this has happened to you, this is an example of how you can use your own experience as empowerment. Sharing your story is the first step. And every time a new woman steps forward, a few others see that they can do it, too.

As I learned when I interviewed McCaskill and Gillibrand, even powerful women senators face sexual harassment on the job. McCaskill recalled her own experience when she was first elected to the Missouri House of Representatives. "As a new legislator, I went up to the Speaker of the House and asked his advice about how to get a bill out of committee. He asked me if I'd brought my knee pads."

Like many strong women, McCaskill believed she could simply outwit the harassers. "At every juncture of my career when I've encountered this, I've always internalized it," she said. "I've always used it as fuel: 'I'll show them. I'll be better and smarter than they are. I'll go farther than they did.'" But the senator acknowledged that it wasn't enough, and told me what I had done in taking the next step was what she wished she had done.

In her 2014 book, *Off the Sidelines: Speak Up, Be Fearless, and Change Your World*, Senator Gillibrand also tells stories of being sexually harassed—right on the Senate floor. One older senator commented, "Good thing you're working out, because you wouldn't want to get porky." Another Senate colleague said to her, "You know, Kirsten, you're even pretty when you're fat." One said, "I like my girls chubby." Another suggested she'd better lose weight to be beautiful again, so she could win the election.

When her book came out, Gillibrand was criticized in the media for not giving the names of the senators who said these things. But she told me she shared those stories for one important reason. "I was trying to teach young women, 'Please don't ever feel underestimated. Just because they say something that is inappropriate or unkind, it doesn't mean it has to affect you. You can push past it.'"

Even though it can be tough to be a badass, whether in the military or on the Senate floor, don't worry, senators. We are listening and are ready to be fierce.

THREE

Don't Rob My Dream!

've been a fighter my whole life. When someone tells me I can't do something, I do it better. When someone has called me a blond bimbo, I've studied harder. When I had to get into world-class shape to compete as a short girl in the Miss America pageant, I willed myself to learn how to run (and I was a fat kid who dreaded running one block!), working up to six miles a day with my toes bleeding. When my own grandfather told me I was too short to be Miss America, I said "No, I'm not" and empowered myself through research. I found out that the very first Miss America in 1921 had been two inches shorter than me. The fire in my belly, which urges me to push and pull and grapple and claw and fight to the bitter end, has been with me since day one. I don't know anything else. I have always believed and fought for the American dream.

But there's something else, too, and maybe you can identify with this. I didn't just want to be driven; I wanted to restore my sense of joy too, after what happened to me. In the early days after my story broke, I felt insecure and self-conscious, and my natural instinct was to keep my head down. I was vulnerable.

Less than two weeks after the first news reports came out, I was scheduled to take my daughter to a Justin Bieber concert at Madison Square Garden in New York City. Given the circumstances, it would not be an understatement to say that I wasn't looking forward to attending a big public event. But to my delight, it couldn't have been more uneventful—which was incredibly empowering. While I wasn't sure what to expect, it ended up proving to me that I could leave the house, move on with my life, sing out loud, and not be fearful. While I didn't know every Bieber song, I have to say that he gives one heck of a concert. And on that night—that special night—I was liberated. Being with my teenage daughter, seeing the joy on her face, dancing and singing at the top of our lungs, I knew that life would go on. Not only that, but I would triumph. I could be happy.

THIEVES IN OUR WORKPLACES

"What do you want to be when you grow up?" We ask our children this question all the time. There's something profound and almost magical about those early dreams. For many of us, our first expression of what we want to "be" sticks. In effect, the dream comes true. When you've wanted something and prepared for it your whole life, you're on top of the world when you achieve it.

Now imagine having it all taken away, in an instant, arbitrarily, because your boss or someone you work with makes an inappropriate advance. You complain; you go through the channels as you've been told to do. But the channels (usually HR) fail to protect you. There is retaliation; you're fired, laid off, or forced to quit. And just like that, your career—the one you've been planning and training for over all those years—is over. You're labeled a troublemaker, blackballed in your industry, and you have absolutely no recourse. The culture is stronger than the law.

Sadly, I know this to be commonplace because I've spoken to many, many women who've told exactly this story. Blindsided early in their careers, they were heartbroken. And I was heartbroken for them. Listening on the phone to a young entrepreneur who told me through tears, "My dream job was a nightmare," I had no words to comfort her. After nearly a year of harassment by a lascivious colleague whose words and antics everyone just laughed off, she took a complaint to HR.

After that, she said, everything changed. No one would speak to her; she had to live with resentment every day, even as she put on a cheerful demeanor to do her job. She told me she was eventually pushed out and is still unable to find another job. The interviews initially go well, and then it's like the prospective employer finds out she did "that thing"—sticking up for herself and filing a complaint after being wronged—and now she's "one of those." I was outraged on her behalf. Her young career was sidetracked solely because, as I've seen time and again, the company seemed to want to protect the harasser more than the woman who complained, and so many others stood by and let it happen. It's incomprehensible to me why we sideline the people who stand up for themselves, while making excuses for those whose words and actions are morally corrupt. It seems completely upside down. Supporting a woman who finally decides to come forward makes the workplace better for *everyone*.

My mind goes back to my first job in television. It's a very competitive industry, and I experienced my share of rejections before I landed a job. It was for a local station, and the pay was less than $20,000 a year, but I felt as if I'd won the lottery. There was only one small blip in getting hired. When my future boss read my application and saw that I'd been Miss America, he told me that he wasn't sure if he could hire me, because he said his wife didn't even allow him to watch the pageant. But I persevered and sent my tape to him overnight anyway. Luckily, my grades, skills, and TV reel won out, and he was a good boss and mentor.

I truly believe that he was the rule, and not the exception. In fact, most of the men I've worked for and with over my career would not dream of treating women disrespectfully—they would, in fact, stand up for them if they saw others doing so. Unfortunately, the Neanderthals in our workplaces are often people of power and influence who are able to get away with their behavior because so many are afraid to challenge them. For them, young women are prey, and they don't care if their abusive behaviors destroy these women's lives.

"If this hadn't happened to me, I'd be running a top firm by now,"

Sophia said to me, describing how she'd been harassed by her boss and fired twenty years earlier. "I've struggled in every job since. That man killed my dream."

Her dream was to have a career in advertising, and Sophia was thrilled when she got a job at a New York agency. She was twenty-three years old, an overachiever with several internships under her belt. Sophia described herself as upbeat and jovial, able to get along in a work environment that was relaxed and easygoing. "I was not a person who couldn't take a joke," she said, even though some of the behavior harkened back to an era she thought was over—such as hiring strippers to perform for the boss's birthday.

On her first business trip, she was happy to be invited to have a cocktail with two top executives from her firm. But she says she wasn't prepared for what happened over drinks. At one point, she said, they started to write a list on a cocktail napkin of the things she could get in exchange for sexual favors, such as a raise and an office with a window. Sophia was uncomfortable, but she thought they were joking, so she played along.

Then new management took over, and was not happy to hear the stories about the sexualized culture—and began questioning people about it. Suddenly, Sophia found herself in the role of witness, and she says many of the guys in the office turned against her. So did her boss. In spite of her impressive work record, she says he put her on probation and then fired her.

Sophia was devastated. She hired a lawyer and filed a complaint with the EEOC, but the outcome was discouraging. She ended up with a small amount of money and a career she says could not be salvaged. Today she talks of the "ripple effect" of sexual harassment. "I feel as if I have this terrible scar," she said all these years later. "If employers find out, they won't want me."

Sophia's collapsing self-esteem is consistent with findings of a 2011 study published in the *Society and Mental Health Journal* that sexual harassment *early in the career* has long-term effects on depressive symptoms in adulthood. In Sophia's case, long after she achieved some success in her field and even started her own company, she remained stuck in a mentality that she's still not good enough. Having been disposed of so unfairly and randomly, she says she's been constantly on the lookout for other employers to throw her out "like trash" too.

FIGHT OR FLIGHT

"Why didn't you just leave?" This was said to me, and I've heard it said to others. During the 2016 presidential campaign, Donald Trump commented to the reporter Kirsten Powers of *USA Today* that if his daughter Ivanka were sexually harassed, "I'd like to think she would find another career, or find another company." Powers wrote, "His reply was startling, even by Trumpian standards."

The following day, while appearing on *CBS This Morning*, Eric Trump was asked by Charlie Rose about what his father had said. Eric defended him: "I think what he's saying is, Ivanka is a strong, powerful woman, she wouldn't allow herself to be objected [*sic*] to it . . ."

So there you have it—two statements, two myths: One, that women who are harassed should just find another job or career. Two, that strong women don't get harassed.

I decided to react to the statements and tweeted:

Sad in 2016 we're still victim blaming women.
Trust me I'm strong.

It was one of the most retweeted tweets I've ever sent. But when asked again to clarify his comments in a *Washington Post* interview, Donald Trump seemed perplexed by the uproar. "I'm surprised people are talking about that," he said.

Well, people *were* talking about it because those two statements were from the Dark Ages. It's easy to say, "Just leave" if your father is wealthy and powerful, and can get you a job in any industry. What about a woman who supports herself and her family, and doesn't have the option to just go elsewhere? What about a woman who loves her career, and doesn't want to give it up? What about a woman who has followed the American dream and worked and studied and busted her ass for years to achieve success in her field and deserves to be there? It's also ludicrous to say that being strong shields you from harassment. Trust me, most of the women I've talked to are strong, and being strong or weak does not determine whether or not you will be sexually harassed!

One of the strong women I'm speaking of is Fredericka, who had a good job in law enforcement, and whose dream was to someday get into the FBI. She excelled in her work and was physically fit and strong. She was going places. But that was before she says her boss got drunk at a company party, isolating her on a back patio, kissing her and propositioning her. Fredericka says she pushed him away and told him that she wasn't interested in sleeping with him. But he wouldn't stop. Later, she says he cornered her in his office, kissing her and rubbing his erection against her. Like I said, she was strong and she fought back. But he was her supervisor and he held all the power. After that, "he made my life a living hell," she told me. In the end, Fredericka decided to leave. But that meant giving up the profession that she loved because she was stigmatized and blackballed. She told me she is haunted by the unnecessary agony that took away her career. For her, and so many others, being strong isn't enough.

HARASSED OUT OF SCIENCE

So many women these days are striving for a new kind of American dream in STEM fields (science, technology, engineering, and math). But discouragingly, in a study of women in these fields, the *Atlantic* found that women are literally being harassed out of science. One of those women is Nathalie Gosset. Nathalie, who for twelve years worked for the University of Southern California's Alfred E. Mann Institute for Biomedical Engineering, had advanced quickly in her career to become a senior director of marketing and technology innovation evaluation. She loved her job, and as the only woman in management, she did not feel undercut in any way. For Nathalie, it was all about the team, and her team was outstanding. There was never a hint that any of the men had a problem with their female leader. "My brain and communication skills were the great equalizers," she said. "The men working for me saw me as a leader, and I inspired a sense of equality. It was all about what our team could do."

Then a new boss came to town. In the beginning, Nathalie didn't have much interaction with him. But after the first year, he held more frequent meetings in which Nathalie says his language was shockingly vulgar. She claims he openly talked about his sex life in group meetings, making her cringe. She noted that her male coworkers seemed uncomfortable at first too, but eventually somehow got used to it. "It's the contamination factor," she said. "If the boss is loose and vulgar, it gives permission for others. I could feel the culture shifting."

Nathalie said that in the beginning, she felt that she "just needed to be quiet, because I thought eventually he'd run out of things to say, and stop." But he didn't. She finally felt she had to say something, and reached out to HR—the proper thing to do. Unfortunately, she says, the response was less than supportive. The HR representative wondered about Nathalie's motives and perceptions, and even asked her, "Are you sure it was *him*?"

Nathalie was flummoxed. Was she sure it was *him*? That seemed to defy logic. Nathalie also says the HR representative wondered aloud if Nathalie had "unresolved father-daughter issues."

After the HR report, she says her boss began to shut her out, refusing to speak to her, making it hard for Nathalie to do her job. She recalls that he also came into her office several times and threatened her and rallied the other employees against her.

Soon after, Nathalie was told that her job function had been eliminated, and she was presented with termination papers. She was out the door in just ten minutes after twelve years.

This becomes not only a story of injustice to one woman, but also a depressing story for all women who work in STEM. Nathalie had always been active in encouraging young women to go into this field. She still believed in it, but what could she tell them now? What would she tell her own college-age daughter?

In the months after she was fired, Nathalie felt traumatized, and suffered panic attacks and sleepless nights. She frequently burst into tears. She felt crushed by the unfairness of the situation—her career derailed because of a guy who she says couldn't handle the fact that a woman stood up to him.

In October 2016, Nathalie hired Lisa Bloom and filed a lawsuit claiming sexual harassment, workplace discrimination, and wrongful termination. Her former boss has not issued a statement, but USC released this statement challenging Nathalie's claim, stating, "The allegations in the case of Nathalie Gosset are without merit. The University will defend itself and those named in the suit vigorously." The entire legal process is still ongoing as of this writing.

Some stories of women's success in STEM have gone unreported until recently—like the story of Katherine Johnson, one of the African American female mathematicians at NASA featured in the movie *Hidden Figures.* When we think our challenges are impossible to overcome, Johnson and her female colleagues show us that nothing is impossible. These women worked at NASA in the 1960s, when their division was racially segregated and they had little chance of advancement. But Johnson proved herself to be so brilliant that the astronaut John Glenn relied on her as the "human computer" to make sure all of the calculations for reentry into the earth's atmosphere were correct during his first solo spaceflight orbiting the earth. In 2016, when *Hidden Figures* was nominated for Best Picture at the Academy Awards, the actresses who starred in the film wheeled Johnson, then ninety-eight, onto the stage. For that moment, a female African American scientist from the 1960s was a rock star. While I watched with my children I was incredibly moved and elated to see her receive this long-overdue recognition. Now, I can only hope that we keep that image alive, so that young women today can take their rightful places in the world of science and fully realize the American dream.

WOMEN OF A CERTAIN AGE

Harassment and discrimination go hand in hand, and nowhere is this more exemplified than in tech industries. The young male culture of the tech world can make it particularly hard for older workers to gain a foothold, and this is especially true for women.

But the problem is pervasive in all types of workplaces, not just tech. The National Bureau of Economic Research conducted a massive field experiment, involving more than forty thousand résumés and responses in a variety of fields. The study showed that older women get fewer callbacks than older men, as well as fewer than younger men and women. The study's authors, David Neumark and Ian Burn of the University of California, Irvine, and Patrick Button of Tulane University, designed forty thousand fake résumés that accurately presented typical candidates at various ages and levels of experience. There were three age brackets: twenty-nine to thirty-one, forty-nine to fifty-one, and sixty-four to sixty-six. The researchers sent applications to jobs in four categories in a dozen cities, in response to online ads. "Workers" age forty-nine to fifty-one got 18 percent fewer callbacks than those age twenty-nine to thirty-one. Those who were sixty-four to sixty-six got 35 percent fewer callbacks. But even the middle group seemed to have aged out— *when the candidates were women.* In one study example of a women-only job search, those who were age forty-nine to fifty-one applying for administrative jobs received 29 percent fewer callbacks than those aged twenty-nine to thirty-one. In other categories in which the genders were separated, older men got many more callbacks than older women.

In the tech industry, where the numbers of women are actually on the decline over the last decade, combining age discrimination (worse for women) with sex discrimination can mean a near-total shutout. That's what Claudia says she experienced at age forty-eight. When the family engineering business where she'd worked for many years was sold to a thirty-year-old man, he didn't even try to hide the fact that he was seeking to hire younger people—not just because they were cheaper, but because he thought they were better, more creative, and more in line with the type of company he wanted. When Claudia

brought him the résumés of experienced people with exceptional credentials, he rejected them, telling her, "I want someone young."

She watched this boss push out several other women who had
apparently reached their "sell-by" dates, but she was still unprepared
when it happened to her. Since she was an at-will employee, she didn't
believe that she had a good legal case to fight her termination. She just
left, feeling deeply demoralized.

"I was raised by a hardworking mother who, with the exception of
vacation days, only missed two days of work in twenty years," Claudia
said. "I followed her lead and became a strong, independent woman.
I was happy and upbeat. I had so many things to be grateful for—a
home, a wonderful husband, a mom who doted on me, a job I loved.
This incident turned my life upside down."

According to a PBS report, older women now make up half of the
long-term unemployed. So what is the definition of "older"? Joanna
Lahey, an economist and expert on age discrimination, says it can
begin as young as age thirty-five for women. "There have been several studies done where companies are asked, 'Well, why do you think
other people might discriminate against older workers?' And reasons
given include worries that they're not good at technology, that they
don't have computer skills. There are worries that they're not active,
that they're slow, that they're not willing to embrace change."

Lahey noted that women are far less likely to sue for age discrimination than middle-aged white male workers. But it's worth it for
women to start making their case. If "aging out" starts at thirty-five
for women, someone has to put on the brakes.

Keep in mind that age discrimination is just one of a long list of
gender inequalities that women experience, both in and out of the
workplace. In fact, a study released in October 2016 found that the
United States ranked thirty-second in a global index of gender equality, below Kazakhstan and Algeria. That is unacceptable, proving we
have a lot of work to do!

One way to do that work is to inspire young people to fight for
equality and respect. The impact of sexual harassment on young

women just starting out in their careers can be dramatic and lasting. Juliana, now in her forties, has achieved success and satisfaction in her career in public service, but she has never forgotten the experience of being a vulnerable twenty-one-year-old subjected to sexual harassment in her first job working for a studio executive. Going into that job, she remembered, "I was on top of the world. I thought I was going to conquer the movie business." Instead, she was demoralized and intimidated by her powerful boss, who would call her a dufus and tell her, "You don't think; that's my job." Furthermore, his overt sexism and vulgar references to her body—"You have the best tits in Hollywood"—made her so miserable that she finally quit. "What happened to me in those two years shaped my view of the world," she said. "I never got over it. It's always been in the back of my mind. My optimism was shaken to the core."

Juliana wishes we would see these young women like herself, listen to them and understand that their worldviews are being shaped by these experiences. "They're at their most vulnerable, and the power differential is great," she said, emphasizing that sexual harassment is not about sex but power. "The disparity of power in our culture makes the issue worse," she said. "People are desperate for employment, and it makes them vulnerable."

When Juliana was trying to figure out what to do in her own situation, she went to two lawyer friends, a woman and a man, for advice. Her woman friend told her not to do anything if she wanted to continue to work in the business. Reporting the harassment would ruin her. Her male friend had the opposite advice: "Go for it." Later she better understood why her female friend advised caution. "As a woman, she was already preconditioned to stay safe, keep it under wraps, protect oneself, take it and move on. Whereas the male lawyer was like, 'Go get 'em tiger,' because that's what men are trained to do—take on the conflict."

She views what she experienced, although easily referred to as sexual harassment, as "actually a type of psychological warfare in which the only possible winner was the guy with the power. The ability to manipulate people is key to being a successful sexual harasser. If you aren't able to make your victim feel that she is responsible for the behavior, that somehow, someway, the victim encouraged the contact, the touching, the comments, engaged the harasser, then the harasser isn't really that good. That's why most victims walk away in shame and blame themselves, and why most victims don't ever report the harassment. Instead, they think, *If only I didn't respond with a smile, if only I had said something in a firm tone objecting to the vile behavior, if only, if only, if only, if only . . .*"

Juliana believes it is important to teach and encourage women to speak up. But her public service work has also given her tremendous compassion for all those who don't feel as if they have the option of quitting or speaking out because they need to keep their jobs.

In advocating for change, Juliana challenges us to think about what we want for our daughters and the women of their generation, who enter the workplace with the same level of excitement and optimism she once had. Are we willing to accept that they too will be permanently harmed by people in power sexually harassing them just because they can?

WARRIORS ON CAMPUS

If adult professional women have a hard time being respected and believed, it's much harder for young women on college campuses. I want to speak to those young women now. For many of you, your independent lives start in college, where you can find yourselves navigating some pretty tough terrain. It's both a training ground for adult life and a setting that can be dangerous. As parents, educators, and students, and as a society that cares about our young people, we must fight together to change this.

I can still remember the wonderful sense of freedom I felt when I left home for college at Stanford University. California was a long way away from Minnesota. And even though it wasn't my first time away from home—I had spent all those summers at the Aspen Music Festival when I played the violin—college was the first time I could really be myself, away from my parents. It's an incredibly important time for young people as they learn to spread their wings, independent of parental oversight. Like most college students, I sometimes tested my limits and did things my parents probably wouldn't have always condoned, but that's part of growing up. I took risks because like so many other young people, I, too, thought I was invincible. To a certain extent, that's what college is all about: learning to live as an adult, sometimes making mistakes and picking yourself up again. But to the young people reading this and to their parents, know that it's also a time to be aware and prepared.

Kids today face so many additional challenges when they go off to college than kids in my generation did. Public stories about campus assault, fraternity parties that end in death, and social media shaming campaigns against young women are scary indicators that we are sending our kids to places that may not have the appropriate safety nets to catch them if they fall.

A large study released by the Department of Justice in 2016 shows that campus sexual assault is a major problem. The DOJ polled thousands of students in nine universities about their experiences with this issue. The survey included colleges and universities in different parts of the country, both two- and four-year schools. The results were astounding. One in five undergraduate women said they had experienced sexual assault, and only 12.5 percent of students who said they were raped actually reported it. Who is not shocked by these statistics?

One young woman told me of an experience that seemed all too typical. "When I was a sophomore in college (nineteen at the time)," she related, "I was sleeping on a couch with a couple of my college girlfriends after a party, and I woke up to discover a man with his hand shoved down my pants. I was so completely terrified and shocked that I did not realize I was awake, and thought at first that I must be in the middle of a nightmare. I could not see the man, as the room was dark, but I could feel his large hand when I reached down to pull his arm off my small body. I suddenly jerked up to realize that the man had sneaked into the room I was sleeping in, and had laid his body flat on the ground in order to reach over the couch on which I was sleeping and grab my private areas, without anyone seeing him, including me. The man had shoved his arm under all my covers and blankets, pulled up my shirt and pants, and assaulted me—all while I was asleep and did not feel his presence until it was too late. When I awoke, he jumped up to his feet and quietly ran out of the room without closing the door behind him."

She told me that she kept silent about the assault for three years. She says she felt intimidated. She was studying at a school with a primarily male student body, and didn't want to call attention to herself in this way. But a few months before graduating, she finally decided to report her assault to the university. "By going public about your mistreatment, you gave me the courage to take the steps to report my mistreatment," she told me. "I held my head high as I sat through meetings with the university's lawyers, multiple Title IX staff, and representatives from university fraternities (that was a tough one) who questioned my motives for coming forward. I did not sue anyone or any institution, nor did I want to. I merely wanted to go on record about my assault on the campus of a school where I was not the first young woman to have her private parts touched by a predator."

It's not surprising that she was so reluctant to report her assault. According to organizations that study this issue, young women in these situations fear that they will be grilled about their own behaviors, and ultimately blamed with questions like these:

What were you wearing?
How much were you drinking?
Did you flirt with him?
Were you walking alone?
Are you sure you said no?

They're asked, "What did you expect, dressed like that?" They're challenged, "Why were you at that party drinking—didn't you know what could happen?" It's confusing and demeaning. And parents might not always be sympathetic. "How could you put yourself in that situation?" they might ask. "I thought you had a good head on your shoulders."

We can tell our daughters to be careful. We can *beg* them to be careful. We can even give them strategies to avoid sexual assault. But these numbers wash over us in an overwhelming wave. The hard reality is that some of our daughters will be sexually assaulted on campus. It's a fear that eats at us. If we're being honest, we worry about our daughters. But in my mind, we need to worry about both our daughters and our *sons* to change the mind-sets that create victimizers, victims, and silent bystanders.

My daughter is a few years away from entering college, but already I'm thinking about it and trying to plant the seeds, building her confidence and self-esteem so she'll be prepared to stand on her own. But our advice to our kids also needs to be more specific, to address the realities they may face on college campuses. We have to prepare our daughters like the other warriors in this book—with real tools and weapons in their arsenals. If my daughter was about to leave for college today, here's the advice I would give her:

Know who your friends are: It's easy to assume that a campus is just a big family, and everyone is equally trustworthy. But you can't let your guard down merely because you're in a group of randomly affiliated people who happen to go to your school. Be sure you have your friend posse, a group of people you can trust to be on your side in every situation.

Take steps to protect yourself: Let's face it: anyone who's ever been to college knows that drinking alcohol is a major part of the social life. But imbibing can also become a major factor in campus sexual assault. Make some rules: Never take a drink from a stranger. Don't leave a drink unattended. Create a protective net before you go to a party; establish a "safe word" with friends, who can help if necessary, and get you out of a situation if you feel that you've had too much to drink, or are being threatened. It's a word that you can say to a friend who will recognize it as a call for help. It's a word you can text to a friend who will know you aren't safe. It's a word you can call or text to your parents—even if they are far away—to let them know something isn't right.

Stay in touch: For many of us, going off to college is the first time we live away from home for an extended period. Sure, we may have gone to summer camps, but college is different. No camp counselors to look after you, or parents to come home to every night. This is why I believe it's so important for parents to establish a relationship of trust with their kids, to encourage them to always be honest with us, even if the news they're telling us isn't good. I believe that kids are safer when their parents are in the loop. Hopefully, you have this kind of relationship, or can start to build it now. (Parents, this trust building starts young. See chapter 9 for more on this topic.) For the kids now away from home, here's my advice. As much as you want to assert yourself and be independent, keep in touch with your family and your roots. Make that weekly phone call. Use your parents as a sounding board. Let them help you problem-solve issues that arise for you, not just in the classroom, but on campus too. There's something about just talking to Mom or Dad that can remind us about how we grew up, and what our expectations have been.

If you're a student reading this and rolling your eyes because it sounds like typical stuff that parents say to keep their kids close, let me add a little perspective. We never stop being our parents' children, even when we get older. And their advice can mean a lot; I know I feel that way about my parents. It's funny how struggle and crisis can crystallize the meaning of this most important relationship.

That was especially crucial for me in the spring of 2016. I needed guidance and support like never before. I can still see myself sitting on my back hallway bench in the dark of the night when the call came in. Both of my parents were on the line. They wanted to let me know they were in my court—that no matter what, they stood with and beside me as I was contemplating jumping off my cliff. Even though I was approaching fifty, my parents' support and advice *meant* something.

Sure, I was adept at making decisions on my own. But that didn't mean I couldn't gain wisdom and courage from those irreplaceable stalwarts in my life.

Find a passion beyond partying: Getting involved with organizations and pursuing meaningful projects will make you stronger and better able to cope in social situations. It will ground you, and increase your sense of worth. Being more involved in a variety of activities can also keep you out of trouble, and create new friendship groups, more people you can trust and lean on if necessary. Choose activities that empower you and give you a forum to speak out about issues you believe in. Always ask how you can be your best self.

These are tools that can help on a personal level. But we also have to ask what colleges and the larger society can do to make campuses safe for our children. I believe that such an improvement begins with a no-tolerance policy for sexual harassment. Experts have said sexual harassment on campus is a gateway crime to assault. Research by Cornell's ILR School shows that public harassment—vulgar words and displays directed mostly at girls—has an emotional impact that is similar to sexual assault. It leads to the same kind of feelings of low self-esteem and depression, and it also makes girls feel less safe. It fills them with self-doubt about what they wear, where they go, and what they do on campus. Hollaback!, an organization devoted to ending public sexual harassment, surveyed college students, and found that 20 percent of them said harassment caused an inability to concentrate in class, while 23 percent said that harassment prevented attendance in class. That's awful! It obviously has an impact on these young lives, and we need to start taking it seriously, long before these behaviors make their way into the workplace.

Some colleges are stepping up and creating mandatory sexual harassment training for students. For example, the University of Kansas requires all students to take sexual harassment training. Its firm policy states: "The University of Kansas is committed to a safe environment where every community member (students, faculty, and staff) can pursue their education without interference. Sexual violence is one of the most unreported crimes on college campuses. Because the University is committed to preventing sexual violence, a mandatory Sexual Harassment Education Training is required annually for all students." Failure to complete the training by the deadline results in a hold on a student's record that will prevent enrollment for the following year.

This training is a fantastic idea. Programs like this send a clear message that any form of sexual harassment will not be tolerated. That's how the culture begins to change: when institutions make it their policy to fight harassment. I'd like to see sexual harassment training on every college campus. And this training should not be just abstract preaching; it should really show students what harassment looks like and how it feels. I highly recommend you watch a series of short films called #*ThatsHarassment*, produced by the actor/director David Schwimmer, Israeli American director Sigal Avin, and Mazdack Rassi of Milk Studios. The idea originated with Avin, who had produced a similar series in Israel. "When she called and wanted to see if something like it would resonate in the United States, it was a no brainer," Schwimmer told me. "It was perfect timing"—with so much talk about sexual harassment. "I knew we had to act fast to get these made."

The films are some of the most striking and realistic interpretations of sexual harassment I've seen. They consist of scenes that typify everyday harassment—in a doctor's office, by a boss, by a coworker, by a politician to a journalist, by a photographer to a model—with the aim of showing what sexual harassment looks like in seemingly normal encounters. The films resonated with me. Often people tell me they don't really understand what sexual harassment is. These videos show it in clear ways, in scenes that have a tremendous emotional impact. You can't watch without feeling tremendous unease, disgust, and sympathy for the women.

In perhaps the most dramatic film, called *The Photographer*, a young model is humiliated by a photographer, clicking away as he urges her to get more sexually into the shoot, keeping up an increasingly threatening banter, ordering her to touch herself and telling her he's sexually aroused. When he finishes, the camera pulls back to reveal a large group of people watching impassively. No one says a word. While the viewer feels agony for the mortified young woman, none of the people working on the set have a reaction. Schwimmer noted that seventy-five models auditioned for *The Photographer*, and every one of them had a story about something similar happening to her. It's real.

Schwimmer told me that the reaction to the film series has been "a lot of gratitude and an enormous outpouring of people who want to share their own stories on our Facebook page. People express a desire that more be done." Also, he said, the films allow a dialogue to be opened. He's found that although there's a lot of support from men, there's also confusion. They're not always clear why it's sexual harassment. "We want people to talk about it and inspire a discussion."

Schwimmer is also active in the Rape Foundation, a highly regarded organization in Los Angeles devoted to support for rape victims and sexually abused children, which is partnering with the fraternity system to educate young men. He brings a lot of passion to these issues. "It's the way I was raised," he said. "My parents were very active and politically strong feminists. I'm driven about using my celebrity as a man to change the culture—and to try and reach other men with the message."

I believe that colleges must also take on the environments that allow these behaviors to flourish. That might mean challenging some of the negative elements within the Greek system (excessive partying and hazing, for example). One positive example is the Men's Project, a six-week program at the University of Wisconsin–Madison designed to help young men redefine healthy masculinity and empower them to be more self-aware and promote gender equity.

Public events can also have a tremendous impact. It's On Us, an effective campaign to stop sexual assault on campuses, hosts events in which survivors share their stories and prominent people speak. At an April 2017 It's On Us event at George Mason University in Virginia, former vice president Joe Biden spoke very bluntly, addressing the men in the audience. He told them that if a woman is dead drunk, she cannot consent to sex. Young men need to hear this kind of message from adult men more often.

I want to say strongly to college women that you can be a part of this fight. Stand up for yourself! Organize Take Back the Night events. Lobby your school about offering sexual harassment training. Demand accountability when assaults happen. Expose any demeaning and dangerous practices on your campus. Use social media to assert your rights and your dignity. Be a warrior on your own campus. Do it for yourself, and for all the young women and men who will follow you.

That's exactly what happened when the women's soccer team at Harvard took back their power. In October 2016, the *Harvard Crimson* published an article reporting that the 2012 Harvard men's soccer team had created a "scouting report" for the incoming women's team, giving each woman a score based on her physical appearance, accompanied by a critique. For example: "She seems relatively simple and probably inexperienced sexually, so I decided missionary would be her preferred position."

When the story came to light, the men's soccer team was suspended for the remainder of the season. But the women's soccer team, including some of those who had been "scouted" in 2012, had their own way of taking hold of the narrative and asserting themselves. In an open letter published in the *Crimson*, they fought back, with strength and dignity. The letter stated: "We have seen the 'scouting report' in its entirety. We know the fullest extent of its contents: the descriptions of our bodies, the numbers we were each assigned, and the comparison to each other and recruits in classes before us. This document attempts to pit us against one another, as if the judgment of a few men is sufficient to determine our worth. But, men, we know better than that. Eighteen years of soccer taught us that. Eighteen years—as successful, powerful, and undeniably brilliant female athletes—taught us that."

Most significantly, they wrote that the men's comments did not have the ability to take them down: "This document might have stung any other group of women you chose to target, but not us. We know as teammates that we rise to the occasion, that we are stronger together, and that we will not tolerate anything less than respect for women that we care for more than ourselves."

I found that same fighting spirit in a blog post by a young student and intern who titled her piece "A Note from the Next Gretchen Carlson." An aspiring journalist, she wrote, "As a green, wide-eyed student and intern, I simply didn't know that the Old Boys' Club and locker room feel of many workplaces was still present at the type of place I could see myself working. . . . I often wonder at what decade we'll agree it's no longer appropriate to defend degradation in the workplace. I can't decide whether sexual harassment or the excuses made on behalf of the perpetrators is scarier to me."

But it was her conclusion that lifted my spirits and heartened me about the next generation. "Even as I fear," she wrote, "I understand that the very nature of a journalist is to speak truth to power. If the power I speak to comes out of my own office, then so be it."

FIND YOUR POWER

Throughout my entire journalism career, I've kept a plaque on my desk with the quote, "A person who risks nothing does nothing, has nothing, and is nothing." But you don't have to start with a big public gesture to find your own personal power. Start with small inspirational steps.

I believe that a big step in being strong is visualizing ourselves as women being strong. We have to imagine ourselves in the position of winning, or speaking up, or telling the truth. I have always used visualization to help me gear up for hard challenges, even if it meant standing in front of a mirror and practicing what I was going to say and do, looking myself in the eye and saying, "You can do this"—and most important, seeing myself doing it!

It's a sad fact that only about 60 percent of people in this country still believes in the American dream. My advice? We need to fight for it. When I put my kids to bed at night, I tell them that the American dream can be theirs with hard work and perseverance and should never be taken for granted. So too with our fight as women. When we stand together and advocate for ourselves, we are fighting not just for our own lives, but also for all of us as a whole, in a society that ultimately encourages us to be our best selves. We *can* still achieve the American dream. Let's do it together.

FOUR

You Have the Right

Begin with this mantra that I created:

I have a right to fulfill my dreams.

I have a right to pursue any career I choose.

I have a right to excel without malicious interference.

I have a right to be treated with respect in my professional and personal lives.

I have a right to not be touched unless I want to be touched.

I have a right to work in an environment free of visuals that demean and objectify women.

I have a right to not be stalked.

I have a right to be called by my name, not diminutive nicknames.

I have a right to work without hearing comments about my body or appearance.

I have a right to not be pestered for dates when I make it clear that I have no interest.

I have a right to advance up the ladder based on my hard work and abilities.

I have a right to speak out without fear of retaliation or intimidation when I am demeaned, harassed, or assaulted.

I have a right to be myself, not be defined by stereotypes.

These are meaningful, powerful assertions, but it took some time for them to form on my lips. When I began this journey, I had no way of knowing what was going to happen to me. I didn't know how much control I would have, if any. I often felt insecure and unsure of what the future would hold. Sometimes a wave of hopelessness washed over me, so strong it took my breath away.

I've since learned that the best antidote to fear is finding tangible ways to take back your power. I created this twelve-point playbook as a practical guide to get you started on that process. We can do this together.

1. EYES WIDE OPEN

Advocating for yourself in the workplace starts with knowing your rights. What *are* they? It's time for a straightforward, understandable description of the laws (free of legalese). But you have to know that the law is not enough. You also need to understand and abide by company policies, correctly read the political atmosphere, and have a plan. And you have to enter the workplace with your eyes wide open.

I still have vivid memories of interviewing for TV jobs. By nature, a job seeker is a supplicant, and the more you want or need the job, the stronger a company's hand. In the initial glow of being hired, it's easy to assume that a company has your best interests at heart. The last thing on your mind is the thought that you might someday make a complaint. The first thing on your mind is your salary and benefits package, your job description, and what the company expects of you.

But before you sign up, take some time for due diligence:

What can you learn about the company? Do you know people who have worked there and can give you a fair account of the working environment? Has the company been in the news for workplace violations or employee complaints?

When you take a tour of the workplace, what do you notice? What's the mood? Is there a diverse staff makeup? Are there women managers?

Carefully read your contract, and ask questions about things you don't understand. Make a note if there is a required arbitration clause for complaints.

Carefully read the employee handbook, if there is one. Some companies have very specific steps to take if you experience sexual harassment, and your case is jeopardized if you don't take them.

Also, be aware of how your status might affect your ability to complain. Although there are laws that forbid sexual harassment of employees, your status might affect your ability to get relief. For example, interns are especially vulnerable. In many states, interns, who are not technically considered "employees," are not protected under workplace law from sexual harassment. In one 2014 case, a New York federal district court ruled that Lihuan Wang, an intern at a TV broadcaster named Phoenix Satellite Television US, could not bring a sexual harassment claim under New York human rights laws because she was not paid, and therefore not considered an employee. Wang's supervisor allegedly cornered her in a hotel room, where he had asked her to come and talk about her job performance. There, she claimed, he tried to kiss her and squeezed her buttocks. And when she repelled him, he no longer wanted to hire her for a full-time position. The man was later fired from the company, but Wang herself had no recourse against him. Here again, the laws don't work in women's favor. However, the good news is that as a result of the spotlight that Wang's case shined on the issue, some states have passed laws to extend workplace protections to interns. And in 2016 the US House of Representatives passed a bill to protect unpaid interns from discrimination, including sexual harassment. A second bill, specifically designed to protect interns working for the federal government, was passed in 2017. Both bills have been sent to the Senate, where as of this writing there is no word on their status. So, to really be sure of your rights, if you're an intern—paid or unpaid, in the public or the private sector—you need to check your state and local laws. And the larger point is, always go into a job (even as an intern) knowing where you are, what the company stands for, what it thinks of you, what it expects of you, and what your rights are.

2. DOCUMENT PROBLEMS

"Document, document, document," stresses the attorney Lisa Bloom. The first time you experience inappropriate behavior, even if it seems minor, start writing it down in a journal. Do not keep this journal on your work computer or in your office where your employer can gain access. (If you're fired, you will lose access to your computer, your office, and email and social media accounts that were set up by your company.)

Your journal should be as detailed as possible, with names, dates, and witnesses. This serves as contemporaneous "proof" if you make a claim. For example:

> *February 1 2017, 10:13 a.m.:* Joe K. slapped my bottom passing me in the break room.
>
> *February 1, 2017, 12:05 p.m.:* Saw photo on bulletin board [attached]. Joe K., Mary B. commented on it.
>
> *February 2, 2017:* Bill P. tossed popcorn down my front during a meeting. When I protested, he asked, "Are you on your period?" This exchange was witnessed by Joe K., Carol S., Fred R. and Mary B.
>
> *February 8, 2017, 4:00 p.m.:* Joe K. and Bill P. openly watching porn in the office. Asked them to turn it off and they just laughed. "We're all adults here." Mary B. also observed this and commented it made her uncomfortable.
>
> *February 9, 2017, 9:30 a.m.:* Complained to Mr. D. about the popcorn and the porn. Mr. D. said, "I'll speak to the boys. But you could do yourself a favor and try to lighten up."

In addition, send emails to yourself, detailing in narrative fashion your experiences. This also creates a contemporaneous record. Again, be sure to keep it at home or on your person. One woman had a folder with details of her harassment in her locker at work. When she was suddenly fired, she could not gain access, and the binder was thrown out.

Also collect written proof. If the harasser is texting, emailing, or sending cards or notes to you, keep copies. Don't delete them, even if you're angry or frustrated. Print them and keep copies in your safe home file, making sure to note the date and time. Also take screenshots of texts, print them, and store them in your safe file. This is compelling evidence. If you receive inappropriate voice mails, keep these as well. If there are offensive signs, posters, or drawings on display in your workplace, take photos and print them.

In your safe file, keep copies of your performance reviews and other personnel documents. These can be used in case of retaliation if your performance reviews were always positive until the aftermath of incidents you are reporting, or if your employer tries to make an issue of your job performance.

Again, your right to access your personnel file varies by state. Even if you have the right to view your file, during company hours on the premises, you might not be allowed to make copies. If that's the case, take detailed notes with direct quotes.

3. TAKE OFFENSE

"No offense intended," a man once said to me after calling me a bitch. I shrugged and walked away. A typical response. Now I'm saying, *Do take offense.*

In the 1970s, assertiveness training became popular as women sought to take back their power. Being polite and compliant in abusive situations wasn't working for them. But to this day, many women find that when they are assertive with men who are putting them down, they're tagged as "ballbusters" or "man haters." As discussed earlier, this leaves women in a no-win situation. If they don't say anything, the behavior continues, and if they speak up, they're called names. My attitude is that we need to collectively decide to stand up for ourselves. Call me a ballbuster if you want, but I'm going to stand up for myself.

Forget about staying silent and hoping it will blow over; that stance sends an unintended message that the behavior is OK. Some harassment situations, whether on the street or in the office, can be stopped short by a confident retort:

> "My name is ———. Please don't call me honey."
> "That makes me uncomfortable."
> "I'm not interested in dating you. Don't ask me again."
> "Stop touching me."
> "Back off."
> "That wasn't funny."
> "Stop staring."
> "You're in my space."
> "Don't rub my shoulders."
> "That's offensive."
> "No!"
> "Don't!"
> "Stop it!"
> "Don't ever speak to me that way again."
> "You need to leave."
> "You're embarrassing yourself."
> "That's harassment."

You have a right to say what you mean, and to be heard.

I realize that many women may be nervous about saying anything at all. And they may be right to be, because let's face it: not every person who is confronted, even in a polite way, is going to respond well, especially if the power imbalance is great.

Brianna, who is African American, had risen up through the ranks of a national restaurant chain, and was one of only a few women to be promoted to manager of a large restaurant. Almost as soon as she started working there, the general manager gave her a diminutive nickname. Brianna was trying to assert herself as a manager and earn the respect of the workers. She found the name insulting, but she didn't want to get off on the wrong foot. "I very professionally pulled him aside," she said, "and I asked him to call me Brianna. He looked offended, and I didn't want it to escalate, so I said, 'I notice you seem offended.' He said, 'I just thought it was a term of endearment.' I told him, 'As an African American female, I can tell you it's not.'"

There's no question that Brianna handled the situation very clearly and professionally. That should have been the end of it, but it was the beginning of a long, difficult time for her. She never found her footing after that, and she says the general manager seemed determined to turn the other workers against her. She heard workers in the kitchen refer to her in insulting ways. Her authority was totally diminished. For example, after she texted the general manager that a crew member was being disruptive and she'd received a complaint from a patron, the general manager told her the crew member had accused her of making fun of his speech impediment—something she would never do.

Harassment can be equated with bullying, and that's very much in the culture. We see it pervading the Internet. For harassers, the anonymity of the Internet is a perfect cover.

A Pew Research study on online bullying showed that women ages eighteen to twenty-four report higher rates of more extreme abuses and related effects online. They report experiencing much higher rates of sexual harassment, stalking, and sustained abuse.

When I had my show, I experienced it firsthand. I used to do a segment called "Mean Tweets," because my daily Twitter feed was loaded with the most vile comments you can imagine. It's notable that so many of them were about my body. What was amazing was that many of the commenters arrogantly identified themselves, and even the companies they worked for! I'd respond to them, "I wonder if your boss would like to see what you sent me," and they'd fall all over themselves apologizing. The point is, they thought they could get away with the harassment, until I turned the tables on them. Women have to be bolder about taking offense.

4. TELL PEOPLE YOU TRUST

Women who are sexually harassed often experience feelings of depression, loneliness, and isolation, not only at work, but also at home, because they don't want (or know how) to talk about it with family and friends. I've heard from women who haven't told their husbands and who've kept their harassment a secret from their closest friends. Believe me, I understand the impulse, but it's counterproductive. Now, more than ever, you need a support system. It's an absolute necessity! Telling others about your experience will make you feel stronger and heighten your resolve. One of the most compelling arguments for women who have come forward even years later was the fact that they told people about it when it happened.

I realize that in some toxic company cultures, speaking to anyone can feel dangerous. Whom can you trust? Who has your back? It's scary to go out on a limb. Other people's motivations are not always easy to read. The woman you chat with about your kids in the lunchroom, or join for girls' night out, might not be your best ally in a harassment situation.

Be observant. Does the harasser put other women you work with in compromising positions, or treat them poorly? Approach these women about their experiences. Say, "I saw what Bill said to you this morning. I thought it was awful. Are you doing OK?" Let them know they have an ally in you, and they might become *your* ally.

I admire Martha Langelan's book, *Back Off! How to Confront and Stop Sexual Harassment and Harassers.* One of her boldest and most interesting suggestions involves group confrontation. Harassers get away with their behavior because they target vulnerable women, often when they're alone. In her book, Langelan describes how to organize a group of women (even two or three) to plan a confrontation, first creating a detailed and very specific list of complaints. "The group can also provide him with a specific list of the alternative, replacement behaviors the women expect from him in the future (for example: do not call any woman in this office 'honey,' use our names; do not touch any of us at any time, keep your hands to yourself; stop displaying pornography, keep it out of the office entirely; keep your sex life to yourself, never proposition any woman in this office again)." As this approach demonstrates, women have power when we use our numbers.

5. TAPE INTERACTIONS . . . IF YOU CAN

I can't tell you how many people have asked me, "Should I get a tape recording of the harassment?" A recording could be the gold standard of proof. However, the use of a tape recorder is a very tricky matter, especially legally. The best way to find out if you have the legal right to make one-party recordings is to check the laws in your state. They vary. Currently, there are eleven states in which it is illegal to record a conversation without the consent of *all* parties. In some cases, it is legal to make a one-party recording, but such a recording is not admissible as evidence in court. In almost every case, it's illegal to tape-record conversations to which you are not a party, or for which you have not secured the consent of one of the parties (such as turning on a tape recorder in the office to pick up general conversation when you're not there).

Even if you live in a state where one-party recording is legal, your company may have a policy that makes surreptitious recordings a fireable offense. Before you even consider doing this, be sure to check the law and your company's policy. And if you do go ahead and record a conversation, the recording needs to remain intact—no editing is allowed. Be sure to keep the recording in a safe place.

Let me add that making one-party recordings illegal is a tremendous blow in the uphill battle women experience while trying to prove their cases. Sometimes it's the *only* proof that will break through the he-said-she said wall of disbelief.

6. KNOW THE POLICIES

Don't get blindsided by failing to follow the complaint procedure established by your company—98 percent of companies have them. Follow it to the letter. There's an important reason for that: the

Supreme Court has ruled that if a company has a procedure in place for reporting sexual harassment, the company cannot be expected to fix the situation unless an employee reports it. The court has ruled that companies have a right to try to address the situation, and if you deny them that right, you might not be able to bring a lawsuit.

That restriction can feel like a Catch-22, because as we all know, once a complaint is made, the repercussions, legal or not, can be severe. And sometimes company policies are not as fair or anonymous as they claim to be. For example, many large companies have "anonymous" sexual harassment hotlines, which are advertised as allowing victims to come forward without fear of repercussions. In some cases, calling the hotline is mandatory. But not only are they not necessarily anonymous, they're also useless to investigators. Women I've spoken to find them intimidating, especially given the fact that they usually go straight to HR.

Sterling Jewelers (see chapter 6) is a case in point. Employees say they were retaliated against after calling the company's anonymous "TIPS" hotline. The hotline was supposed to provide safe access and empower those who had complaints, especially those related to sexual harassment or discrimination. But in Sterling's case, women allege, the company was able to determine who was making the calls, and the abusers learned about them, leading to retaliation. In this instance, the anonymous nature of the calls worked against the women; without a written record of the complaint, they could not prove retaliation.

7. MAKE IT OFFICIAL

In most companies, employees are required to bring a complaint to HR if they expect action. However, as we've discussed, this can be a scary prospect. Many employees fear that coming forward will just make things worse, and in some cases, it does. In an online survey of over eleven thousand people on ToughNickel.com, a website that addresses money, finance, and related workplace issues, only three percent of respondents said they trusted HR very much, while 56 percent of respondents said they very much *distrusted* HR. The greatest concern is that HR will share the most intimate details of your situation with others in the company, such as top executives, legal personnel, managers, and maybe even the harasser. It's intimidating to feel as if people are talking about you throughout the company. Worse still, some of the people in the loop might be friends or allies of the harasser who might try to undermine your complaint behind the scenes. As Anita Hill recently observed in a *Washington Post* interview, "There are still companies that pay lip service to human resources departments, while quietly allowing women to be vilified when they come forward."

Rarely discussed outright, but a very real concern, is whether or not a complaint will get a fair hearing if the accused is a top performer in the company. The dollars-and-cents calculation may never be acknowledged, but it's certainly one reason why repeat offenders stay in companies, and why women who charge harassment are often transferred, fired, or paid off.

Working in HR doesn't magically put you above the fray. HR representatives are people too; they have relationships and biases. In one egregious example, a woman wrote to me saying that the HR person assigned to her case was having an affair with the harasser!

Given the realities of company cultures and human nature, taking the leap to make a report to HR is an act of courage and blind faith. In its June 2016 report on sexual harassment, the EEOC suggested that companies take extra steps to demonstrate their seriousness. Among the commission's recommendations:

Appoint an ombudsman to oversee company efforts. I think this is critical. Companies need an independent outsider to review complaints so they can be fairly heard. Most of the women I interviewed were intimidated by having to go to a company executive—and in many cases, they had reason to be. A company committed to ending sexual harassment must take this important first step.

Authorize dozens of key employees throughout the organization to handle complaints. That way people don't feel that there is only one way to be heard, even if it's by a person who might have an association with the harasser.

Train people in civility. That is, don't train them in what *not* to do, but in how to be civil to colleagues, and how to speak up as a bystander.

An important step is working to change the culture within corporations by *celebrating* women (and men) who have the guts to come forward—not penalizing them. This culture shift would also include celebrating the bystanders—the employees who witness misconduct and speak up despite their own fears of being looked at as complainers or troublemakers. Here's the key: if companies can create environments where speaking up is seen as a positive, the whole dynamic surrounding the issue can change.

It's a myth that women casually complain to HR. There's nothing casual about it. Notice how many steps we've gone through before even reaching this point. Usually, it's a torturous decision, made after a buildup of numerous incidents. It's no wonder so many women wait for months and even years before finally complaining. This delay leaves them open to harsh criticism: "If it was so bad, why did you wait?" They are damned by speaking up, damned by staying silent. Yet anyone who's been there can tell you that it's a very lonely and difficult decision.

Naomi had been experiencing worsening sexual harassment for some time at the large chemical firm where she was a manager. She had begun to have recurring nightmares of being caught in a giant tidal wave. Minor harassment was part of her regular work life, and she'd even grown used to it. When she started with the company, she says it was well known that the lab manager had a goal of sleeping with every woman in the lab. She often got assigned to cleaning tasks in the lab, and would be asked, "Naomi, have you done the dishes yet?" She didn't hesitate to speak out, and would ask, "How would you feel if someone said that to your daughter?" She firmly believed that she could overcome anything by being good at her job. But when she was promoted to another division, her boss said when she arrived, "It's about time we got a damn good-looking woman in here." Comments like this were ongoing, and Naomi said—in an understatement—"It's hard to concentrate when someone is hitting on you all the time."

Naomi recounted an incident in which an executive came into her office after hours and complimented her on her lip gloss. Standing in the doorway, he asked, "Can I pat you on the fanny?"

"That's damn inappropriate!" she exploded.

She told me, "Suddenly I was pissed off for every time it had happened. The anger bubbled up in me. I decided then and there to talk to the director of HR."

Even if your meeting with HR is face-to-face, write a letter detailing your complaint. Be specific about every incident you've recorded in your journal, along with supporting materials. There is no such thing as overkill. All the details are significant, as they add up to a complete picture. Label your letter for what it is—a complaint of sexual harassment. Be direct and specific. This is not a place for vague language; you want to leave no doubt about the nature of your complaint. I've seen cases in which HR asserted that a woman never actually said she was sexually harassed. The language matters. Here is a sample letter of an effective complaint made to a fictional company:

August 12, 2016

TO: Department of Human Resources
XYZ Company
RE: Formal Complaint of Sexual Harassment

I am making a formal complaint of sexual harassment at XYZ Company by my supervisor, Joe Smith.

I have been an engineer in the compliance department since October 5, 2012. During that time, I have been promoted twice, and have received favorable reviews throughout my employment.

On December 15, 2015, at 4:45 p.m., I was called into the office of my direct supervisor, Joe Smith. He invited me to dinner the following evening to celebrate the holidays. He said, "We've worked hard this year. We deserve to have some fun." I politely declined, with the excuse that I had to be home with my children, since we had preparations for the holiday.

He replied, "Let's just get a drink, then."

I reminded Mr. Smith that I was married and would prefer to keep our relationship professional. He said, "Oh, come on. You know there's a spark between us."

I was very uncomfortable and embarrassed. I didn't want to insult Mr. Smith, or make him angry. I told him how much I enjoyed working for him, but repeated that I wanted to keep the relationship professional. I felt shocked because I had never said or done anything that would give him the wrong impression. Before I left his office, he said in a playful voice, "You can't fault a guy for trying. I hope this isn't the end of the story."

I was very upset after this meeting, and I immediately worried about my job security. I love my job and have always been happy at XYZ, but I wondered if now I would feel uncomfortable. That evening I told two people what had happened: I sent an email to Deborah Taylor, a personal friend who does not work for the company [attached]; and I also told Jane Jones, my coworker and friend in compliance. I also began keeping a journal to record any further incidents [attached].

On February 12, 2016, our department held a daylong retreat at a local convention center, which concluded with a reception and dinner. At the reception, Mr. Smith, who had been drinking, took me aside and, putting his arm around me, asked in a low voice whether I had had a chance to consider his proposition. I pulled away from him and reminded him that I was married and did not want a personal relationship. He said, "It's hard to see you every day, knowing how you've rejected me." Again, I sent an email to Deborah Taylor, describing this incident [attached]. At 11:00 that evening, Mr. Smith left me a voice mail [attached], apologizing if he offended me, but saying he was working on handling his feelings for me.

After that incident, the atmosphere at work changed. Previously, Mr. Smith had given me important projects. Now I noticed he was giving the same projects to my coworkers, but not to me. On April 9, 2016, I asked his permission to take a half day the following week so I could attend my daughter's recital. In the past, I had received such permission without a problem, but he said to me, "I don't feel inclined to do you any favors."

Mr. Smith's change of attitude toward me was noticeable to others. On May 2, at 9:30 a.m., my coworker Ben White asked me, "What did you do to piss off the boss?" Another coworker, George Kent, told me on May 18, at 4:50 p.m., that Mr. Smith had told him he was losing confidence in my work. I asked him if Mr. Smith had said why, and he said, "Something about you not being a team player."

On May 20, I asked Mr. Smith for a meeting, and we met in his office at 5:00 that afternoon. I told him he seemed to be unhappy with my work, and I wanted to clear the air. His behavior toward me was very cold. He said, "You had your chance."

On July 9, at 10:45 a.m., I received a copy of my performance review, which, for the first time was not good. Mr. Smith gave me low marks for teamwork, and wrote a comment that I was unable to take direction. He recommended that I not receive a regularly scheduled raise.

I was very upset about this. My anxiety level was high. I had trouble sleeping, worrying about my job. I felt that my status at the company was in jeopardy. I am making this complaint of sexual harassment because the problem I am experiencing is the direct result of Mr. Smith trying to date me and my rejection of him. There is substantial evidence of persistent retaliation. The attachments to this complaint demonstrate that this has been an ongoing harassment/retaliation situation for nearly a year.

I am asking HR to investigate my claim against Mr. Smith. Thank you for your time.

Sincerely,
Mary Heller
Attachments: Journal notes, voice mail, emails

Proceed cautiously. As stated before, HR is not necessarily your friend. It is the company's representative, and a complaint might lead to places you never intended to go. By the time Brianna, the restaurant manager, finally complained to HR, she was initially met with a supportive response. "I've only heard great things about you," the HR director told her warmly. She assured her she'd take care of it. But within days, Brianna says the corporate office had shut her out, reassigning her to another, less prestigious restaurant, and finally firing her on what she believed was a trumped-up charge.

When you speak to HR, you will probably be told that the employer will protect your confidentiality, if possible. Realistically, however, this probably is not possible, because the investigative process is bound to reveal your identity. For this reason, don't go to HR if you're not sure you want to make a complaint. HR is not a place to go to get general advice about your situation, or support for a hard time you're experiencing, or just to blow off steam. Once it's out in the open, your employer has an obligation to investigate, whether you want it to or not.

Having said all that, the greatest fear nagging at the back of women's minds as they consider whether to report sexual harassment is this: *What if I put myself on the line and jeopardize my work status because it is the right thing to do—and nothing happens!* I know what it's like to feel that fear. It keeps you awake at night. Deciding what to do feels like the most terrifying bungee jump. You might die; if not literally, then in terms of your career and your relationships. You have to choose for yourself whether it's worth it, whether you're going to be a warrior or walk away. Choosing to be a warrior is not all high-minded marching into the future. It's gritty and hard. People hate you. They blame you. Many women I've spoken with made claims against very popular or powerful people, and their coworkers despised them for it. If your case goes public, it will be "litigated" in the media. People will say the worst things imaginable about you. Your parents and, worse still, your *children*, will be exposed to it.

After the principal of her school touched her and made lewd comments on several occasions, Robin complained to the school board, which conducted its own investigation. She felt as if they all were inside a tight circle, and she was on the outside. "I don't understand why you don't like him," one member said to Robin. "He's a good man." After that, "I became the enemy." Nothing happened, and life went on as before. The principal was not even disciplined. Deeply depressed, Robin retired.

In a more positive scenario, a legitimate investigation will be launched. Take the opportunity to directly ask for remedies you would like to see made. These include:

- Transfer of the harasser.
- Suspension of the harasser.
- A formal reprimand in the harasser's personnel file.
- An apology by the harasser.
- Training or counseling for the harasser.
- Removal of unfairly negative reports in your personnel file that are related to the harassment.
- Restoration of your position, if you were moved or demoted as part of the harassment.
- Compensation for losses, such as sick days taken because of the harassment.
- Improvements in company training to prevent harassment.

Make sure you have a plan before going to HR or telling a supervisor or company counsel. (See more about consulting a lawyer on pages 97–99.) Often, women take it and take it and take it, and then finally erupt and go to HR before they've thought things through. Once you make a claim, you can't go back and collect evidence and create a plan. And if you have an arbitration clause in your contract, the minute you make a claim, the company will move to put you in arbitration as soon as possible to keep everything under wraps.

8. AVOID TRAPS

Zoe was a young middle school PE teacher, coaching the girls' teams. She loved her job, and loved the kids, but she says she didn't appreciate the behavior of the older male athletic director. He didn't refer to her by name, but called her "Sweetie," "Darling," or "Honey" when he addressed her. She hated that, but let it go, telling herself that he was from another generation. But with time, she says, he exhibited some behaviors that freaked her out. On one occasion, after she had returned from a sick day and had a hoarse voice, he put his arms around her, and said as if she was a child, "We have to get you better, Sweetie."

When Zoe finally decided to complain to the school principal, he was very supportive and upset by her report. But then he did something that put Zoe at a definite disadvantage. He scheduled a mediation talk between her and the athletic director to "clear the air."

The idea that a company would put an accuser across the table from her harasser is very troubling. This might be an appropriate method if the dispute involves differences of opinion about work issues, but in a sexual harassment case it amounts to further abuse, especially if the accused is someone in a position of power over the accuser. Intimidation is a very real factor here; the accuser might be physically or emotionally terrified of the accused, and also fear for her job if she doesn't make nice. Furthermore, it sends the message that this is a conflict that is up to both parties equally to work out, rather than a complaint that one of them has done something wrong.

These traps and unhelpful responses that, in effect, punish the victim all over again can happen even in large companies. Carmen, the flight attendant supervisor mentioned in the introduction who complained along with two other women to HR about the repeated sexist comments and behaviors of a supervisor, reported this bizarre response: "We scheduled a meeting with the vice president of human resources. We met with her and thought the meeting went well, but we were wrong. The three of us, along with our other staff members, had to attend numerous sessions on sexual harassment in the workplace. At no time did the VP in question attend a class. Things continued to get worse, and finally the three of us who reported his actions were summoned to corporate. *We* were accused of doing the harassment." Carmen says the company turned the tables on the victims, unbelievably saying *they* were the perpetrators because their complaints had caused disruption. And this is the twenty-first century!

9. DOCUMENT ANY RETALIATION

"I am still crying as I write this," wrote one woman who reached out to me. "It's been thirteen years, and I can't get over it." The harassment she experienced at work was bad enough, but she said she suffered the most pain because of the retaliation. "When my abuser was fired, that's when the worst torture began," she said when I spoke with her. "I was treated like a leper. Even people I'd been friendly with ignored me." But there was more. She says that her harasser, who had many friends in the industry, took it upon himself to destroy her name in the business.

I've heard similar scenarios described countless times. There are two kinds of retaliation: direct and environmental. Direct retaliation occurs when people in authority take negative actions against you because you complained or refused inappropriate advances. These actions can include giving poor performance evaluations, demoting you or transferring you to a less desirable job, being physically or verbally abusive, unreasonably denying requests, failing to give you reserved bonuses, threatening you, turning others against you, spreading lies about you, and even firing you.

If anything about your work conditions worsens after you've made a complaint, document the instances clearly to build a case, because retaliation is illegal. For example, if your performance reviews have always been positive, but suddenly you receive a negative evaluation, that could be retaliation. I've often found it baffling how many times women talk about the most egregious forms of retaliation, such as demotions, poor reviews, and being frozen out of meetings. Can't the retaliators see that these are documentable actions? I think sometimes people in power are so arrogant that they feel untouchable, and they really don't believe anyone will stop them from doing exactly what they want to do. They often have an outsize view of their indispensability to the company. If they have previously used their power to harass women, they already have a sense of entitlement that empowers them to continue harassing.

So we need to be vigilant about reporting retaliation. Stand up for yourself and call it like you see it. Don't beat around the bush or be vague:

"My performance reviews have always been excellent. I don't deserve this poor review, and I believe it's retaliation because I complained."

"I deserve this promotion, and I believe I am being held back because of my complaint."

"Before I complained, I attended every manager's meeting. Now I am not invited. That's retaliation."

"Joe K. told me I'd be sorry I made a complaint. That's threatening me. It's retaliation."

"Here is email proof that I was given the wrong time for an important conference call with a client. I believe it was deliberate retaliation."

Environmental retaliation is harder to prove and more difficult to stop. You can't *make* coworkers like you or talk to you, especially if they think shutting you out improves their own job security. Even when coworkers sympathize and privately offer support, many of them just want to keep their heads down and not get involved. If you have supporters on the team, enlist them to help you break through the freeze.

The risk of backlash from other employees is especially high when the accused is a beloved figure in the company. Jada's boss was practically a legend in his field, and she was thrilled to get a job as his assistant after she graduated from college. "I thought my boss hired me for my skill set, but he was interested in more," she said. She repeatedly rejected his advances, but it didn't stop. She finally reported him to HR and he was asked to leave the firm. The backlash from her coworkers was brutal, far worse than the original harassment. "He was their hero," she said, "and I brought him down. They hated me for it." The irony is, he had behaved the same way with other women at the firm, but they were now defending him.

I have to emphasize that there's no soft-pedaling the prevalence or severity of retaliation. As one woman wrote to me, so movingly, "It's so horrible. Can you imagine if our daughters encountered this? We all love our kids so much and want a better world for them. The after-effects of trying to stand up for yourself and fight for a career came at me because people think they need to retaliate for the benefit of the harasser, just to prove a point or feel better about themselves, and it is so wrong."

For Lisa Bloom, retaliation is especially sinister when the accused is a person in authority. "Powerful people say, 'If you go against me, I'll destroy you,'" she says. "This is who they are—a person with no boundaries. It's a part of their personality because no one ever held them to account before."

10. GO LEGAL

Most lawyers I've spoken to advise women to retain a lawyer before they make a complaint. There is no question that an experienced sexual harassment attorney can help you avoid the many pitfalls you face when you go it alone against your company. However, lawyers cost money, and many of the women I've spoken to were able to engage a lawyer only when they knew they were filing a lawsuit and were able to make a contingency arrangement.

Having said that, employment law is a vast and complex area, and a good lawyer can be invaluable in the long run. Plus, in my experience, lawyers who practice this kind of law tend to be passionate advocates who are angered by injustice. Just the kind of person you want in your corner! Here are the questions to ask when interviewing lawyers:

- Does the lawyer specialize in sexual harassment?
- Has the lawyer represented plaintiffs in cases against companies like yours, of similar size and industry?
- What are some of the cases the lawyer has handled successfully that are similar to yours?
- Does the lawyer practice at both the state and federal level? Has he or she been involved in cases with the EEOC?
- Does the lawyer believe you have a strong case?
- Is the makeup of the firm such that you believe your case will be a priority? Is it easy to reach the lawyer on the phone or email?
- What is the fee structure—contingency, straight fee, or some of each? What is the approximate cost of each stage—filing a complaint with HR, filing an EEOC complaint, handling arbitration, filing a lawsuit, settling a lawsuit, going to court?
- What is the lawyer's philosophy about settling versus going to trial?
- If your company has forced arbitration, what are the strategies the lawyer will use to get you the fairest hearing?
- What are the remedies, apart from financial, that the lawyer is prepared to seek? For example, is it possible to get your job back if you were fired, or to get back pay and benefits?

Also ask yourself:

- Do you feel a personal connection with the lawyer? Do you seem to be on the same page? Are you comfortable sharing your most personal experiences and history with this person?

- Does the lawyer thoroughly explain what you're up against, and give you a balanced reading of the pros and cons of taking various steps?

Hopefully, a good lawyer will tell it to you straight about what you can expect. Can you be made "whole" by winning or settling a case? Will the compensation be worth the potential loss of a job or career? For the most part, the answer is disappointing. For example, a study of fifty harassment settlements in Chicago courts found that amounts averaged around $53,000, with a median of about $30,000. Those who took their cases to court and won did somewhat better (more than $200,000), but not enough to compensate for the loss of a career. Before you sue or settle, be armed with the facts—especially if you work for a small company, where federal law might limit awards to $50,000.

Deciding to hire a lawyer and file a legal case can be a big reality check. One woman told me an all-too-familiar story. Although she said she had many witnesses to a coworker physically assaulting her at a company party, none of them were willing to come forward. "Nobody defended me!" she cried, years later, still heartbroken by the lack of support. Instead, the corporate office indicated that she might have been drinking too much. She told me she could feel them looking for ways to blame her. Her lawyer delivered a final blow when he told her that without the testimony of witnesses, there wasn't enough evidence to make a case.

11. SECURE YOUR RIGHT TO SUE

There is one more hurdle to cross. Before you can bring a discrimination or harassment lawsuit under federal law, you must file an administrative charge with the federal Equal Employment Opportunity Commission or a similar state agency. This is a legal requirement: If you file a lawsuit without first having filed a charge (called "exhausting" your administrative remedies, legally speaking), your lawsuit will be thrown out. Depending on your state, you have 180 or 300 days from the date of the sexual harassment incident(s) to file. So, even if you're not sure you're going to file a lawsuit, the clock is ticking.

The EEOC will notify your company and conduct an investigation, but keep in mind that it might be cursory because of the enormous case load. Don't expect the EEOC to sue on your behalf; relatively few cases are selected for this remedy. More important is to get a ruling from the EEOC in the form of a "right to sue" letter, which will allow you to proceed with a lawsuit. Once you receive a "right to sue" letter, you have only ninety days to file a lawsuit.

It's important to reiterate that when you file an EEOC complaint or lawsuit, it is illegal for people in the company to threaten you or retaliate against you. Be sure to document such instances. Rebecca, who filed an EEOC complaint after receiving no satisfaction from her company, was immediately challenged by the executive who had assaulted her. "You think you can sue [large corporation] and keep your job?" he taunted. As of this writing, she's hanging on at the company, but she might ultimately have little recourse but to sue or leave the company. It can be extremely frustrating for women who feel strongly about the legitimacy of their cases to realize how toothless many of the remedies are.

In addition to the federal law, there may be state or local laws that provide legal remedies for sexual harassment. The time to file these claims varies from place to place. For example, under New York City human rights law, you have three years to file in court. Under the New Jersey Law Against Discrimination, you have two years to go to court. Both of those laws provide that you can *voluntarily* choose to have the administrative agency investigate first, but you don't have to. Some state and local laws require an administrative filing before you can go to court. To be sure that you do not lose your rights, you should see a lawyer familiar with the law in your locality as early as possible.

12. BE THE CHANGE

Sexual harassment thrives in an atmosphere where women's rights are not valued. I've heard many tales of large companies expressing their commitment to respecting all employees, championing diversity, and having a no-tolerance policy for harassment. These boilerplate assertions are sometimes like a pretty facade put up around a corporate identity, which can collapse amid the reality of what might be going on in the office.

For one thing, it's the company's job to make sure employees understand the sexual harassment policy, not just assume that the words speak for themselves. In one study that really caught my eye, researchers at the University of Missouri asked why, if 98 percent of organizations in the United States have sexual harassment policies, sexual harassment is still so prevalent. Good question. They found that although the words in policies focused on behaviors, most people thought they meant *perceptions* of behaviors. According to Debbie S. Dougherty, one of the study's authors, this led to confusion and a sense of victimization, especially by men. "In this somewhat paranoid scenario," she observed, "a simple touch on the arm or a nonsexual comment on appearance ('I like your hairstyle') could subject 'innocent' employees (usually heterosexual males) to persecution as stipulated by the policy." As a result, the organization's sexual harassment policy was perceived as both highly irrational and as targeting heterosexual male employees. The study went on to say that the result of these perceptions meant that employees were more likely to see the "female targets of sexual harassment framed as the perpetrators and male perpetrators were framed as innocent victims." If this is true, it helps explain why people are reluctant to speak up for others in the workplace—they're preprogrammed to believe that men may be getting a raw deal.

Sexual harassment training is one vehicle for change, used by about 70 percent of companies. But how effective is the training? Many are just corporate cover-your-ass measures, in anticipation of possible future litigation. Or worse, they're a slap on the wrist for those who have been accused of harassment. At the very least, there should be a standard of effectiveness for these programs.

The EEOC's 2016 report on workplace harassment was critical of most harassment training approaches. It suggested more effective ways of getting the message across, such as gathering small groups of employees to discuss what they know and do not know about workplace harassment, in order to identify areas that might need more training or attention. It also recommended creating training programs that target bystanders, rather than just employees who face harassment.

True workplace change starts with a top-down commitment to equality and a positive workplace culture. The *Harvard Business Review* reports that sexual harassment costs organizations $22,500 a year in lost productivity for each employee affected. Calculating this cost, we can see that it makes financial sense for companies to take this issue seriously—in addition to the moral imperative for doing so.

Here's a simple test: when you're looking for a job, check the many online resources for places named the best companies for women to work for and to advance up the corporate ladder. These ratings are based on actual women's recommendations, and they provide valuable clues about what you can expect.

By the time sexual harassment is a reality in a company, there are signs that other things have already gone off the rails. So, before we get into what you can do to advocate for yourself if things go wrong, let's talk about what companies can do to prevent that from happening in the first place. Imagine, for example, the impact it would make if a company's president gathered the staff together and spoke directly about sexual harassment, saying something like: "Today I want to address an issue that is very important to our company—that is, the way we treat one another. You've all heard the term 'sexual harassment,' and you know it's not something that can be tolerated. But what does it mean? Today we're going to talk about that and try to clear up any confusion you might have. We place a high value on our employees being happy at work, so we're going to talk about the kind of environment that allows that to happen." This approach, coupled with mandatory sexual harassment training, can go a long way to creating a positive work environment.

Talking about it helps. Companies need to understand that these discussions are outside most employees' comfort zones. They won't talk about sexual harassment unless they are pressed to do so by management.

"Mandatory sexual harassment training does work," as Cliff Palefsky, a noted San Francisco employment lawyer who has been fighting discrimination, sexual harassment, and other employee-rights cases for his entire career, told me. "It's one thing to say, 'If you do this, you'll get sued or fired,' stressing sanctions. It's a more effective tool to explain, especially to men, why it's inappropriate or unfair, even when you mean well, when you do things like ask a subordinate for a date. Women should not be put in the position of fearing repercussions. In the workplace, your subordinates are required to be friendly and congenial, and that can be misunderstood. Men need to be educated to read the signals."

Jeffery Tobias Halter, a gender strategist and president of Y Women, has some tough talk for corporations about their commitment to eliminating sexual harassment. "It boils down to this," he told me. "Your company is only as good as your worst manager." For this reason, the senior leadership needs to draw a line in the sand: zero tolerance. That means addressing it head on. "When I was coming up in business, we were taught not to talk about sex, religion, or politics," Halter said. "But whether you like it or not, people talk. Business leadership needs to step up and create a civil environment—a safe environment."

That, Halter believes, means talking. "Men are scared to death to say anything about race and gender in the workplace," which is why the training work he does engages people in conversations about differences. "You can ask any question of anyone if you assume good intentions and do it in a genuine manner."

He gave me an example of how executives can find out what the women in their organizations are really experiencing. "Take a woman to lunch," he suggests. "Say, 'Tell me your experience about being a woman working here.' The first time, you'll probably get silence. Wait ten minutes, then ask again, 'Please tell me what I don't know about the experience of being a woman working here.' You'll get a little more. Then wait another ten minutes and ask again. This way you'll hear stories of what women experience and hear things you'd never thought of before."

He uses this simple exercise in his training, and finds it to be quite powerful. Women, he says, often have difficulty talking about their issues because they're not given permission to do so. When properly trained, a company's leadership can play an active role in opening up the dialogue.

It's an urgent matter for companies to get this right—to act decisively before sexual harassment occurs—because, as Palefsky said, the sad truth is that once sexual harassment is going on, "it's almost impossible to put Humpty Dumpty back together again."

The goal of any twenty-first-century company that seeks to attract the best and brightest women should be to fully embrace women's opportunity: paying them what they deserve, opening promising career paths, encouraging them to be the best they can be, and rewarding them when they excel. Women employees should be able to "lean in," as Sheryl Sandberg put it, without being resented for their success or placing their health and safety at risk.

FIVE

"Asking for It"

When I was Miss America, I got used to a certain amount of lewd treatment on the road. It bugged the hell out of me that, for example, I was sometimes introduced by my "vital statistics" rather than my accomplishments. After a lifetime of being judged on my violin talent, I found it jarring to be evaluated strictly on my looks. By the way, I didn't always measure up so well in the eyes of the perfectionist public, who thought "America's ideal" should be taller, thinner, prettier, and *nicer*. Most of the time, I shrugged it off. It was hurtful and sometimes disgusting, but I figured it went with the territory. I do remember feeling ashamed when the pageant organizers told me I had to smile more or be "friendlier." I sometimes felt as if I were a painting hanging on the wall for people to study and evaluate.

My experience is relevant to the myth that some women who put themselves out there are asking for harassment. This idea holds that they're asking to be treated like sex objects, and therefore their harassers should be absolved.

One of the first things that frequently happens when a woman claims sexual harassment is that the accused—and often, at a workplace, the company too—tries to find ways to challenge her credibility. The research in such cases can be brutal, seeking out any evidence that the woman might have been complicit, or have had some sort of past that would challenge her credibility. Our expectation of women to be perfectly pure and virginal is, ironically, part of the packaging of ideal womanhood that opens the door to harassment in the first place. I experienced this idealized pedestal as Miss America, but this idealization is, in itself, a disempowerment of women. In my time on that pedestal, I came across people who didn't believe that I was worthy of autonomy and respect.

At the end of my term, when I had an opportunity to meet with an important television executive, I thought he was interested in my talent and potential. I went to New York and spent a day with him, and he couldn't have been more encouraging. He called some top TV shows and told them I was a great talent, and I was flattered by his attention. I thought I was lucky that he believed in me. After a full day, he took me out to dinner and sat there advising me in a fatherly manner.

After dinner, he offered to have his driver drop me at my friend's apartment where I was staying. He and I got in the back seat, and I suspected no ill intent. But as we neared my destination, he lunged at me. His mouth pressed against mine, and he jabbed his tongue down my throat. Shocked and horrified, I wrestled out of his grasp. I gasped for the driver to stop, and I tumbled out of the car onto the street. I ran to the apartment building, and by the time I got inside, I was sobbing. I felt stupid and unnerved. Why would he do that? How had I believed he was truly interested in my talent?

Today, I know the answer, having spoken with many young women who have found themselves in similar situations. For young women feeling empowered and full of dreams, this kind of duplicity simply isn't on the radar. They're not on the lookout in what seem like benign situations, and they often have a high confidence in their worth, and believe that others do, too.

Not long after my encounter in New York, I was in another office— this time with a top public relations executive in Los Angeles. He was eager to show me how my Miss America experience had set me up beautifully for a media career. I was very interested in what he had to say. As Miss America, I had enjoyed the public side of the role—the speeches and presentations—and I was beginning to think that a media career was the right fit for me. We had a very good meeting, and when he suggested we get dinner, I thought nothing of it. I got in his car, and he immediately grabbed the back of my head and pushed my face so hard into his crotch I couldn't breathe. I somehow was able to forcefully push him off, and feeling sick to my stomach escaped from the car as fast as I could. Again, I thought, why had this happened?

Until I wrote my memoir, *Getting Real*, in 2015, I had never told anyone about these occurrences. Why? Maybe I thought I didn't have the right to complain, that I had somehow brought this unwelcome attention on myself. I was embarrassed, ashamed even. Who would believe me? I didn't want to be part of any statistics. I could rise above it. At the time, I didn't fully grasp that these were predators, and that I was not to blame for their behavior. In fact, I didn't even know what to call what had happened to me. When a friend declared, "That was assault!" I was surprised. Thinking about it now, I wonder why I didn't call it what it was. What makes women camouflage the brutality of these instances? If we don't feel confident in coming forward, we somehow pretend it didn't happen. Out of sight, out of mind. It somehow disappears.

As I look back today, older and wiser, I think I might see the signs that these men did not have good intentions. I hope so. But it's not always clear. I will say this: When a powerful person in a professional setting sexually assaults you, you feel all of your self-confidence drain out of you in a nanosecond. You question who you are. It almost feels as if you have to start over from scratch to build up your sense of worth.

And it never really goes away. Women who have been assaulted in this way suffer from a form of PTSD. Twenty years after that man shoved my face in his crotch, when I was a successful broadcaster and a mature, confident woman, I saw him walk by my office door one day. He was visiting someone in my company and I immediately went into panic mode, slamming my door and hiding in my office until I was sure he was gone. I was sweating and upset, literally back in the moment of the assault. Even though it had been two decades since the incident, I was completely debilitated. PTSD is real.

After my Miss America year ended, I returned to my studies at Stanford University, relieved to be just another student, anonymous in my casual clothes and without makeup. I could let go of all the publicity and the need to be "perfect" in every situation. I was also able to reflect on some of the discomfort I'd felt being on display. I signed up for a class in feminist studies because I really wanted to discover who I was as a woman in the world. The course turned out to be an outlet to express some of my deeper thoughts about being Miss America. I shared that perspective in a paper I wrote for the class:

> What I gained is of import to me. However, for this paper I wish to focus on what I feel, in retrospect, got lost during that year. In looking back on my experience, I now realize that being Miss America exacerbated all of the inferiorities women face on a daily basis in a man's world. While women are expected to manage their emotions, stick to women's work, do emotional labor and serve men, Miss America is really expected to fulfill these duties. It was as if it was OK to treat Miss America with such disrespect. Before I knew it, I had become a target on which men could and did project their true perceptions of women.

I continued, writing that before I became Miss America, I had never thought of myself as a "bimbo," and I hadn't thought others regarded me that way, either. But sometimes it had felt as if being Miss America was synonymous with being a bimbo. Let me be clear: My purpose wasn't at all to trash the institution of Miss America, which I honestly think provided me with a tremendous amount of opportunity. Rather, it was the culture that was in my sights. I had to face the fact that because I had put myself out there, in the minds of some people, I was asking for it—agreeing to be objectified. Agreeing even to be sexually assaulted. In that context, imagine if I had made formal complaints against the powerful men who assaulted me. Those people probably would have accused me of coming on to them. What was I wearing? What did I say? To what lengths would I go to get a job in TV? Or maybe they thought I deserved it because I'd walked on a stage in a bathing suit. The truth is, a modern woman is always fair game for these accusations, as the writer Marge Piercy put it so vividly in a poem titled "The Grey Flannel Sexual Harassment Suit":

> The woman in the sexual harassment
> suit should be a virgin
> who attended church every Sunday,
> only ten thousand miles on her
> back and forth in the pew.
> Her immaculate house
> is bleached with chlorine tears.

FAME SEEKERS OR TRUTH TELLERS? YOU DECIDE.

On October 7, 2016, an outtake from a 2005 *Access Hollywood* appearance showed Donald Trump speaking proudly about his approach to women in the most vulgar manner. His claim that his celebrity status gave him license to "grab 'em by the pussy" is burned into all of our brains. The tape broke a spell among women who said they had been sexually harassed or assaulted by Trump, and many of them courageously came forward: the Miss USA contestant who said he had kissed her twice without permission; the woman who said he had groped her on a plane; the receptionist who said he had kissed her in a Trump Tower elevator; the *People* magazine writer who said he assaulted her at Mar-a-Lago when she was there to interview him and his wife; the Miss Teen USA contestants who said he walked in on and observed them while they were dressing; the *Apprentice* contestant who said he had kissed and touched her against her will—and on and on. These were damning accusations, which Trump roundly dismissed as lies by women seeking fame. Neither Trump's own videotaped words nor the stories of his accusers had an effect on the election. And politics aside, it left so many unanswered questions. Were the women not credible? Did the public buy Trump's assertion that they were lying? Did people just not care?

Those who believe that the women were just fame seekers should meet Natasha Stoynoff, the former *People* magazine writer, who is the opposite of someone who wants notoriety. Natasha is a serious journalist who now writes bestselling books and screenplays. She says that she made the decision to go public in 2016, eleven years after her incident, following tortured consideration. When I met with her in 2017, she was still rattled by what she says happened to her, which had come roaring back into her life during the presidential campaign.

Here's what she says took place: In December 2005, Natasha, who had been on the "Trump beat" for years for *People* and had even attended his wedding to Melania, was at Mar-a-Lago interviewing Donald and Melania Trump for a feature on their first anniversary. Melania was seven months pregnant. Natasha thought the couple looked very happy, and Trump seemed to be a proud, doting husband.

At one point, they took a break in the interview so Melania could change her outfit for photos. Keep in mind that Trump, Melania, and Natasha had been together on many occasions, and they were friendly, if not friends. A comfort level had developed. So when Trump offered to show Natasha around the mansion, she thought nothing of it. They stopped at one room he particularly wanted her to see because it was "tremendous." It never entered Natasha's mind that anything was amiss. But when they entered, she says, Trump shut the door behind them. Then he pushed Natasha against a wall and kissed her forcibly.

As she recounted the scene eleven years later in *People*, "Now, I'm a tall, strapping girl who grew up wrestling two giant brothers. I even once sparred with Mike Tyson. It takes a lot to push me. But Trump is much bigger—a looming figure—and he was fast, taking me by surprise and throwing me off-balance. I was stunned. And I was grateful when Trump's longtime butler burst into the room a minute later, as I tried to unpin myself." The butler told them Melania would be down shortly, and they could resume the interview.

As they returned to the terrace by the pool where the interview was being conducted, Natasha was shaken to the core. "I felt sick inside," she told me all those years later. "I was there in a professional capacity. I had assumed he saw me as a professional. I wanted to impress him with my ability as a journalist. In that moment, he took it all away, made me nothing more than a sex object. That's what hurt the most. I felt worthless."

And, she claims, Trump couldn't resist a final jab before his wife returned. As Natasha, with trembling fingers, fiddled with her mic, she says he leaned forward. "You know we're going to have an affair, don't you?" he teased her with an air of certainty. "Have you ever been to Peter Luger's for steaks? I'll take you. We're going to have an affair, I'm telling you."

Because Natasha was a professional, she finished the interview. She forced herself to smile and behave normally. But when she returned to her hotel room, she burst into tears. "It was like the five stages of grief," she said. "Shock, tears, anger that he'd taken my power from me, self-blame—had I done something wrong?—and fear. Would he retaliate? I was worried that if I made a fuss about it, he'd do harm to my job."

That night she had a call scheduled with a former professor, and she found herself spilling the whole story to him on the phone. He advised her to stay silent. Trump was a very powerful man. He could make serious trouble for her if she exposed him.

Back home in New York, Natasha struggled about what to do. She told a few close friends and colleagues, trying to make sense of it, but she didn't want to be at the center of a scandal. And she didn't really want to go public anyway. She felt protective of Trump's wife. "I was very conscious of Melania," she said. "I didn't want to hurt her life."

The *People* feature about the Trumps' blissful wedded life ran, and Trump left Natasha a voice mail telling her the article was great, and she was terrific. She was painfully aware of how different his reaction might have been if she'd gone public.

Natasha took herself off the Trump beat, making a career sacrifice. Some months later she says she ran into Melania on the street in

Manhattan. Melania was holding baby Barron, and she greeted Natasha with a hug. "Natasha, why don't we see you anymore?" she asked. Natasha had no answer.

Life went on, but Natasha says she never forgot about the incident. It was like an ember that burned and occasionally flared up, but by 2016, she felt she'd mostly buried it. Then, the *Access Hollywood* tape aired. She watched, shaking and in tears, as Trump bragged to Billy Bush, "I just start kissing them. It's like a magnet. Just kiss. I don't even wait. And when you're a star, they let you do it. You can do anything." Natasha says her reaction felt like a form of PTSD; hearing Trump, she was back in the moment, back against the wall with his tongue down her throat. Later, during a presidential debate, when he denied ever kissing women without their consent, she felt disgusted and angry. It had happened to her!

It was a decisive moment. She decided to speak out, and *People* was on board. To the magazine, she was still a colleague who deserved its support. In her October 2016 essay for *People*, Natasha described her experience at Mar-a-Lago in 2005. When Trump's supporters criticized her, many friends and colleagues spoke out, saying she had told them her story contemporaneously, in contradiction to claims that she was just seeking attention during the campaign. Trump's reaction was telling. At a campaign rally in West Palm Beach, following the publication of Natasha's story, he mocked Natasha and dismissed her claim, saying, "You look at her . . . I don't think so."

Natasha had just finished coauthoring a *Chicken Soup for the Soul* book on body shaming, so his response didn't shock her. But she was surprised by Melania's reaction. She denied ever seeing Natasha on the street, and even had her lawyer send a "demand for retraction and apology" to *People*, which she also tweeted: "The true facts are these: Mrs. Trump did not encounter Ms. Stoynoff on the street, nor have any conversation with her. The two are not friends and were never friends or even friendly. At the time in question, Mrs. Trump would not have even recognized Ms. Stoynoff if they had encountered one another on the street."

Natasha felt for Melania, but she was also deeply disappointed when Melania defended her husband's words in the *Access Hollywood* clip as mere locker room talk, shrugging it off as something boys do. "I wasn't in a locker room," Natasha said. "I was at work."

As for the charge that Natasha was just looking for fame, nothing could be farther from the truth. What she wanted was dignity. Like so many other women, Natasha became a very reluctant warrior in this arena. "I still want it to go away," she admitted to me. "But I also want women to know they can speak out."

When the *Access Hollywood* tape aired during the campaign, and then women like Natasha came forward, many people turned a blind eye. Not me. Of course, I was close to the issue, but as a parent I decided I needed to make this a teachable moment for my kids, and I hoped millions of other parents felt the same way. We can't pretend that our kids don't have eyes and ears, that they aren't exposed to these stories. It was a difficult conversation, but I told them, "This is not the way to treat people." And we talked about it and shared why those behaviors were not acceptable. By the way, that conversation had *nothing* to do with political parties! It had *everything* to do with making sure my kids learned the right lesson about respect.

"WHAT GIVES YOU THE RIGHT?"

Heather McDonald is a successful stand-up comic with a raucous wit and a tendency to speak her mind, sometimes in an edgy way. I mention this because when we spoke, she herself made the point: "I'm a female who's an R-rated comic. How can I be sexually harassed? That's like asking how can a prostitute be raped." But these notions of who does and does not have the right to speak out is precisely what gives Heather's story so much authority.

Heather's experience began when she got a gig producing a podcast called *Juicy Scoop* for PodcastOne, which was owned by Courtside Entertainment Group. The chairman, Norm Pattiz, seventy-three, was a regular presence at the studio.

"You could tell the vibe at the place was hinky," Heather told me.

She says that Pattiz once brought a gun to a meeting and bragged about being an honorary LA sheriff. But she claims his sexual overtures made things really uncomfortable. She says he'd frequently make provocative comments, and would make her give him tight hugs when they met. At first she let these incidents go, thinking, "It's just his old man ways." She thought that he was annoying, but basically harmless. As often happens, the full impact of these behaviors kind of sneaked up on Heather. She didn't get how miserable the atmosphere was until she left and realized how happy she was to be free.

The final straw came one day when Heather was in the studio taping a commercial for a bra made of memory foam. In the middle of the taping, Pattiz knocked on the studio door and called out a compliment about how popular her show was. Heather called back that she had to finish the ad, but he came in and hovered. Heather felt flustered and even a little scared. She stumbled over the words. "You're making me nervous now," she told Pattiz. "I have to do one more take."

"Wait a minute," he said. "Can I hold your breasts?"

"No!" Heather cried.

Pattiz held out his hands, telling her they were "memory foam" hands.

"I pushed him away, and I kind of laughed because I was so embarrassed for him," she said. "But I was also intimidated."

Later that day, Heather called Pattiz and told him she wasn't going to do a podcast anymore. She said it was because she wasn't making enough money. He didn't take it well. PodcastOne was responsible for making her podcast available, and he made it very hard for her to get out of her contract.

Even as Pattiz was making life so hard for her, Heather was reluctant to tell people the real reason she'd left. "People said, 'Don't say anything. He could ruin you.' So I kept it to myself."

Pattiz finally gave her permission to do the podcast elsewhere, and that might have been the end of it. But Heather, observing that I and others had spoken out, decided that she too had an opportunity to stand up for herself and make a statement. And she had the goods—a tape of the episode in the studio, which belonged to her. So in brave fashion she played it on her podcast. Now people could hear for themselves about Pattiz's "memory foam hands." They could also hear Heather's extreme discomfort. Proof.

Pattiz wrote her an email that day: "I was only joking. If you were offended, I'm sorry."

Heather suffered some consequences for her bold action; there were some canceled gigs, and she was never again able to book a show on PodcastOne. "Some people wrote to criticize me for airing his 'alleged' comments," she said. "Alleged? They were on tape!" But the overwhelming response was positive. People told her that because of her, they felt the courage to stand up for themselves. "Choosing to speak my truth proved to be the popular choice," Heather said. Her publicist said, "It's not good for your career to be defined by this story." But she told me, "I'd love for young girls to see me this way."

And as for the question, "Should an edgy comedian be able to say she was sexually harassed?" The answer is, "Damn right."

I love this attitude, and I'm behind Heather 100 percent. She's right: Why should women feel apologetic or go into hiding? Instead of considering their behavior to be negative, we should honor people who come forward. Since this happened to me and I've become known for it, I've realized that it's a fantastic way to be a role model for the younger generation. Let's celebrate the warriors who come forward! I was very touched by the message Lena Dunham sent me, someone who's popular and has influence with many young people. She wrote, "You amaze me. I'm so thankful for the tide you've turned. Whenever you're down, please remember the army of women you lead. All of whom have your back. Always, Lena."

HE SAID, SHE SAID

I've come to despise the phrase "he said, she said." It's a convenient formulation that equates victims with harassers. In fact, it trivializes workplace harassment, and has become synonymous with "Don't take that risk; they won't believe you." Can you see how the very phrase instantly makes a woman less credible? The worst part of it is that in many cases, people actually do believe the accuser, but out of loyalty, fear for their jobs, or resentment, they maintain a stance of denial. And if there's no tangible proof, that's the end of the story.

Tamra was a young woman living her dream in California, with a great job as the assistant creative director for an up-and-coming advertising agency. She was very good at it, and saw herself advancing in the field. She hoped to someday become a creative director herself, and her boss was a mentor to her. All was well until about a year into her time at the agency. They were at a colleague's party, and she says that her boss offered to drive her home. Walking to his car, he propositioned her. And do you know what her first thought was? "Damn, all I worked for is going to be gone." She might not have realized how true her instinct was.

Although she very politely turned him down because he was her boss, he continued to pursue her sexually. "It was relentless," she said. "I thought it would stop. I even resorted to sending myself a bouquet of flowers from a fictitious new beau." Nothing worked. Eventually she confronted him, and then he turned on her. "He told everyone I was a liar, and crazy." She says that he systematically set out to ruin her reputation, and the other employees fell into line, treating her like a leper. "You're an evil woman," one of them told her.

This story has a twist. When Tamra finally reported her boss to HR, they believed her and her boss was fired. But that only made things worse for her, because her colleagues did not believe her. Now, not only was she considered a liar, but she'd brought down the man they all admired. She says HR was uninterested in the sabotaging behavior of the other employees; its staff was done with her after they'd performed their legal obligation.

The agency brought in a new creative director who happened to be a friend of her old boss. He basically ignored Tamra, and she finally spoke up for herself. "Do you know what it was like for me?" she asked, her voice full of the torment she was feeling. He lashed out, saying, "Do you know what it was like for *him*?" Unable to tolerate the work environment any longer, Tamra quit, only to discover that her good name had been destroyed in the industry. She hasn't worked in advertising since.

But the high-profile sexual harassment case brought by Anucha Browne Sanders against a former basketball star proved to be a different story. Browne Sanders, senior vice president of marketing and business operations for the New York Knicks, faced a "he said, she said" dilemma against the former NBA star Isaiah Thomas, who had become president of the Knicks. Browne Sanders claimed that her job environment changed after Thomas came on board in 2004. She said that Thomas made unwelcome advances, including touching, vulgar comments, and general hostility. He frequently called her a bitch and even called her a "ho." For a long time, Browne Sanders tried to work through it, considering Thomas's behavior a professional challenge she had to figure out. After all, she'd been in the sports industry for most of her life. But she ultimately determined that Thomas just didn't want to work with her, and he made that perfectly clear. Having run out of options, she complained to the management at Madison Square Garden, the Knicks' corporate owner, and was told that this was mostly a style problem, and she should try harder to work with Thomas. The lack of action on the part of the company led her to hire an attorney and file a sexual harassment and hostile work environment claim.

In January 2006, in the wake of her lawsuit, Browne Sanders was fired by the Knicks. She then filed a $10 million lawsuit against Thomas and Madison Square Garden. Because she was not subjected to an arbitration clause, she was able to get her case heard in court before a jury of her peers. And the jury ruled in her favor. On October 2, 2007, the jury awarded Browne Sanders $11.6 million in punitive damages. Unlike so many others, she did not leave her profession, but went on to further successes. Today she is the vice president of women's basketball championships for the NCAA.

Thomas's career with the Knicks ended in 2008 after the team suffered disastrous losses. In an ironic move, he was rehired by Madison Square Garden in 2015 to be the president and part owner of New York

Liberty, the Women's National Basketball Association's (WNBA) New York team. Although his ownership bid was suspended, he remains president as of this writing. Neither Thomas, Madison Square Garden, or the Garden's owner, Cablevision, have ever acknowledged any wrongdoing.

The "he said, she said" dilemma, which is common in rape cases, is exacerbated by the occasional public examples of false accusations, such as the University of Virginia case published in *Rolling Stone* magazine. However, according to social scientists, only between 2 and 8 percent of rape allegations are provably false. (There are no comparable statistics for sexual harassment.) In court, where the standard of proof is that which is beyond a reasonable doubt, rape cases that lack hard evidence can be difficult to prosecute—a reality that is more true when the defendant is a beloved figure, such as Bill Cosby. In spite of the fact that more than fifty women so far have made allegations against him, his 2017 sexual assault trial involved only one of them, Andrea Constand, with supportive testimony from one other woman. Although the law in Pennsylvania, where the case was tried, does allow for more witnesses to testify, the judge would not let the others tell their stories. They were silenced in this court of law.

Cosby arrived at the court every day accompanied by Keshia Knight Pulliam, who played his youngest daughter, Rudy Huxtable, on *The Cosby Show*. It is a strategy often used by the defense to show that the accused couldn't be so bad if women are supporting him. Pulliam said in a televised interview, "That's not the man I ever experienced." Well, I got that. I also met Cosby as a young woman when I was Miss America. He couldn't have been nicer. But here's the important point: neither Pulliam's experience nor mine is relevant to the accusations. Harassers and abusers don't treat every person they come into contact with in the same way. Harassers don't harass everyone. They often choose their targets carefully. And while we live in a country that rightly presumes that a criminal defendant is innocent until proven guilty, I believe this kind of female "support" sends a mixed message not only to other women, but also to men.

Unfortunately, the jury could not agree on the facts and a mistrial was declared. I am haunted by the reality that once again, a woman was not believed—at least, not by all the jurors. The prosecutor announced that a new trial has been scheduled for November 2017. I can't help but wonder if the result might be different if more of his accusers are allowed to take the stand and tell their stories at the next trial.

BY ALL THAT'S HOLY

Sexual harassment is an immoral act—so let's talk about morality. I have spoken frequently about the importance of my Christian faith, but by no stretch of the imagination have I been perfect—far from it. I've made a lot of mistakes. And apparently so have many other Christians when it comes to sexual harassment. A study by NationalChristianPoll.com in 2008 showed that more than a quarter of Christian women had experienced sexual harassment, often in a church or ministry setting. And no doubt within this group, the incidents are probably underreported. Although there is no more recent data, the results of this study are revealing of the way the Christian women surveyed often responded to harassment.

Of those who personally experienced sexual harassment, 50 percent said they avoided the perpetrator, 45 percent ignored it, 38 percent shrugged it off, and 31 percent prayed. A female minister noted that women in these settings tolerate a lot of inappropriate activity for fear of antagonizing the men in their workplaces.

A woman inspired by my story wrote about being harassed for years by her minister and boss. He created a climate in which sexual jokes, unwanted hugs, uncomfortable stares, and vague come-ons were a daily factor of her life. She agonized over speaking out: "I didn't realize how much my Christian commitments would complicate my situation. I wanted to act with as much grace and compassion as possible, in case my boss was actually just mistaken about what was appropriate for the workplace. (After all, he was a pastor, used to having close relationships with the people he worked with, right?) What I didn't realize was that he took advantage of the grace 'nice people' like me extended to him. I was also very concerned about treating him justly, and even after I recognized that his behavior counted as sexual harassment, I didn't want to report it, because I felt like the damage it would do to him and his ministry would be unduly harsh."

Nancy French, a bestselling conservative Christian author, who coauthored Sarah Palin's memoir, revealed in 2016 that she had been sexually abused by her preacher when she was a teenager. "I told myself I simply had a relationship with my preacher," she wrote. "I didn't know the word 'pedophilia.' Sexual abuse robbed me of my ability to feel the right things at the right times. It awakened me to things I shouldn't have known. My home—which should've been a place of comfort—became a place of abuse. Shame lodged into my soul like a gigantic, immovable beam." She never spoke of it, and eventually adopted the belief that the Republican Party was a place where she could express her values. Unlike the Democrats, who seemed to accept behaviors of men like Bill Clinton and Ted Kennedy, she says, the Republicans had a moral compass she could believe in.

Until 2016. "When the Trump videotapes broke, I watched the news and Twitter feeds of prominent evangelicals to see justice be done. But what I saw was all too familiar, and yet somehow still shocking. 'This is how men talk,' one said. 'Let him who is without sin cast the first stone,' another said. . . . It confuses me to hear the values preached from the podium, but ignored in real life; it feels odd to just repurpose a political party into an extension of the Trump empire without acknowledging the values which had so recently dwelled there."

When I spoke with Nancy, who was at home in rural Tennessee, where she lives with her husband and children, I was inspired by her strength and resolve. It was sad, too, because in going out on a limb and speaking her truth, Nancy says she suffered a backlash from the community of Christian conservatives to which she'd belonged for most of her adult life—especially for not supporting Trump. "I'm still conservative," she told me. "I just feel like the party has left me. I feel like I've been kicked out of the nest, and don't have a tribe, don't have a nest anymore."

This was her moment of truth, and it was deeply painful and all too real. "My party [the Republicans] will give lip service against sexual harassment and sexual abuse," she said. "We will say that we are the party that celebrates God. We will mock the Democrats for taking God out of their national platform. We will laugh about the Democrats' proclivities for hedonism. All of that stuff is a sham. All of it. It was all fake. And I fell for it. So, I just feel like an idiot. I realize, now, that I've been duped."

Back when Nancy says that she was being sexually abused, she didn't have the awareness or the language to evaluate what was going on. In the rural South of the 1980s, there was little acknowledgment of issues related to women and health. "I remember the first time I heard the words 'sexual harassment,'" she recalled. "It was by this woman who was at my high school. We were rednecks. In my junior high, we did not have seventh-grade science; we had 'hunter safety.' We would take our guns, we would go shooting. I was the best shot in the seventh grade. You really can't overstate the level of rural that we were. So, this woman came to talk to us about sexual harassment, how it's not appropriate. It was the biggest joke. We'd never even heard that there was such a thing, or that it was wrong. I just didn't have the proper vocabulary to describe the things that had happened to me."

When I finished speaking to Nancy, I reflected on this troubling cultural situation we've placed ourselves in, of choosing sides and hanging on for dear life, even when "our side's" actions are wrong. I often say in my speeches that sexual harassment is not a Republican issue. It's not a Democratic issue. No harasser stops to ask what party you belong to before he acts. It's a human issue, a women's issue, a man's issue. It's everyone's issue. So I deeply admire people like Nancy who've summoned the courage to speak up at what could be tremendous personal cost to themselves.

SIX

Forced into Silence

When you start a new job, you never expect to get into a dispute. You're just happy to be there, bringing home a paycheck and having a career. Maybe at the back of your mind you think that if something goes wrong, you'll have the ability to get a fair hearing, but that's not where your head is at in the early days. Now imagine that you find yourself in a situation in which you're being sexually harassed or discriminated against, and just when you muster up the courage to come forward, you are shunted into a secret hearing, and nobody will ever hear one damn thing about your case. Suddenly you're hearing a new term you haven't heard before: "mandatory arbitration."

You learn that buried in your employment contract is a clause that already predetermines how disputes will get settled at work. It's a system in which all too often you may be the one to lose your job, get less of an award (if anything at all) than in an open-court system, and in many cases, the perpetrator will be able to stay in the same position at the company without anyone ever knowing. Because in many mandatory arbitration proceedings, any details about the case are *shrouded in secrecy* forever. What's fair about that?

The issue of forced arbitration feels kind of eye-glazing, right? "Probably won't ever happen to me." But what I found out was that it is the centerpiece of one of the biggest fights we may face in the workplace. We talk a lot these days about our First and Second Amendment rights, but when we sign arbitration clauses, did you know we are being forced to give up our Seventh Amendment right? I want you to know about this so you can be equipped with all the necessary information to make the best decisions. As part of my new work in the last year, I've added my voice to those in Congress who are working to be fierce advocates for a change in the law.

On March 7, 2017, I went to Washington, DC, to participate in a press conference organized by Senator Al Franken. The purpose of Franken's press conference was to reintroduce the Arbitration Fairness Act of 2017, a bill to stop the unfair use of forced arbitration clauses in employee and consumer contracts. I was there to cast a light on one untenable aspect of forced arbitration in companies: the way it is used to settle even the most egregious cases of discrimination and sexual harassment, denying women their right to seek justice in the courts.

Appearing with Franken were other senators and one congressman supporting an end to arbitration, including Senator Patrick Leahy of Vermont, Senator Richard Blumenthal of Connecticut, and Congressman Hank Johnson of Georgia. This wasn't their first attempt; a similar bill introduced in 2015 did not pass the Senate.

In an era described by many as "populist," one would think this would be a popular bill. And that's why I'm working hard to make it a bipartisan effort. Historically, Republicans have not been in favor of rescinding arbitration rules. But at the time of this writing, I've been meeting with Republican senators, working on building Republican support for a compromise.

So, let's talk about this mysterious arbitration clause and how it might affect you. If you look at your employee contract, chances are good that you have one. They are increasingly common in companies seeking to limit their liability in disputes, and are in fact buried in many contracts that we sign, whether it's for nursing home care or even cell phone service. But they are nearly ubiquitous in employee contracts. These clauses often seem designed to protect the company more than to fairly mediate a dispute with an employee. You may not have even noticed such a clause when you signed your contract, and if you did, you probably thought nothing of it. After all, how many employees, excited about new jobs, are thinking about the possibility that things could go wrong?

Arbitration clauses are often shrugged off as boilerplate language that doesn't mean much in a practical way. They get great press from the courts and government agencies because they are said to reduce the glut in overburdened courtrooms. Sounds good on the face of it, right? Everyone knows how crowded the courts are, how bogged down we've become in our litigious society. But efficiency cannot be the primary value we hold in legal disputes. The primary value is justice—and too often, justice is denied in arbitration. For this reason, the fight against forced arbitration may be the civil rights issue of our time.

FORCED ARBITRATION'S MISCONCEPTIONS
Let's look at some of the misconceptions about forced arbitration.

#1 Arbitration Is Voluntary
The argument that victims of harassment have "agreed" to give up their constitutional rights, when in fact they have been *compelled* to sign an employment contract with an arbitration clause, is flawed. When employers make arbitration clauses mandatory in contracts, they insist that employees waive their rights as a condition of getting the job.

If you're told that unless you sign an agreement, you will be fired or not hired, does that sound voluntary? Ask Jennifer Fultz. Fultz had been working for four and a half years at a call center in Rockford, Illinois, run by Expert Global Solutions, handling help-line calls for JPMorgan Chase. In June 2016, Expert Global Solutions was acquired by Alorica, a large outsourcing firm. Soon afterward, Fultz was called into a meeting with the HR manager. She was handed a form titled "Agreement to Arbitrate," and told to sign it.

Fultz hesitated. She didn't fully understand what she was being asked to sign, and she asked the HR manager if she could see a lawyer to discuss it. This felt like a reasonable and responsible request, but instead of working with Fultz, the HR manager curtly informed her she had thirty minutes to sign. If she did not, the company would consider her to have voluntarily resigned.

Fultz didn't know what to do. She placed a desperate call to her father, seeking advice. "What would you do?" she asked him. Her father, an advocate of employee rights who owned his own small company, encouraged her to do what she thought was right. A few minutes after hanging up, he texted her, "Don't sign it."

Fultz refused to sign, and asked HR to call the police to escort her out; she wanted documentation that she was being forced to leave. A police officer showed her out, but she wasn't cited.

It was a brave act for Fultz, who as a single mother needed that job. She filed unfair labor practice charges with the National Labor Relations Board, which filed a complaint against Expert Global Solutions and Alorica. Her case hit the media, and Fultz became another reluctant face of the issue. All she wanted was her job back and assurances that Alorica would discontinue forced arbitration. As of this writing, Fultz's employer has not made a public statement about her filing.

It's disingenuous to say an employee can "voluntarily" waive rights before she even knows what such a waiver might entail. In a normal legal setting, the choice to waive rights takes place in the context of a specific case in which the consequences are clearly outlined. As Nancy Erika Smith points out, "The idea is that you are agreeing to give away your constitutional right in exchange for work. They used to say, 'Children agree to work.' They used to say, 'People agree to work one hundred hours a week.' They used to say, 'This person agreed to work for twenty-five cents an hour. How dare you tell me he has to have a minimum wage?' These arguments were always made, but we overcame them because we decided that we don't want that kind of society."

Smith also points out that forced arbitration actually has a stifling effect on the progress of discrimination law in our society. It's as if there is no record. "Since discrimination law is very new, the development of the law is essential," she said. "We look to court cases to develop the law. Arbitration prevents that. There are no opinions or rulings that have precedential value. Every arbitrator can make whatever arbitrary decision they want. It's a place without law."

#2: Secrecy Is a Good Thing

One of the biggest problems with forced arbitration is the complete lack of transparency. As we stated earlier, the procedures and outcomes are shrouded in secrecy, so it's impossible to know who's doing what to whom in companies. This protects serial harassers from being confronted by other women, and limits the pressure to remove them from the company. In contrast, public lawsuits shine a bright light on what goes on behind the scenes.

Harassers often hide behind arbitration and confidentiality clauses. The public never knows how many charges are filed and secretly resolved. In such cases, the victim may get a few bucks, but forfeits her job, and sometimes her career.

As I was interviewing women for this book, I frequently came up against this frustrating aspect of forced arbitration. Often women couldn't tell me their stories because they were sworn to secrecy by arbitration awards. We can't know if they were satisfied with the outcome, or felt unfairly treated. We can't know if they found justice, or were sidelined. We can't know which companies and individuals were found liable, and how much money it cost. We can't know if the alleged perpetrators are still in the same workplace. When companies use arbitration, a veil is drawn over everything. Other employees have no idea how many claims have been made against the company or individual executives. This undoubtedly stops other people from coming forward. In a nation that values transparency, especially in matters of law, this secrecy feels un-American.

Supporters of forced arbitration will try to convince accusers that secrecy is a good thing for them. Nancy Erika Smith believes that women often accept this as true because they feel ashamed. She cites a successful sexual harassment case in the early nineties, *Lehmann v. Toys 'R' Us*, in which the plaintiff, Theresa Lehmann, filed the case under her own name. The appellate division, the second court level, changed it to TL, her initials, when they published their opinion about her case. When a reporter called Smith asking what she thought, she told him, "Three men in the appellate division decide that she should be ashamed because she's a victim of sexual harassment." Smith believes that women will continue to be shamed unless they go public with their harassment claims. She also applauds the movement among young women to name themselves as rape victims. "We've got to change our heads about this," Smith told me. "We should not be shamed when we're sexually assaulted. We should not be shamed when we're sexually harassed."

And in cases of forced arbitration, we have to be clear that secrecy is meant to benefit the company, not the individual.

#3: Arbitration Is Just Like a Court Proceeding

Having your case heard by an arbitrator is not the same as going before a judge in court. For one thing, your family and friends are not there to give you moral support. You're on your own, with only your lawyer, sitting in a law office. But the legal differences are also substantial. There is limited discovery and no right to appeal a decision, even if there are legal flaws in the process.

"Think about it," Cliff Palefsky said. "The court has to enforce the arbitration ruling even if there are errors of fact or law. Even if the arbitrator gets it wrong! This is not a justice system. It is a dispute resolution system, which is misused and mischaracterized as justice. It's the *opposite* of justice." Worst of all, forced arbitration deprives people of the right to have their cases heard by a jury of their peers. Victims of sexual harassment are not second-class citizens, and they should not get second-class justice.

One woman told me that she had no idea she had an arbitration clause in her contract—it really *was* in the fine print. After she made a complaint to HR, she says she was completely shut out by everyone she worked with, even former friends. "Nobody spoke to me," she said. Suddenly she felt that she had no value. She was always a very high performer, so this was a new experience. She withstood the retaliatory atmosphere for a few weeks, and finally walked out and went to a lawyer. Only then did she find out about the forced arbitration clause in her contract.

This woman is forever prevented from publicly speaking about the outcome of her arbitration proceeding. But she privately painted a vivid picture of the experience for me. She described sitting across a table facing the people she'd named in her complaint, describing their angry glares. This went on for a full day. In a courtroom setting, the intimidation factor is limited by having the parties seated side by side; they can't loom over you. But this woman says she found the arbitration hearing very hostile to her. These were people she had worked with and once respected! To sit for hours across from their hostile faces was like torture.

Without full discovery, there can be no fair or thorough hearing. "The plaintiff has the burden of proof," Palefsky points out. "You need access to documents, and you can't get those without discovery. The employer can say, 'We were getting complaints from her customers,' but they are not required to show proof. In most cases, there's no cross-examination. There are no depositions. The company has all the documents and all the witnesses, and they're untouchable."

If the experience of arbitration bears little resemblance to a courtroom, the results are also different. According to a 2011 Cornell University study led by Alexander Colvin, individuals are much more likely to lose under arbitration than in federal court. Of the personal cases Colvin studied, only 21.4 percent won in arbitration, compared with 36.4 percent in court. Even for those who win, the damages paid as a result of arbitration are far less than those paid in court proceedings—an average of $36,500 in forced arbitration, compared with $176,426 in court.

#4: Arbitration Protects Both Parties Equally

This is not always true. In almost every way, the company has an advantage. It's an entity; you're only an individual. The company may have been through the process before, and is probably familiar with the proceedings. Even if you have a good lawyer, that might not be enough to balance the scales.

The process begins with selecting an arbitrator. You might have a say in who that is, but as Smith points out, most available arbitrators are from the ranks of retired judges—overwhelmingly older men who grew up in an era when sexual harassment wasn't even illegal. They got on the bench when there were few women or minorities in the workforce, and most judges came from a pool of large law firms. Even today you don't see a lot of public defenders sitting on the bench. So there's an inherent bias. There's also a repeat bias. If you're an arbitrator who certain companies often hire, there is an expectation that favorable rulings could mean repeat business. A relationship has been formed.

To add insult to injury, another little-known factor is that you might have to pay. Some contracts require workers to pay fees for arbitration, which is not cheap. And if your company headquarters is out of state, you might have to pay travel expenses as well. The process, which is sold as easier for plaintiffs, in reality can often be much more difficult.

#5: Arbitration Is a Preferred System

"Today there is a false presumption in favor of arbitration," Smith says. She points out that the Federal Arbitration Act, which was passed in 1925, makes arbitration a viable process, but does not assert that it is preferable to a jury trial. "Our Declaration of Independence mentions jury trials. Our Constitution mentions jury trials. So, this false 'preference' for arbitration is driven by judges who, when they retire, go out and make lucrative careers as arbitrators. The back pages of every law journal are filled with advertisements by ex-judges looking to be hired."

Smith says the way arbitration is practiced today bears little resemblance to the original intent of the Arbitration Act of 1925, which established the practice. It was designed to allow sophisticated parties—think general business contracts—to mutually agree to waive rights to a trial in order to expedite proceedings and reach an agreement. It was not designed for discrimination cases, in which one party is able to force the other into "agreement."

What angers Palefsky most about forced arbitration is that judges, who should understand and respect the primacy of the justice system, are key players in it, essentially diminishing what the courts do every day.

Lest we forget, we have rights under the Constitution, and no arbitration agreement should be able to dictate that we waive our statutory rights. This is particularly important for all discrimination claims, including sexual harassment. It means, in effect, that if you already have a right determined by law—such as the right to not be sexually harassed in the workplace—your company cannot force you to take a complaint about the abuse of that to secret arbitration.

SEEING THE LIGHT

We can find some good news in the massive class-action arbitration suit filed in 2016 by thousands of employees of Sterling Jewelers, the parent company of Kay, Jared, and Zales jewelry stores. The class-action suit stems from arbitration that was first filed in 2008. At the time, the complaints had little chance of a public airing. One woman reported that her manager told her, "Sterling is highly protected . . . we have our own resolution program, which means you cannot hire an attorney. . . . You're not going to win." But now the class-action suit includes as many as 69,000 women. With an agreement between the plaintiffs' attorneys and the company, 1,300 pages of sworn statements were released to the press, with the caveat that the names of managers and executives who were accused of harassment be redacted.

According to the complaint, the culture at Sterling was shockingly regressive, and it started at the highest levels. Among the behaviors described were "frequent references to women in sexual and vulgar ways; groping and grabbing women; soliciting sexual relations with women, sometimes as a quid pro quo for employment benefits; creating an environment at often mandatory company events in which women are expected to undress publicly, accede to sexual overtures and refrain from complaining about the abusive treatment to which they have been subjected. It has even included sexual assault and rape."

With some of the secrecy around arbitration already breached with the release of these documents, it will be interesting to see how much additional secrecy can be maintained as the case goes forward. With Sterling's stock taking a hit with the revelations, the public will be watching and demanding answers.

There are other signs that the role of arbitration is getting a fresh look at the highest levels. The EEOC has voiced a concern that the widespread use of forced arbitration could undermine progress in workplace equality. To quell that, President Barack Obama signed an executive order in 2014 prohibiting contractors who do business with the federal government from forcing their employees to arbitrate sexual harassment claims or many other kinds of discrimination claims. During the 2016 presidential campaign, Hillary Clinton affirmed her support for the measure. But during his first months in office, President Trump rescinded the order.

So here's how the issue stands now: For individuals, the bad news is that you probably have no recourse but to sign an arbitration agreement if it is required by your employer. But that doesn't mean you are totally helpless. It might be possible to negotiate within the agreement—for example, getting the company to cover expenses, or making sure you have a full say in the appointment of an arbitrator.

As a community, the best thing we can do is be educated and involved in protecting our civil rights. I strongly believe that this issue can be nonpartisan, with Republicans and Democrats coming together to make sure the fundamental liberties enshrined in the Constitution are upheld.

SEVEN

Men Who Defend

Some people say New Yorkers aren't the nicest strangers on the street. Always in a hurry with somewhere to go: yes, but that's me too, so I actually find New York City energizing, albeit totally different from my hometown in Minnesota.

But after I became one of the prominent faces of the sexual harassment issue, I started seeing a different side of New Yorkers. Last summer and fall I spent a lot of time in the city, and I began to notice a pattern. As I walked the streets to and from the train station to meetings, people stopped me to let me know what they thought: "You go, Gretchen." "Thank you for speaking up, Gretchen." "You have balls, Gretchen," and so on.

But here was the surprising part: the majority of those approaching me were men. Yes, women did stop me, but more were men. Many of them said, "Thank you for doing what you did for my daughters." And that became a common theme. Many of them wanted to shake my hand when they said it—"for my daughters."

Every single encounter was meaningful to me because each felt so incredibly personal. On almost every occasion I had to work hard to fight tears, but these men helped me realize what I had done was important not just for women, but for everyone—men included.

When I was growing up in a small town in Minnesota, I was lucky to have men in my life who unabashedly rooted for me, particularly my father and my maternal grandfather. Thanks to them, I never felt less capable or equal than my brothers or other boys. I was a tomboy who preferred playing football in the yard with my brothers to playing dolls, and no one ever told me I shouldn't. And I gave as good as I got in those football skirmishes! I grew up expecting to stand side by side with my male counterparts, and when I became involved in issues of sexual harassment and abuse, I realized how important it was to bring men's voices to the table.

As I've said, after I left my job, I heard from thousands of women, and their huge, supportive response was very meaningful to me. But do you know who else I heard from? *Men.* I call them enlightened men; men who defend women, men who care. Like the broadcast journalist Jake Tapper. I didn't know Jake before this happened, but he reached out to me and thanked me, saying that his daughter would grow up in a better world because of what I did. It moved me to the core.

Many other men reached out as well. They wanted me to know that they supported me, that they were appalled by sexual harassment and assault, that they wanted to be part of the solution, not the problem. Their words, in texts and emails, from both friends and strangers, meant a lot to me and inspired me. Here are a few:

I am so happy that my daughter (and son!) know you. That is truly the highest compliment I can ever pay anyone. They will know henceforth that no matter your gender, or the height of your achievements, no woman should ever have to be made to feel less, or robbed of an opportunity, because of some misogynistic jackass who can't read the Constitution.

It's not very often that I write to someone I don't know, and no, I don't know you. But I felt I should try to connect and thank you. I have a family with three children. I have worked in a variety of companies over the last twenty years. And I see that very soon my oldest daughter will be off to university and eventually the workforce. There are many good behaviors I can role model for my children, but I as a parent have always struggled with how I was going to explain to her how to handle inappropriate behaviors in the workplace that I have witnessed. My son knows that I have high expectations for his behavior, and my oldest daughter as well, but I really had no role model. I do now. I can point my daughter to you and tell her, "You see what this woman did? It takes courage, but this is what you must do."

I know I am a former soldier, but seeing you on YouTube shows the strength you have more than anything I have done . . . Always be strong and never back down to anything. You are such an inspiration to women across the world.

As a father of two daughters in the workplace, I often cite professionals like yourself as excellent role models and mentors. You have much to be proud of, enjoy your success, you deserve it.

It's heartwarming to hear from men, because harassment is not just an issue for women. It's a societal issue, and women alone are not going to solve it. We need men to be on board too. That means taking women seriously in hiring and promotions, treating them with dignity and making sure others do too, and a whole host of other actions and attitudes.

This point of view has been a long time coming because there is such a high social barrier for men in making women's issues their own. The breakthroughs have come because men have stepped up and talked about their role in stopping harassment. In a TED Talk that went viral, with over three million views, Jackson Katz, an international thought leader and educator on gender equality, stated clearly, "I don't see these as women's issues that some good men help out with. In fact, I'm going to argue that these are men's issues first and foremost."

Katz says that calling them "women's issues" gives men an excuse to not pay attention. "A lot of men hear the term 'women's issues,' and we tend to tune it out. We think, 'Hey, I'm a guy. That's for the girls,' or, 'That's for the women.' A lot of men literally don't get beyond the first sentence as a result. It's almost like a chip in our brain is activated, and the neural pathways take our attention in a different direction when we hear the term 'women's issues.'" He has made it his mission to help men change that inner conversation.

A big part of this movement involves men believing that it is to their benefit to make the issue of sexual harassment their own. I was struck when reading a *New York Times* interview with Michael Kimmel, a sociologist and the executive director of the Center for the Study of Men and Masculinities at Stony Brook University. In the piece, he defined very succinctly the internal conflict men face when thinking about themselves. "If you were to ask men, Republican or Democrat or anywhere in between, what does it mean to be a *good* man, they'll all tell you pretty much the same thing: honor, integrity, responsibility. But ask what it means to be a *real* man, and we're talking about never showing your feelings, never being weak, playing through pain, winning at all costs, getting rich, getting laid."

This conflict starts young, and by adulthood it becomes almost instinctual. In the worst-case scenarios, we see the "real man" ethos at political rallies and in male-dominated industries. I've certainly seen it in my Twitter feed! But the "real man" cannot exist without the "good man," and it is the "good man" who will rise above limiting stereotypes and create change.

It helps when those male voices come from the highest office in the land. On June 14, 2016, President Obama opened the first United States of America Women's Summit by telling the crowd of five thousand, "I may be a little grayer than I was eight years ago, but this is what a feminist looks like." Then in August, on the occasion of his fifty-fifth birthday, he wrote an essay for *Glamour* magazine emphasizing how important it is for men to stand up for women. "Michelle and I have raised our daughters to speak up when they see a double standard or feel unfairly judged based on their gender or race—or when they notice that happening to someone else," he wrote. "It's important for them to see role models out in the world who climb to the highest levels of whatever field they choose. And yes, it's important that their dad is a feminist, because now that's what they expect from all men. It is absolutely men's responsibility to fight sexism too. And as spouses and partners and boyfriends, we need to work hard and be deliberate about creating truly equal relationships."

MAN UP

Jake Tapper credits his wife, Jennifer, with opening his eyes about women's experiences. "Not that I was sexist," he told me. "I had good women bosses, including Diane Sawyer, whom I respected, and I had promoted women. But my wife educated me about the day-to-day ways women aren't treated fairly. I've been awakened."

Jake vividly remembers his first date with Jennifer. When she learned that his middle name was Paul, she told him that one of her greatest heroines was Alice Paul, the suffragette. Fast forward, when their first child, a girl, was born, they named her Alice Paul Tapper. "She lives up to the name," Jake said. Now with Alice Paul and his son, Jack, at home, he's more serious than ever about being someone who "can set an example of what a twenty-first-century man behaves like."

Jake, who is the chief political correspondent for CNN, the anchor of the daily news show *The Lead*, and the moderator of a Sunday show *State of the Union*, has been upfront when it comes to speaking up about outrages against women. "Don't get me wrong," he told me. "I wasn't always a choirboy. I was in a fraternity at Dartmouth, and we all said stupid things. It's not that I haven't ever had a sexist thought. But I recognize those aren't the good parts of me."

In particular, Jake distinguished himself in the aftermath of Trump's *Access Hollywood* tape. His interview on *State of the Union* with the former New York mayor Rudy Giuliani is a model for the way men can speak back to attempts to excuse bad behavior. In the interview, Jake reminded the mayor that Trump's comments weren't carelessly delivered by an eighteen-year-old, but were made by an older man. "It's really offensive on just a basic human level," he said. "Who did he do that to?"

"This is talk," Giuliani said in defense of Trump. "Gosh almighty, he who hasn't sinned throw the first stone here. I know some of these people dropping their support—"

Jake interrupted. "I will gladly tell you, Mr. Mayor, I have never said that. I have never done that. I'm happy to throw a stone. I don't know any man, I've been in locker rooms, I've been a member of a fraternity, I have never heard any man ever brag about being able to maul women because they get away with it, never."

In an effort to protect Trump, Giuliani appeared to be demeaning men, saying it is common for them to talk that way. Jake wasn't having it. I imagine that most men watching this exchange, even if they supported Trump, did not see themselves in Giuliani's depiction. This "boys will be boys, men will be men" excuse is, frankly, embarrassing. But the instinct to stick up for one of your own is a powerful silencer for men who would speak out. "It's much easier to look away," Jake told me. But he has made it a principle not to do that.

Over the years, he has developed a sensitivity to unfair and inappropriate behaviors, and is determined to "impact my little corner of the world." He realizes that the stories that become public are just the tip of the iceberg. "For every one story we hear about, there are dozens if not hundreds [of women] that went along because they're afraid for their jobs, living paycheck to paycheck," he said. Why does it continue to be a problem? Jake has one theory. "For certain men, there is no group left they feel comfortable attacking except women. They'd never say anything anti-Semitic, racist, or bigoted. But all the rules go out the window when it comes to women."

For the future, Jake believes, change will come only by raising an enlightened generation, and he focuses on his daughter and son. "Fathers who become feminists because they have daughters are wonderful," he said. "But sons are important too. They need to understand that girls need to be treated with dignity."

Another man who reached out to me was Paul Feig, the director, producer, and screenwriter who brought us such popular hits as *Bridesmaids* and the *Ghostbusters* remake. "A huge part of the equation is men helping to lead the way alongside women—enlightened men," he told me. In some respects, this has been the story of Paul's life. Growing up an only child, Paul was a sensitive kid who felt uncomfortable around the typical boys' groups, which felt off-putting and somewhat bullying. (His acclaimed show *Freaks and Geeks* was in large part based on his own experiences.) He felt more comfortable around a "nerdy" crowd, particularly in drama club, where there were a lot of girls. His female drama teacher was, he says, the biggest influence in his young life. He believes that being friends with girls and then women—not "just dwelling in a male world"—gives him perspective.

Paul fights for equality in the movie industry. He looks back fondly on the great films of the thirties and forties, when men and women were portrayed as equals and intellectual sparring partners—think Tracy and Hepburn. But he believes that the introduction of the blockbuster mentality in moviemaking changed all that. Blockbusters are basically made for fifteen-year-old boys; they project a "dude mentality."

This being the norm, Paul stands out as someone who pushes different narratives. His work has been characterized as norm-bending and gender-bending. When he first started telling people that he was making *Bridesmaids*, they were dismissive. "It was unheard-of for a movie to star six women." It became a huge hit. But Feig sparked real controversy with his remake of *Ghostbusters* with female leads. He described to me the ferocious assault that went on for two years. Many men were outraged, as if he were ruining *Ghostbusters*. "The dam burst," he said. "My Twitter feed became an ugly place, with a deluge of blatant misogyny. These were not true fans of *Ghostbusters*, but just guys who were mad to see women in those roles. It showed me we're more behind than I thought." More positively, though, Paul cites the tremendous outpouring of messages he has received from women and girls who have been thrilled with the movie. All of this is very important. "The way movies, comedies, portray women affects the culture, and bleeds over into workplace settings," he said.

Paul has thought deeply about the reasons male culture (he, too, pointed to the *Access Hollywood* tape) is still so mired in sexist language and behaviors. "A lot of verbal sexual harassment is guys who think they're being funny," he said. "'Just joking around.' And when they're challenged, they'll accuse you of being 'politically correct.' Like that's a bad thing. Political correctness exists for one reason: to not hurt people's feelings."

Paul believes there are two separate cultural tracks, both of which lead to sexual harassment. "One is, 'Let's all have fun and say anything we want.' The second is, 'I'm going to take advantage of my power.'" He calls it the Morons and Monsters theory. The Morons are the guys who don't know that they're being offensive and harassing, and the Monsters are the ones who demean women for power. He believes the first one is harder to change because it requires people to stop, think, and resolve to be different. As severe as abuse of power is, altering the common mentality—often portrayed as lighthearted and joking around—is more important to creating a cultural difference.

On a personal note, I want to thank Paul for the kind words he said about me when I asked him to introduce me at the Matrix Awards in New York City in 2017. Paul called me, as one of the honorees, "the bravest woman I know," going on to say, "And I know a lot of brave women." My eyes welled with tears—and this was before I had to speak! It had been an emotional year. I was so grateful to be recognized and respected in such an incredibly meaningful way. It's something I will never forget.

I feel it is especially important for younger men to be on the forefront of changing sexual harassment in society. That is why I was so impressed to read a piece by Yashar Ali, a writer, politico, and commentator who often takes on issues of bias. A few years ago, Yashar wrote a piece called "A Message to Women from a Man: You Are Not 'Crazy,'" which is still a viral post today. It opens:

You're so sensitive. You're so emotional. You're defensive. You're overreacting. Calm down. Relax. Stop freaking out! You're crazy! I was just joking, don't you have a sense of humor? You're so dramatic. Just get over it already!

Sound familiar?

If you're a woman, it probably does.

The impetus for writing this piece (which was followed by others) was hearing from women about the ways their experiences had been sidelined—what Yashar calls a form of gaslighting, where you are manipulated into thinking your reactions are crazy. "I wanted to rebrand the word 'gaslighting' to make it useful for people now," Yashar told me. "When I wrote it, I knew it was going to be a big deal. I put it in a drawer for three months before I posted it, and within an hour of posting, 140,000 people had read it. It's still read by a half a million people a week."

Yashar realizes that a big part of the reason his piece had such a dramatic impact was because it was written by a man. He's on a mission, unafraid of repercussions, and he always defends women against sexism on Twitter—which is how I came to be aware of him.

I was curious about how this young man, who is Iranian American, came to be such a strong advocate for women. "It has to do with growing up in a family in which we were never told women were less than equal," he said. "My mother was a very confident person, the director of public health at the University of Illinois." Yashar also said that he and his sister were taught to trust their instincts. "My parents never gave me flack for my beliefs."

"Sexism is sexism," he told me. "It's like the Zika virus. Once it was only affecting six babies in Brazil. Now it's in Miami and Hawaii. If we don't stop it, it will spread. And the fear men have of speaking up for women is outsized. I have never lost a friend or a colleague because I've spoken out."

Yashar's solution to make sexual harassment go away in companies is simple and direct: "Publicly apologize, and get rid of the offenders. To deal with sexism, be swift, harsh, and without any reservation. Send a message: 'We don't tolerate it.'"

There is no question that men who model attitudes of respect and equality for women were often raised with strong role models themselves, which underscores the important role we can play with our own children. The political consultant, author, and commentator Matthew Dowd grew up in a Detroit Irish Catholic family, with six brothers, four sisters, and a "strong mom" who was summa cum laude at the University of Detroit and a schoolteacher before she started having children. "The lessons she taught, I carry with me to this day," Matthew told me. "Particularly this one: 'No one is better than you, but you're no better than anyone else.' It was ingrained in us that we treat each other with respect, and that informed how we treated everybody else."

Matthew emphasizes that fathers have a vital role to play in patterning behavior. "By our behavior, we show our daughters how they should be treated. When men don't pattern respect, girls grow up to settle for bad behavior.

Part of that modeling involves being the one to stand up when you witness sexist or demeaning behavior. "I've watched situations change instantly when someone stands up, because people always follow the leader," Matthew said. "We don't have to give up and say things are impossible to change. Civilization *does* change, and we can be part of it." That change, Matthew believes, in part involves men breaking out of the box of what defines their manhood. "In our culture, we're presented with a false choice—either be a guy's guy, or treat women with respect. It's as if you have to pick one or the other; that you can't be a strong man *and* treat women with respect."

Once again, patterning behavior is the key. "My daughter has seen me cry," Matthew said. "At the same time, if someone did something untoward, her dad would be the first to push back." Patterning is also important for sons. "My oldest son, Daniel, has an incredibly big heart and is the most sensitive person you'll meet in your life. He also served two tours of duty in Iraq, where he carried an M16 rifle."

STAND UP!

Larry Wilmore stands out for me as a man who unapologetically supports equality and respect for women, using comedy to bring the point home. His Comedy Central program, *The Nightly Show*, which, sadly, was canceled in 2016, was a rare oasis in the late-night arena, where he actually talked about issues that affected women.

Larry was relentless in covering the rape allegations against Bill Cosby. "People worshiped him," Larry told me, which complicated calling him out. "But these allegations had been going on for many years. I was astounded by how many women made accusations and were not heard. How can you not be moved by how many people were *not* moved by their stories? When we protect powerful men, we make women invisible."

On one segment, Larry set out to define rape for Cosby. He explained that a rapist is a person who "commits an unlawful sexual act with or without force on another person without their consent, and [being] physically or mentally incapacitated, whether by alcohol, drugs, or being asleep, is unable to consent."

He went on. "By denying their victims their sexual agency, a rapist increases their own deluded sense of self-worth, which is why a rapist can tell someone else to pull up their pants even though he himself never did"—referencing Cosby's frequent criticism of young black men and the way they dress.

When we spoke, Larry pointed to growing up with a single mother as his initiation into "a world I did not understand." He said, "I witnessed how hard it was for her." Later, when she told him she had been abused as a child, he was forced to process the reality that exists for many women, and he struggled to understand it. Invited to a *Vagina Monologues* "night for men," he was in the audience when the question was asked, "How many people know someone who has been sexually abused or have been abused themselves?" He looked around and saw that almost everybody was raising their hands. "I almost started crying," he said. "Because in the world, nobody raises their hands."

Experiences like this influenced his late-night program. "I used *The Nightly Show* as a platform to force people to take a stand," he said. "I never saw sexual assault and harassment as a partisan or black and white issue. It's one hundred percent a human issue. I have a daughter, but even if I didn't have a daughter, I'm a human being and shouldn't be silent."

The *Access Hollywood* tape highlighted the underlying intentions that women experience but can't fully identify or prove. The exchange between Trump and Billy Bush was itself ugly, but Larry was particularly struck by how the two men treated the woman they had been discussing afterward. "It was revelatory," he said, characterizing all the women "who don't have enough evidence, but know something is not right. They can't even verbalize what's going on, but they can feel it. As a writer, I see people's intentions." He sees the way harassers won't say enough to get them in trouble, but they make their intentions clear. "That's why so many cases of sexual harassment go unreported."

As for women in the workplace and the role men can play, "It's a listening issue. Women are not listened to. We have to teach young men to respect women. Don't say, 'We have to teach young women to respect men.' There's no equivalency. The issue here is how men treat women. That's what has to change."

Another prowoman comedian is Pete Dominick, who was once a regular guest on my show, where I had a Friday "Man-el." What I loved about Pete was that he had a way of representing a male point of view without "mansplaining." He was also razor sharp and funny, a stand-up comedian with a social conscience. These days, Pete hosts a daily three-hour show called *Stand Up! with Pete Dominick* on Sirius Radio. Recently, the tables were turned, and I was on his show one morning.

Pete really tries to understand gender issues from a male perspective, and he's a big proponent of women's rights. Every day on the air, he speaks about his two daughters and how he's dedicated to raising them as independent, confident, powerful women in a world where they can pursue their dreams fully.

Sexual harassment and assault, he says, "is a disease that comes from the past and lives in the present. It will only really change when men understand (A) what women are dealing with; and (B) decide the standard you walk past is the standard you accept. If I allow that behavior, I'm condoning that behavior. I'm part of the problem."

Getting on board means recognizing that the problem really exists. On the air, Pete shared his experience. "When I talk to women about this issue, about sexual assault, about rape, it seems like too often—I want to be careful I don't use absolutes—but far too often women you get close enough to to have that conversation with will tell you, 'Oh yeah, I've been raped. Yes, I've been sexually assaulted.' This is an issue that women understand, unfortunately, far too intimately, that men don't believe, don't want to believe happens as much as it does."

Later, I sat down with Pete to talk more about why he is so impassioned by the issue, and what he and other men can do. "Every day on the radio I interview smart women about important issues," he said. "If I had any thought that women are fragile, the anecdotal evidence of brilliance—including my wife—shows otherwise." Pete always speaks out if someone is being disrespectful or inappropriate around women or about them. "I don't tolerate certain behaviors and language," he said. "It doesn't always win me friends, and I don't care. . . . Men are having a difficult time knowing what they can and can't say," he added. "I say, 'It's about time you learn how to talk to people.' It was never OK with women before, and now they're speaking up and changing things. If men don't know how to behave, they should learn how to behave. I don't want people treating my daughters that way."

But just as important as speaking out, is taking action. "It's one thing to say the right things—we also have to advocate for women in the workplace and defend their interests," he said. He does this in his own workplace and in volunteer efforts. "I'm paying it forward for my daughters."

BEING "THAT GUY"

W. Brad Johnson, PhD, and David Smith, PhD, first came to my attention through their book, *Athena Rising: How and Why Men Should Mentor Women*. They bring an interesting perspective. Both are naval officers, psychologists, and professors at the US Naval Academy. And both are committed to bringing women to a place of equal standing. Realizing that women's advancement and equality issues are usually advocated for by other women, they call on men to be "that guy"—the one who stands up for the women in their midst.

They call their book "a call to arms," writing, "For too long, most of us have been a part of the problem . . . we're all silent beneficiaries—or whistling bystanders—in a world that persists in keeping women on the sidelines, excluded from key leadership roles, and earning less pay for equal work."

Brad and David shared some of their thoughts with me about the task they have set for themselves—not just in the world of the navy, but also in the larger culture. "The nature of work is gendered as masculine," David said. And in the military, he said, this is dramatically evidenced by the legal structure of career paths that have been designed since World War II around a particular type of person: a man with a wife at home. Policies and practices are created to fit that person. The upshot is that women in the military are penalized for having children. It's designated as a women's issue, but it's really a family issue.

"It's personal for me," Brad said. "My son and daughter-in-law are both lieutenants in the navy; they're pilots. And they're getting to the point of discussing having a family. One of them will have to step away. More often it's the woman. We have a lot of work to do to level the playing field. Meanwhile, we give the message to women, 'We want you here,' but we don't think of how we're pushing them out the door."

When the story broke in April 2017 about a Facebook group, Marines United, sending out nude photos of servicewomen, Brad and David were disappointed that so much of the public focus was on the generals. "What about all the other guys?" they ask. "The bystanders who are aware of it and say nothing?" Focusing only on the leaders ignores a more pervasive problem: the everyday guys who don't have the moral courage to stand up when they witness bad behaviors.

The two men have created a unique program at the naval academy called Sexual Harassment and Assault Prevention and Education. It's a peer-education program run by students, who spend eighty hours training and then work with classes across four years. The sessions are wide ranging, but a lot of the focus is on helping the students become more thoughtful and purposeful. "We talk about everyday language," David said, "and how we can create a sense of privilege versus those who are 'less than' just by the words we use. When you walk into a mixed gender room, and say, 'Hi, guys,' you're using a masculine term that signals preference, in the same way that when you address a group of females as 'girls,' you are signaling that they are lesser. It might seem like no big deal, but language makes a difference in the culture."

ON AND OFF THE FIELD

We cannot address the role of men without talking about the culture of sports. I've been a big sports fan since I was a child. One of the greatest thrills of my young life was meeting Fran Tarkenton, the famous Vikings quarterback, and getting his autograph. I'm married to a sports agent. Both my son and my daughter play sports. Having said that, there is no question that the sports culture can be a breeding ground for negative male behaviors. Increasingly, though, it can also be the place where a change of culture is most promising. Kathleen Neville, a leader in the movement against sexual harassment who has written two books on the subject, including one detailing her own experience, has been working with the NFL since 2010 and wrote the first sexual harassment policy for the league. Her ally in this cause is Troy Vincent, the former great cornerback for the Miami Dolphins, Philadelphia Eagles, Buffalo Bills, and Washington Redskins, who is now the executive vice president of the NFL's football operations.

Vincent is dedicated to changing a sports culture that has defined masculinity in ways that give permission to abusers and harassers.

Under his leadership, not only has the NFL strengthened its code of conduct, but it has also instituted training in personal conduct and domestic violence awareness, and has formed alliances with organizations that fight sexual assault. Vincent is also active in A Call to Men, an organization that promotes healthy models of manhood, in sports and in life. (Gloria Steinem was a keynote speaker at the group's 2017 conference.)

Vincent believes that men have to play a role, or else the problem of violence against women is not going to go away. He stated this plainly in a March 2017 op-ed piece about domestic violence during No More Week, part of a campaign to end domestic violence and sexual assault, writing powerfully, "It's no secret that more needs to be done to change the culture of violence so often perpetuated by men in our society. We are taking steps towards this at the NFL, and are continually striving to do more to prioritize these issues—as every corporation, campus, community and family should. Nobody is an innocent bystander. We all play a role. As men, we must speak up and say, domestic violence will not happen in my home, in my neighborhood, on my campus, on my team, in my workplace or in my circle of family and friends."

Vincent challenges men to take tangible steps to make this change happen, including being allies for women; modeling healthy, respectful manhood for young men; refusing to laugh at jokes that disparage women; and having the courage to confront men who are disrespectful or abusive.

He often takes this message on the road. Neville described a recent event at which Vincent gave a presentation to student athletes, calling on the men to lead. "It was so powerful," she said. "You could have heard a pin drop. These big, huge players were crying during his presentation."

FROM BYSTANDERS TO ALLIES

Some men have stood up for women in the workplace and paid the price themselves. In many cases, they've faced the same retaliation as the women victims.

John Shouldis's New Jersey case was a classic of courage. Shouldis was a police officer in Teaneck, New Jersey, who stood up for Teaneck's first female officer, who had filed a sexual harassment claim. He agreed to give a deposition and testify on her behalf, and as a result was subjected to severe retaliation. After he supported his female colleague, Shouldis was repeatedly denied a promotion, deprived of overtime, surveilled as he signed in and out each day, frozen out by other officers, and threatened with expulsion from the PBA local. He was shunned and ostracized on a daily basis. Ultimately, he was reassigned to a patrol car on a midnight shift, and relieved of his other responsibilities.

Finally, it became too much for him. He suffered a nervous breakdown and took a leave. But when he returned, the harassment picked up where it had left off. He decided he had no other option but to sue. It was a traumatizing process, and a full decade would pass before Shouldis finally received justice from a jury—a $4.1 million award for the retaliation he had endured. But despite the victory, there is no question that the experience destroyed his life, made him ill, and ended his career—all because he did the right thing and told the truth on behalf of a female colleague.

It takes courage to be the one to stand up when others are running for cover. I was impressed by the story of another man who told me about the experience that changed his life forever.

"A lot of us want the workplace to be fair and good," Mark, a former media executive and now an entrepreneur, told me. "When it isn't, we all suffer."

Mark, a graduate of a top Ivy League school, was on a career upswing when he took a challenging job with an international company. His job was to lead a small innovation team on the cutting edge of technology. He was excited by the challenge. One of his team members was Sharon, a very well qualified young woman, a business school graduate with good credentials.

The week Mark joined the company, his boss, Jeff, called him in and ordered, "I want Sharon off the team."

Mark was surprised. "Why?" he asked. He didn't see a reason, and Jeff was unable to specify. "If something is not working, let's figure it out," Mark responded.

"Your job is not to figure it out," Jeff said. "Your job is to get her out of here."

Mark left Jeff's office, not overly alarmed. "I thought, 'I'll figure it out,'" he said. Things calmed down after that, and Mark figured that maybe Jeff had just been having a bad day. Everyone on the team, including Sharon, was working extremely hard, sometimes putting in sixty- to eighty-hour weeks.

But about a month later, Jeff went after Sharon again. Mark asked him to back off. Jeff just glowered at him.

The frustrating thing was, there was nothing about Sharon's performance that could explain Jeff's attitude. Mark thought he just didn't like her style. She was hardworking but reserved, and Jeff clearly favored a culture in which people were bold and in your face. Mark had heard other stories about Jeff's behavior toward women in the department. One had left right before Mark came. "She was pushed to the couch," he said, referring to her need to see a psychiatrist to deal with the hostile work environment. She finally decided it wasn't worth it to stay, and she quit. "The workplace hostility was extreme," Mark said. "The message was, If you're going to survive, you have to be as tough as Jeff is."

This is an example of the way harassment doesn't necessarily need to involve sex to be sexual (i.e., gender oriented).

New to the company and its culture, Mark tried hard to balance these competing realities. He was a classic problem solver, a well-trained business executive, and a principled leader, a believer in creating workplace environments that allowed people to thrive. But he was having a hard time making it happen, and the crux of the matter was the hostility his boss directed at this particular woman, a good worker who didn't deserve it.

One day Sharon came into Mark's office. "I've got to talk to you," she said. He invited her in and told her to shut the door. Sharon collapsed into a chair and immediately started crying. "It's so tough working for Jeff," she sobbed. "It's gotten really bad." As Mark tried to calm her down, she dropped a bombshell. She told him she had a medical problem, but was afraid to leave her office for necessary trips to the ladies' room—a situation that affected her health.

By this point, alarm bells were ringing in Mark's head. This was no longer just an uncomfortable workplace dispute. It was a matter of health and safety. As Sharon's supervisor, he knew he had to speak up.

Reluctantly, he went to see the head of HR, who had been his contact when he was recruited to the job. He told her the story and asked, "What can we do to protect Sharon, and protect the company as well?" She assured him that she'd take care of it.

The next day, he was called to Jeff's office. He walked in and found his boss, his feet up on the desk and a scowl on his face. He accused Mark of taking sides against him. Mark tried to reason with Jeff and explain himself, but he wasn't listening. By the end of the meeting, Mark saw that he had now become the enemy in his boss's eyes.

In the coming months, Jeff made it clear that he no longer wanted anything to do with Mark. He even said to Mark, "We don't want you here." Mark deliberated long and hard about what to do. "I really felt alone," he said. "No one at the company was on my side." He finally decided to cut his losses and move on. Sharon remained behind, but she soon left the company.

It was a traumatic experience, and he sought coaching to make sense of the experience, learn from it, and move on. In time, he found work that was equally challenging and far more rewarding. "For the modern workplace," he said, "the bravado of the old world is obsolete. How we relate to and treat each other at work is important." Fortunately, he is able to foster a positive and supportive culture where he now works, within an environment where all employees are well respected. But he is troubled by the lingering consequences of the hostile environment too often present in many large corporations.

As Mark discovered, being a "real man" didn't mean being a tough guy or a brute. So what *does* it mean? I had an interesting conversation with Bob Thurman, a worldwide authority on religion and spirituality, Buddhist science, and His Holiness the Dalai Lama. He put this issue of masculinity in perspective, coining the phrase "cool fierceness" for me. That is, to be fierce doesn't have to mean being angry. "The fuel of rage is frustration where anger takes over, and that's ineffective," he said. And the image of the "angry woman" is counterproductive. "Women," he said, "are socialized to be polite, and the frustration builds until they feel as if they're going to blow their tops." But "cool fierceness" means being strategic, knowing how to advocate for yourself along the way, before you get angry. "It's preemptive ferocity and forcefulness," he told me. "Being fierce means being cool like a martial artist, not reactive when out of control."

BREAK THE "MAN CODE"

Jeffery Tobias Halter, previously mentioned, identified what he calls the "man code," which contributes to the unequal treatment of women. He told me, "This code is embedded in male cultural norms, which become default corporate norms." Halter says one of the precepts of the code is to avoid all things feminine. "Even talking about women's issues and advancement can be considered feminizing. Men are told to be strong, show no emotion, to 'man up.' The mandate to avoid all things feminine also puts women in a double bind of always appearing either too soft or too hard."

Another tenet of the man code, Halter says, is to be a man's man. "That means keeping the company of other men and primarily engaging in male activities: sports and sports talk, drinks after work, and other activities that exclude women. There's nothing inherently wrong with men hanging out together, but when women are consistently shut out of bonding experiences, it reinforces the male culture of the workplace."

Halter believes there is an underlying mandate for men to enforce the man code, which means turning a blind eye to bad behavior. With regard to sexual harassment, Halter says many men get stuck thinking that if they stand up for women who are harassed, they may be breaking the man code.

The solution? "Men need to take an active role and challenge the man code," Halter says. He believes men can do that by creating a new code that enhances everyone's well-being and success in the workplace.

I've often said, "We *need* men in this fight." The responsibility of fixing sexual harassment in the workplace, or pay inequity, or women being blocked from advancement, shouldn't be only on the shoulders of women. As long as so few women sit atop Fortune 500 companies as CEOs, or in positions of power in so many other companies, we need enlightened men to help us lead the charge.

EIGHT

Enough Already!

So many women feel frustrated in their jobs when they're not treated well. And maybe they stay silent. They take it and take it, until finally they can't take it anymore. And they say, "Enough already!"—and make their move. I know that feeling. I've been there several times in my career. You can feel so powerless. But now, looking back, I realize that the one way you can feel *powerful* in your life is to *find exactly what you can control*. Life is full of twists and turns, so you have to focus on the things whose outcome you can affect. For me, it is every day trying to be my best self, and having a good relationship with my children, my husband, and my parents. My biggest piece of advice when you feel like other parts of your life are spinning out of control is to hold on to the things that make you feel good, that are within your reach. So when we say "Enough already," it's not an expression of defeat, but one of self-awareness and power. It's the moment when we finally realize who we were truly meant to be.

WOMEN STRIKE BACK

On the morning of April 6, 2017, I walked onto a stage at the David H. Koch Theater at Lincoln Center in New York City, flanked by my attorney, Nancy Erika Smith, and a firefighter, Patricia Tomasello, for a panel on sexual harassment, moderated by CBS's *60 Minutes* correspondent Lesley Stahl. The event was part of the eighth annual Women in the World Summit, a three-day presentation by powerful women from around the world and the men who support them.

The auditorium was packed, engaged, vocal, and responsive to our lively discussion. It was particularly meaningful to have Patricia on the stage. A twenty-year veteran of the Fairfax County Fire Department in Virginia, Patricia filed a lawsuit in 2016 against seventeen of her colleagues, accusing them of bullying, sexual harassment, and conspiring to get her to quit. The first African American woman to be promoted to fire investigator in the department, she said she endured years of mistreatment at the hands of her colleagues and supervisors in what became a concerted effort to ruin her career. In addition to badgering her for sexual favors, she said they made false claims against her, and even planted marijuana in her vehicle.

Patricia's case illustrates that in spite of women's advancements in all industries, there are places in society where women still struggle to feel welcome. She told the audience that silence about the issue is nurtured in these environments. "If someone speaks out, they're immediately ostracized," she said, and she warns her female colleagues, "You will face retaliation." Yet, even knowing that, she decided to be one of the brave women who chose not to remain silent.

"What I have found out is that in 2017, every woman still has a story," I told the audience, repeating a line I use frequently. "And we've got to change that."

It's wonderful to be in a setting where you can feel the passion and resolve in the cheering voices and clapping hands. Since I began this journey, I have felt the energy around this issue grow. When I decided to write this book, I said to myself and others, "This is not just a book. This is a movement." And every time I take to the stage now to speak, I *know* it's a movement that won't just dissipate with political winds or other news of the day.

It was meaningful that the Women in the World Summit came a little more than two months after the Women's March on January 21, 2017, when two and a half million women and men took part in 673 marches in all fifty states and thirty-two countries. The largest was in Washington, DC, and was particularly poignant coming just one day after the presidential inauguration. The marches were a promise of action, the vow of the movement I'm talking about, and the words I'd been saying over the months before were a part of it. A woman I interviewed for this book declared loudly to me, "Enough already!" It sounded to me like a battle cry. We as women have decided to wake up. We as women are saying "enough." We as women will stand up and speak up.

But it's a long road. Progress doesn't happen as in those old charts of the march of evolution, in a continual advancement. It's choppier, as President Obama put it after the 2016 election: "You know, the path this country has taken has never been a straight line," he said. "We zig and zag and sometimes we move in ways that some people think is forward and others think is moving back." That reality feels frustrating at times, but I also believe that there is a continuity, a forward thrust, that can't be denied.

I've been giving a lot of thought to what it takes to be a movement, to say together, "Enough already," and believe it. What does it mean to have a voice? To use your voice?

It nags at me that women who report harassment and abuse are often not believed. That reality, so ingrained, is a big reason women are afraid to speak. And the worst fear in some cases is that women's own family and friends, the people who love them most, won't believe them.

I see this every day: people being divided into opposing camps on this issue, often depending on their political positions, when it should be something we all agree on as Americans. We should all be making this issue a priority.

We live in a society where the danger of terrorism had been elevated to a primary issue, even though incidents of it are relatively rare. Yet according to the Rape, Abuse, and Incest National Network (RAINN), 351,500 people are sexually assaulted every year. The cumulative effect is in the millions. Where's the public outrage? Where's the political resolve?

Why do women have to fight so hard to be heard and believed? Certainly, the impulse to protect the reputations of powerful people and organizations is a big part of the reason. But I also think it goes deeper into the psyche of the population, especially in America. In a nation that boasts of its democratic principles, people find it hard to accept that such egregious abuse is commonplace. They don't want to believe that women (much less their own mothers, wives, daughters, and sisters) could be treated this way. It spoils the idealized picture. So it's easier to ignore the problem, make excuses for the abusers, or blame the women.

It's true that many women I've interviewed experienced terrible outcomes; there was no silver lining, no big moment when they prevailed. But the fact that they reached out to me told me something very important. It told me that they were ready to say enough was enough. Many of them said it was the first time they'd talked about their experience. And that's a start and a victory. The big question is, what can we do to give them a megaphone? How can we help them use their experience for empowerment, and not defeat?

Time and again, women have spoken to me about feeling powerless, about being lonely, and I've felt lonely myself. But when the reality of sexism seems overwhelming, it helps to reach back in history. Over a century and a half ago, women started asserting their rights in what led to the suffrage movement. They started out few in number with small resources and little support. It was physically dangerous then for a woman to speak from a public stage, but a few of them did. It was as though the world were against them. How on earth did they ever imagine their goals were possible? What gave them the courage to make such seemingly outlandish demands?

What they had was each other, a tenacious band whose bond was unbreakable. Together, they designed strategies, coaxed fearful sisters out of hiding, enlisted like-minded men, and built a movement. They were not afraid. In 1872, Susan B. Anthony was actually arrested for casting a ballot in the presidential election. She boldly used the occasion of her court hearing to give a treatise on women's equality. She died in 1906, before women got the vote, but she seemed to be clear that it was a long journey, saying, "Oh, if I could but live another century and see the fruition of all the work for women!" That century has come and gone, and here we are, holding her torch.

It's clear that sexual harassment doesn't exist in a vacuum, but is rather an element of and an indication of a larger crisis for women seeking equality and respect. Tremendous advances have been made, but hardened attitudes take longer to change. According to a 2016 report by Francine D. Blau and Lawrence M. Kahn of the National Bureau of Economic Research, women have actually closed the education gap with men, and have nearly closed the experience gap. So why is the pay gap still so large, even for the same jobs? People often talk about women's career tracks being broken up because of having children. (I don't think we're ever going to be able to change that reality!) And even though employers aren't supposed to ask, I've spoken to women who have been questioned by nervous bosses about just how many children they're planning to have. Women are still stigmatized for family involvement, while men aren't.

Believe it or not, even in this day and age, there is still an underlying sense that married women don't need their careers because they have an economic fallback. Sometimes that bias pops to the surface. Years ago when my husband, a sports agent, negotiated a new contract for one of his premiere players, someone at work actually said to me, "Oh, I guess you don't have to work anymore now"—as if my own career and ambitions meant nothing! Unfortunately, it wasn't the first time I'd heard it. When I was fired earlier in my career in Cleveland, one of my bosses told me, "You're married now. You'll be all right." I'd never heard any man be told that. So even when it's unspoken, many women sense that it's part of the calculation. Karen, whose experiences on Wall Street were described earlier, told me, "My husband was very successful and known on Wall Street. I know that before my firm fired me, they were thinking, 'She'll be OK. Her husband makes a lot of money.'" What made this attitude especially frustrating for Karen was that she was such a high performer herself. She was regularly cited as an up-and-comer in the industry, while deftly handling the challenges of working in a male-dominated field. "I'd travel all the time with men," she told me. "There were so many men. Me and men. There was always that knock on the door in the middle of the night by my married coworkers. There were comments about what I wore. I sort of just went with it, went with the flow. Didn't answer the door when the coworkers knocked. There was always that sort of sexual harassment that was prevalent, but not articulated. We women just kind of thought it was the way of business." But once Karen got pregnant, her accomplishments were easily overlooked and she was sidelined, even though she was among the highest performers in her firm.

In their book, *The New Soft War on Women: How the Myth of Female Ascendance is Hurting Women, Men, and Our Economy*, Rosalind Barnett and Caryl Rivers write about the less overt, insidious ways in which women are held back in the workplace—which is why they call it a "soft war." That is, while opportunities, even in traditionally male fields, are purportedly open to women, underlying biases continue to get in the way of women being considered "a good fit." It appears we still have a lot of work to do.

Where can we start? Like our foremothers in past movements, we can start with our actions. We can start with our voices. We can start with our mind-sets. In the end, this isn't just about sexual harassment and assault. It's about changing an entire culture. And if we're ready to say, "Enough already," we have to speak up. Here are some ways I believe we can begin.

SLAY THE DINOSAURS

"You take a look at her . . . I don't think so." We all remember Donald Trump's loud retort to Natasha Stoynoff's claim that he sexually assaulted her. Of all the responses, this is one of the most disheartening. Although few people would come out and say it, the belief is deeply ingrained in our culture that to be sexually targeted, you have to be "harassment worthy," meaning good looking. I heard the same crack in many tweets about my own situation, almost always from men. And some of the women I spoke with actually said that their friends and even mothers suggested they should be flattered that their bosses or coworkers found them so attractive.

"These days, women get mad if you compliment them," complained a man I know. But he got it wrong; women don't mind being complimented. They mind being *objectified*. If a stranger tells a woman she looks hot, that's objectification. He doesn't see her as a person, but rather as an object. And every woman I know would prefer a colleague to say, "Your ideas in that meeting were off the charts" to, "You look great in that dress."

The other side of complimenting a woman for looking good is humiliating her for not looking good enough. William Goldman, the famous screenwriter, was one of the celebrity judges at the Miss America pageant the year I won. He later wrote a book—unfortunately, a lot of it about me—in which he disparagingly referred to me as "Miss Piggy." He also characterized me as "chunky." What an insult! Especially since I weighed 108 pounds at the time—the thinnest I had ever been. The most confident woman on earth can be stung by assaults on her appearance. I imagine even Hillary Clinton and Angela Merkel get tired of hearing their looks repeatedly slammed. It's so beside the point. So mean. So *objectifying.*

Right up there with how women look is how they are perceived to act—particularly their tone. Karen, referenced earlier, told me of a regular conference call her company had with the CEO. It was a real give-and-take, in which they could ask the CEO any question on their minds. The calls were frank and sometimes a little rough. "I asked the CEO a question," she said, "and I guess I had a little edge to my voice, but the men always had edges to their voices. He called me afterward and he said, 'I really didn't appreciate that tone of voice.'"

Ah, yes, "tone." I've heard this most of my life, as women do. We twist ourselves into pretzels to appear both warm and friendly and tough and competitive, and it can be a strain. How many of us have had the experience of "forgetting" to smile because we're concentrating on doing our work, only to be called an "ice queen?"

In 2016, the Kellogg company surveyed more than two thousand British women about the descriptions they found the most derogatory. Some of them were distinctly British, but many were familiar to Americans as well, including:

"Drama queen"
"Hormonal"
"Bitchy"
"High maintenance"
"Diva"
"Ball-breaker"

It's interesting that when we complain about these depictions, we hear that it's our problem or we're being overly sensitive—an attitude that gives permission for people to say offensive things about women, minorities, gays, and others. Few of us would tell our children they can say anything they want to say, no matter how rude; yet today a lot of people are loud and proud about their right to be offensive. A New Zealand man named Byron Clark helped turn the conversation around. Referencing an assertion by the author Neil Gaiman that being politically correct simply means "treating other people with respect," Clark created a computer program called PC2Respect that changes all browser mentions of political correctness to "treating people with respect." Thus, a comment that "I hate political correctness" becomes "I hate treating people with respect." It puts things in perspective. When people look at it this way, it may give them pause before they call you a diva.

GRAB THE BULLY PULPIT

"The whistleblower wore high heels." That's how Alyssa Bermudez's story opened in a *Washington Post* article, and after I read it, I thought, "She's a warrior." There she was, tall and beautiful, looking quite fierce as she walked a solitary picket line in high heels in front of the Transportation Security Administration (TSA) building in Washington, DC.

Alyssa's lone picket was a particularly bold way of getting her point across. She made the decision to take on the TSA after the agency ruled that her complaints about sexual harassment were without cause—before, she says, they fired her a week before her probationary period ended. Instead of quietly disappearing, she stood up for herself and other women in the most dramatic way she could think of.

All over America, women are refusing to go quietly when they're harassed, demeaned, and pushed aside. Instead, they're grabbing the bully pulpit.

SPEAK YOUR MIND

Have you seen Ashley Judd's 2016 TEDWomen talk? She opened with a string of insults that had been leveled at her online: "Ashley Judd, stupid, fucking slut. . . . Fuck off, whore. . . . Ashley Judd, you're the reason women shouldn't vote." Her conclusion: "Online misogyny is a global gender rights tragedy."

And to think the reason Judd had been subjected to an incredibly ugly, onerous wave of online bullying was simply because she'd tweeted a criticism of her sports team's aggressive play. The threats of violence—rape, death, sodomy—poured in, so shocking to her that she said *enough already* and decided to take on the cause of cyberbullying.

Another famous woman to join that fight is Monica Lewinsky, who calls herself "patient zero" in cyberbullying. She says that she was called all kinds of horrible names like "a tramp, tart, slut, whore, bimbo, and, of course, 'that woman.'" I can't imagine the courage it has taken for Lewinsky to return to the public stage, but this is a cause she cares about and her new mission. She is determined to do what she can to protect others, especially young women, from the shaming she received and is still recovering from.

It's not a small matter. Some experts state that cyberbullying is just as damaging to women as physical violence. Think about that. Knowing this, we cannot afford to downplay its significance. And although bullying is most often a term we use in the context of children (and we'll talk about that in the next chapter), it happens to adults too. Especially to women. We've all heard about "revenge porn," which is the nonconsensual publication of sexually graphic images online. It has become such a serious issue that thirty-six states have passed laws banning it. Women are also more vulnerable to being stalked online, which, as a former stalking victim, I can assure you is the most terrifying thing that can happen to you.

My stalker terrorized me early on in my career for four long years; following me to my first job in Richmond and then to Cincinnati. No one can appreciate the constant fear of a stalking victim unless you've lived it yourself. And while I'm thankful to the police in both cities, who helped me as much as they could to keep me safe and find unique ways to try and prosecute the jerk trying to destroy my life, the fact remains that the issue of stalking doesn't get as much attention as it deserves—because it's almost always a woman's issue. After enduring all those years of hell, wearing an alarm around my neck 24/7, and constantly looking over my shoulder to see if he just might be there, we finally collected enough evidence to bring him to trial. I can still see myself in the Cincinnati detective's office, crying and shaking as I testified over the phone (thankfully I didn't have to see my stalker face-to-face in Wisconsin, where he was being tried) as though it were yesterday. When somebody strips you of your ability to live your life in any kind of a normal way, that should be punishable by more than just probation—but that's all my stalker got. Only because he violated the probation and tried to contact me did he actually have to go to jail, and then for only one year. I can write about it now and be at peace because he's no longer alive. But to any woman who's ever been in a similar situation, my heart goes out to you, and I know and feel your fear.

REJECT THE MYTHS

Now that we know more about the issues that can hold women back, it's in our power as a society to choose what we believe and don't believe. It's up to us to get even more educated, and to acknowledge that many of our prejudices about stalking or sexual harassment or assault are myths. They're simply not true.

Myth: Women Bring It On

This is the oldest line in the book: that women bring on unwelcome sexual attention because of the way they dress or act. It's an easy out for the harasser and his allies, but according to a study by Colin Key, a psychologist at the University of Tennessee at Martin, people who blame the victim often tend to be harassers themselves. Key and his colleagues asked college men ages eighteen to twenty-eight to take a survey about how likely men are to sexually harass women. The survey asked questions such as whether women use sex to their advantage, and if they actually like sexual attention. Then the men were asked to read eight vignettes of potential sexual harassment and how likely they would be to relate to the men and blame the victims in each case. The men who earlier agreed that women used sex to their advantage and were often to blame for harassment tended to identify most with the harassers in the vignettes.

We must reject the idea that women encourage harassment through their dress and demeanor, and place the focus on those doing the harassing. Harassment is not a cause-and-effect matter. Women don't provoke harassment because they wear makeup or dress a certain way. Most harassment, as we know, is a power play, not a helpless reaction to an attractive woman. We need to reinforce that fact constantly. In the twisted logic of harassers, by sexualizing women, they give themselves permission to treat them as sexual objects.

Here's how I think we can make this happen: We can begin by speaking openly with the men, and even the women, in our lives who might not understand the experience of being sexually harassed, and why even seemingly innocuous incidents can be demoralizing. Focus on how the behaviors make you feel:

"When my coworker tells me I'm 'hot' and he wishes I weren't married so he could date me, it feels like he doesn't respect me for my talents and contributions at work."

"When my coworker hugged me in the elevator, I felt trapped and scared. I didn't say or do anything to encourage him."

"When the CEO introduced me as 'our beautiful new vice president,' I was embarrassed. I thought everyone was staring at me for my looks, not for what I was bringing to the company."

"When my colleagues excuse Joe's constant jokes and innuendos by saying, 'That's just Joe. Ignore him,' I feel as if they're condoning his behavior and even agreeing with him. It makes me uncomfortable."

"When the boss asks the women in our department to be in charge of the Christmas party, and says, 'This is a job for the ladies,' it sounds like he's saying that the men have more important jobs to do."

Myth: Women Make It Up

Contrary to the myth that women make up stories of sexual harassment, in actuality, women not only rarely file false complaints, but they vastly *underreport* sexual harassment and assault. Every study shows that women fear retaliation or further injury. In fact, according to the National Research Council, sexual assault is significantly underreported. As for harassment, while studies show that one in three people have been sexually harassed at work, the actual complaints are a drop in the bucket. We need to kill the myth that women are out there making things up to hurt powerful men.

Let me paint you a picture of a typical striving woman in a company or organization: Chances are she was a real achiever in school, with activities and internships under her belt, and high ambitions for her future. Once in the workplace, she goes the extra mile, proving herself by working twice as hard as everyone else. Because she has always been rewarded for her hard work and abilities, she expects to continue to thrive. And this is the woman whose career is likely to be stalled or ruined as a result of allegations of sexual harassment. She's not a "troublemaker." She doesn't overreact to minor slights. She would walk barefoot across hot coals before she would even dream of complaining about anything. Her eye is on her future aspirations, not on her current grievances. Why on earth would such a woman invent a story that places her reputation and career in jeopardy?

We must reject the idea that a woman in this situation is lying; especially given that exposing a harasser puts *her* career in jeopardy.

Myth: Nonphysical Sexual Harassment Is Not Harmful

Harassment doesn't have to involve sex or sexual language for it to be sexual harassment. The courts are clear on this. The "sexual" can also refer to harassment that is targeted at gender. The law also tells us sexual harassment doesn't have to be physical. According to the courts, the idea that "words can never hurt you" is false. For context, it helps to consider intention. Words spoken and an atmosphere created with the intent of demeaning women is harassment. In this day and age, these behaviors are seldom accidental, since most companies have sexual harassment training. Some men might not like it that they can't make sexually provocative comments to their female coworkers or brag about their sexual exploits, but if these actions are unwelcome, they're harassment.

We must reject the idea that women cannot be harmed by toxic environments.

Myth: Women Who Complain Want Money or Fame

We've all heard of the supposed sexual harassment gravy train, right? Well, actually it doesn't exist. First of all, most women who file complaints want the problem to be solved, including reinstatement if they've lost their jobs. And those that do reach settlements or win their cases typically receive less than $50,000, hardly worth blowing up their careers. As for fame—well, I don't know a single woman who wants that kind of notoriety. The decision to go up against a powerful and well-known harasser is an excruciating choice, made with the knowledge that a woman's own reputation and career could be destroyed. In today's Internet environment, a public claim exposes a woman to severe online harassment and even death threats.

We must reject the idea that women have something to gain by being harassed. In fact, they have everything to lose.

These and other myths are perpetrated not just by the abusers and their allies, but in a culture that is too ready to blame women when bad things happen to them. What would it mean if we shifted our default position from "I don't believe you" to "I believe you?"

GIVE IT AWAY

Once you become empowered, try to find ways to symbolize and ritualize your new life and inner strength. I was happy to find a perfect way to do that, while at the same time helping other women.

I didn't spend a lot of time in my closet in the months after my story became public. I guess part of me didn't want to be reminded that I wasn't working anymore. But also the particular wardrobe—dozens of brightly colored dresses, many brand new—seemed to symbolize the "old" me and weren't what I wanted to wear when I reentered the workplace. Even if I didn't have a lot of use for them, I knew someone else could. So, I decided to give most of them away. Dress for Success is a wonderful organization that takes in gently used clothing and puts it in the hands of women who need a new wardrobe to get into (or back into) the workplace. It was the perfect place to receive my clothes. I was guest-hosting *The View* on ABC after the new year, and decided to unveil all my donations at the end of the show. The producers rolled out two huge racks of dresses—ninety-eight in all. Sitting on the set, I felt emotional; it was such a cathartic experience. It was as if I were shedding my old life and at the same time giving new opportunities to others. They used to call women's work outfits "power suits." I certainly hope I gave ninety-eight women the "power" to take on a new challenge in finding work and starting anew, just as I was with my own life.

HAVE FAITH IN YOURSELF

A disturbing thing happens in environments that are rife with harassment. People begin to see it as a twisted kind of normal. Often the pace is set by a single individual, usually one in a position of power. But other times it's the overwhelming culture of an organization or company that an inexperienced employee is unable to combat. We are so used to thinking that we live in more enlightened times that the reality can feel surreal. At these moments, it is more important than ever for us to believe in ourselves. I found myself thinking about that when I heard Cheryl's story.

"This was something I dreamed of doing my whole life," Cheryl said of her job as an airline mechanic. She embraced it wholeheartedly, starting her new career after being a stay-at-home mom for years, and she was the first and only woman among many men at her station. She was shocked when she heard that her new manager had told the other mechanics, "Women do not belong in line maintenance," before she even got there. Once she arrived, she heard people say that she was "taking a man's job." She says one of her coworkers told her, "Do you know what a disruption you are? We even had to build a bathroom for you!" Another older worker asked her out, and when she said no, he wouldn't talk to her anymore—and neither would others.

Although she was eager to learn, Cheryl often felt as if she was being sabotaged and set up for failure. Her boss would often yell at her for missteps. The most egregious example was when she was given jobs she had not been trained to do, and then was cited if she made a mistake. There were procedures she was not yet skilled at, but she felt shut out, as no one would teach her.

All of Cheryl's efforts to complain to HR went unheeded, and it became clear that they thought she was the problem. Ultimately, she was fired—she says because someone falsely accused her of violating a regulation.

Today, Cheryl and her family are devastated by what happened to her. She's investigating legal remedies, but it's a slow process. In the meantime, she is working part-time and waiting for the day when she will get justice. She is teaching her sons to respect each person's different outlook on navigating life. "I want them to know that a woman's perspective is different from a man's, but that difference should not be discounted. Just because a woman asks more questions should not be a reason to think she is not just as smart," she said. And she is bravely determined to find a way to reach out to other women who aspire to work in male-dominated fields, hoping her story of perseverance will inspire other females to make their mark as well.

I would tell women like Cheryl to have faith in themselves, to rise above what others say about them, to refuse to be diminished by their failures. She was made to feel incompetent, but says the real detriment to her success was purposely being poorly trained. She should not have to wear that negative designation and neither should any other woman working in a male-dominated field.

BE BRAVE

One place where women are speaking out about sexism more than ever before is Hollywood, whether it's sexual harassment, equal opportunity, or pay equity. Robin Wright, known for her role as Claire Underwood, the wife of Kevin Spacey's Frank Underwood on the hit Netflix drama *House of Cards*, is a bold voice for equal pay. In 2016, Wright demanded that Netflix pay her the same as Spacey. She argued that her character was just as popular as Spacey's, and that they were both the main characters. She told Netflix's executives that if they didn't, she'd go public about it. They assured her she was getting the same pay. Many of us were proud of her victory in speaking up. In fact, I celebrated her forthrightness on my show, stating how important it is for women to speak up for themselves to invoke change. Recently, however, Wright confirmed in press reports that she believed she still wasn't being paid the same as Spacey after all. "I really don't like being duped," she said. "It's such a male-dominant workforce still. There's a conditioning. And changing the condition of men is what needs to happen." So apparently, there's more speaking up to do.

Debra Messing is another one of the brave actresses telling her truth about women's treatment in Hollywood. In February 2017, Messing spoke out about the way she believes women are treated on movie sets at the hands of some directors who objectify and humiliate them. She says young actresses are particularly vulnerable.

Messing recalled her first big movie part and all the excitement she felt. Then she was told, although it wasn't in her contract, that she was expected to appear nude in one scene. When she complained to her agent, she was told, "You can say no and they fire you, or you can do it and you keep your job."

For Messing, the worst part of filming the scene was not the nudity, but the sexually harassing treatment of the director, who she says forced her to stand around the set barely covered while he yelled at her: "No, cover your nipples! Cover your ass!" It was traumatic. In spite of her youth and inexperience, Messing believed that this was not art; it was abuse. "The whole thing was a power play, a game," she said. "And the goal, to demean me, to strip me of my pride and power and make me feel on a cellular level his dominance over me. I felt violated."

Why did Messing decide to tell this story after all these years? It wasn't just to complain about a bad experience she herself had had, but to put the culture of Hollywood on notice that women were demanding to be treated with respect.

Stories like hers demonstrate that the emotional trauma caused by abuse, harassment, and retaliation can begin to heal when women find their voices. If you're reading this and feeling like you don't have that courage or power, I want to encourage you to dig deep and know you are not alone. Together, we can find out who we really are and what we're capable of achieving. I believe that every child is born with a special gift. It just takes cultivating. Yes, it's hard work, but let's do this. Do this for *you*. Don't give up on your dreams. Make the most of who you are, and if that means standing up more and speaking up more, let your voice be heard. My passion in life has been to be the best I can be and to live every day to the fullest, and I want that for everyone I know and for all I don't know.

When women decide they're going to live their best lives in spite of the immense pain they've experienced, it is so inspiring. I was touched by the story of a woman who says she was raped by an off-duty police officer. She wrote to me of her suffering, physical and emotional. She was in the hospital for weeks, and couldn't eat or sleep. One day, a friend came to see her and spoke the words that would turn it around. "He got one night. Don't let him get the rest of your life." Since hearing her tell me that, I've thought about her statement every single day. If she could recover and push forward with her life and not let him "get the rest of her life," others can too. If you've experienced any kind of bullying, put-downs, harassment, or abuse, make the pledge today. Don't let him get the rest of your life.

The symbols that remind me every day about my inner strength are three bracelets I wear on my arm, inscribed with words that help me with my journey: "fearless," "brave," and my life motto, "carpe diem." I bought them the day after my job ended, and they remind me of what I stand for and what I want other women to see in themselves. I know that together, we will all say enough is enough, seize the day, and win this fight.

NINE

Our Children Are Watching

These days, I often wake up thinking about my daughter, Kaia. She's fourteen now, right on the brink of young womanhood—bright and talented and earnest, with her whole life ahead of her. It has pained me to have to tell her that the world doesn't always play fair with women. I also think of my son, Christian, who is twelve. What does it mean to teach him to be a man? I want to protect them, but I also want to introduce them to the real world and help them navigate it.

When Kaia returned to school after I no longer had my job, and my face had been all over the news that summer, many people were interested in asking her what had happened to her mom. I was filled with anxiety, thinking about the questions she would face and how brave she would have to be, but to my surprise she came home from school and told me, "Mommy, when people asked me about what happened to you, I felt so proud to be your daughter." And two weeks later, when Kaia told me that she had finally found the courage to stand up to two girls who had been giving her a hard time, she said, "I knew I could do it, Mommy, because I saw you do it."

In the end, that's all that matters. I as one person had somehow mustered up the courage to do something monumental, and if my one act meant that my daughter would now approach life in a braver fashion, it was worth it. So, through my emotions and tears, I felt tremendous pride in that day and moment, because my children had been my number one concern throughout my entire ordeal. The task of raising our girls and boys to be strong, respectful, caring, and courageous is not easy in a world where they see so many examples of the opposite. We can't protect them from seeing what's out there, but we can give them alternative ways to approach a world that is often challenging.

Pride, strength, and self-worth are ideas that we want to embed in our daughters, but to do that, we have to acknowledge the weight of stereotypes and expectations. We need to appreciate how devastating these stereotypes are for young girls, who lack the ability to fully understand that they're not legitimate.

Jodi Norgaard is the founder of Dream Big Toy Company, featuring Go! Go! Sports Girls. The dolls, books, and apps support creative play and social-emotional growth through sport, and encourage girls to dream big.

I first met Jodi in 2013 when she appeared on my show to celebrate the International Day of the Girl. In honor of the occasion, we both appeared on air without makeup as role models in the effort to "let girls be girls" and to underscore the importance of building self-esteem from the inside, not from the exterior. Jodi's determination to change stereotypes has always inspired me because I can see myself and my own daughter in her experience. But when she found out I was writing this book, she reached out to share her own story. It's one she often tells in talks to girls and women:

> Until about the age of eleven, I knew I was strong, smart, and adventurous. When I was in seventh grade, this all changed. In science class, I asked a question. My male teacher didn't think it was a very good question, and he said in front of the class, 'You're blond, and that's why you asked that question.' The class laughed, and I was very stunned and confused. In eighth grade, it happened again. I was in math class, and I asked a

question. Again, a different male teacher didn't think it was a very good question, and he said in front of the class, 'You're blond and pretty, so you can't have brains too.' And again, to the laughter of my classmates. At the end of my eighth-grade year, I had two male teachers ask me to stay after school one day because they wanted to discuss something with me. Of course I did, and they proceeded to tell me how hot I was, and that I would have so many boyfriends in high school and the boys were very lucky. I remember running out of the room to their laughter, feeling terribly uncomfortable. I was so confused because I focused on my strengths and the importance of what my mind and body could do, but I was quickly realizing that others focused on what my body looked like.

Jodi says that she never shared these experiences with her parents, sister, or friends, because she was embarrassed. But for the next four years she was silent; she stopped asking questions. "I wanted to slide under the radar, which I did successfully," she said. "By the time I entered college, I started to find confidence again, but I had a heightened radar for sexual harassment. And when my sweet, blond, blue-eyed daughter, Grace, was born, I thought, 'I am going to fight like hell so that she never loses her strong, smart, and adventurous girl.'"

Jodi's heart still breaks for her younger self. But when she told the story in a talk, a young girl asked her, "Do you think you would have accomplished so much if you hadn't had this experience?" She replied that she didn't know. The experience weakened her for four years, but she feels fortunate to have found strength and determination.

"I look back on my twelve-year-old self with so much compassion," Jodi told me. "It was confusing to me when others commented on my blond hair and the way I looked. I knew what my mind and body could do, as opposed to what I looked like. I didn't understand why they were saying I was asking questions because of my appearance."

The inspiration for her toy company came when her daughter was nine years old. One day, they visited a toy store. "My daughter had just finished playing soccer, and she looked like a normal girl," Jodi said, "but when we went into the toy store, all the dolls looked unreal and sexy. I remember one was named 'Lovely Lola.' I flipped my lid. Why were we marketing dolls to girls based on attractiveness?"

That night Jodi spilled out her frustration to her husband. "I think I can do something here," she said. "Let's research creating a sports doll."

He replied, "You're on to something."

The more she researched the market, the more confident Jodi grew that she needed to pioneer a big change. "There's something wrong when you see a doll and the first word that comes to your mind is 'sexy,'" she said. "Imagine! [In 2014] Barbie was on the cover of the *Sports Illustrated* swimsuit issue, which is marketed to grown men!"

Jodi's first sports doll, Tennis Girl, debuted at the US Open in 2008 and sold out in six days. In the coming years, she added other dolls and slowly built momentum. But it wasn't until 2013, when she pitched to Walmart buyers at the Toy Fair, that her dolls turned a corner. "This is a winner," the buyers said enthusiastically. "We'll take it." By 2015, the dolls were being packaged with books.

Jodi sold the company in 2016, but she remains a consultant. Her major focus now is giving speeches to inspire and empower women and girls. "The one word that keeps coming up is 'confidence,'" she said. "Girls need confidence to resist the pressure to conform."

A couple of years ago, Always, the Procter & Gamble company that makes feminine hygiene products, launched a powerful campaign based on research showing that more than half of the girls surveyed claimed their self-confidence levels dropped around puberty and when they got their first period. To create a conversation about girls' self-confidence, the company created a powerful video. A documentary filmmaker asked women, men, older girls and boys to act out what "throw like a girl" and "run like a girl" look like. They acted out the stereotypical notions: limp arms, goofy expressions, and a lack of forcefulness. The interviewer then asked prepubescent girls to do the same thing. Their response was completely different. They threw and ran with complete confidence, strength, and passion. The point was made: before puberty, girls viewed "throwing like a girl" as a positive; after puberty, they believed that it showed weakness. The video made such an impact that "throw like a girl" became a meme—a way to turn the stereotype on its head. When I first saw the video at my daughter's school, I cried. I couldn't believe that there was such an immense change in the perception of what a girl was supposed to be like, and that both boys and older girls saw throwing or running "like a girl" in a negative light.

I began to question what happens to girls that changes their view of themselves when they reach puberty. I couldn't stop thinking about that video, and I had to know what happened that changed their understanding of the world with regard to themselves and their own self-esteem (not to mention what made the boys think poorly of something done by girls).

I try to tell Kaia every single day she can be whatever she wants to be. She loves science, and I keep saying that's wonderful. I put her in places where I think she will continue to grow with strong self-esteem. But culturally, there is a lot that I can't control—for instance, social media and what happens at school. After all, kids don't live in a family bubble.

Recently, I read about an appearance that Jameis Winston, a quarterback for the Tampa Bay Buccaneers, made at an elementary school in St. Petersburg, Florida. Winston had recently settled a lawsuit in which he had been accused of rape. His talk was supposed to be inspirational; you decide.

Here's what Winston said:

"All my young boys, stand up. The ladies, sit down. But all my boys, stand up. We strong, right? We strong! We strong, right? All my boys, tell me one time: I can do anything I put my mind to. Now a lot of boys aren't supposed to be soft-spoken. You know what I'm saying? One day y'all are going to have a very deep voice like this" (speaking in a very deep voice).

And then he said: "But the ladies, they're supposed to be silent, polite, gentle. My men, my men . . . supposed to be strong. I want y'all to tell me what the third rule of life is: I can do anything I put my mind to. Scream it!"

How is this defensible? You can say, well, he's only twenty-three years old. You can say he didn't really mean it the way it sounded—as he later explained by way of apology for his "poor word choice." But if I heard that such a performance had been given in front of my son or daughter, I'd be in the principal's office screaming bloody murder.

Although Winston later apologized for his "poor word choice," I wonder how much damage was already done to the kids in that room. I suspect that most of them did not hear his apology.

Research shows that negative, stereotypical messages have a direct impact on girls' performance. And this impact grows as they get older. A study by the German psychologist Marina Pavlova was quite striking in this regard. Pavlova divided students into groups for a test. The groups were given different messages suggesting that men or women were better or worse at taking the test. When told that women typically did worse on the test, the women's scores declined. They also declined when the message was reframed to say that men did better than women. When told that women typically did better on the test, the women's scores improved. If such results occur in a relatively innocuous, non-threatening environment, imagine how proportionately greater the impact is in the rough-and-tumble world of an average middle school!

The roots of negative stereotypical thinking take hold young, as early as age six, according to a new study by researchers at New York University, the University of Illinois, and Princeton University. The NYU psychology professor Andrei Cimpian, the lead author of the study, pointed out, "Even though the stereotype equating brilliance with men doesn't match reality, it might nonetheless take a toll on girls' aspirations and on their eventual careers."

To test this theory, researchers created experiments with groups of children between the ages of five and seven. In one, the children were told a story about a person who was "really, really smart," and then were asked which of four adults—two men and two women— the story was about. Five-year-old boys and girls viewed their genders positively, but the six- and seven-year-old girls were more likely to choose the men as "really, really smart."

This story pained me. I wondered, what happened between ages five and six that made the girls less secure in terms of female brilliance? I'm haunted by this change that comes over girls. Why does it happen? There must be something that goes on when they start school—messages, subtle and overt, that get implanted. It's one of the reasons my husband and I became proponents of single-sex schools, especially for our daughter. Some studies show that when boys and girls are in class together (especially math and science), the gender differences are exacerbated, whereas in single-sex schools, girls are allowed to excel without barriers. It's something to think about.

BRAVE NEW WORLD

"The genie is out of the bottle, so please don't be scared," Allison Havey tells parents. A journalist and producer, and the cofounder of the RAP Project (or Raising Awareness and Prevention Project), Allison is dedicated to helping kids and teenagers negotiate the treacherous arenas of social media and self-image. Although the RAP Project is headquartered in the United Kingdom, it has expanded its reach to a global audience through its website.

As the mother of a twelve-year-old and a fourteen-year-old, I am as prone to being scared as the next parent. We were one of the last families in the sixth grade to allow Kaia to get a cell phone. Then immediately the questions started: "When can I get Instagram? When can I get Snapchat?" When Christian was in sixth grade, we went through the whole thing all over again. It's tough to stand your ground when everyone else is doing it, especially since social media is the way kids communicate.

In her book with RAP's cofounder Deana Puccio, *Sex, Lies and Social Media: Talking to Our Teens in the Digital Age*, Allison revealed the age requirements for various social media, which I found sobering. Facebook, Instagram, Snapchat, and Twitter all list the age requirement as thirteen! Allison told of her young daughter casually mentioning that an Instagram user had asked her to enter a contest, giving three competition requests: "(1) Please send a photo of your hairdo, (2) Please send a photo of you wearing pajamas, (3) Please send a photo for best swimsuit."

When we spoke, I asked Allison if, given the way kids are communicating, she thought we'd gone backward in terms of respectful and positive behaviors. In some ways, we have. "It used to be skipping school and smoking," she said. "Now it's sexting." It's shocking for parents to realize that they have to talk to their kids about porn when they're as young as ten!

Since the Internet and social media are a reality, Allison says schools and parents need to begin having important, frank discussions. "We don't want to terrify the kids," she said. "We want to empower them." Her suggestions include:

- Talking about the kinds of communications they're having with their friends, and pointing out where it is and isn't respectful of them.
- Talking about porn, and how it doesn't reflect healthy relationships or what love is. (I just took Allison's advice and did this.)
- Teaching boys to resist peer pressure to behave in misogynistic ways by telling them that not all boys feel that way—thus giving them permission to behave differently.
- Encouraging kids to delete texts and sexts that make them uncomfortable.
- Teaching them to be leaders and speak out when other kids are behaving inappropriately. Telling boys, "Chivalry is sexy."
- Modeling mutual respect as parents, because "seeing is believing."
- Encouraging them to use their brains to analyze offensive advertising, so they can discern the difference between real and unreal images.

As parents, we must be vigilant. I believe that social media is the crisis of the current generation. It's hard enough to hold your own in the classroom or on the playground. It's hard enough to be a middle schooler without worrying about being "liked" on an app. When you add the surges of meanness and sexualizing behaviors on social media, parents can feel as if they have no control over the messages their kids are receiving, or those they're sending to others. We can't ignore it and hope for the best. We need to teach our kids good social media behaviors, and help them evaluate how to respond when someone is mean to them or to others. Kids are killing themselves over this!

Title IX statistics show that eight in ten students experience some form of harassment in school, and for 56 percent of girls, this is sexual harassment, including sexual comments, jokes, gestures, or looks; claiming that a person is gay or lesbian; spreading sexual rumors about a person; touching, grabbing, or pinching someone in a sexual way; intentionally brushing up against someone in a sexual way; and flashing someone.

HELPING BOYS BECOME GOOD MEN

We can't forget about our boys. I often say that I work as much for my son as for my daughter. It's equally important that he sees a role model of a strong woman, and that he also observes the respect that his mother receives from his father and other men. Because just as negative stereotypes start young for girls, they also start young for boys.

Kathleen Neville, the expert I mentioned earlier who is working on sexual harassment training for the NFL, deals with this issue. She became interested in analyzing the roots of the type of male misconduct that is expressed on adult sports fields or in workplaces. She thinks one breeding ground is early childhood. For that reason, she told me, "Waiting to educate people about sexual harassment when they are adults in the workplace is too little, too late, to change behaviors."

In her research thesis, Kathleen laid out the importance of this perspective, noting that her earlier writings on sexual harassment had focused on adult behaviors, but people were not asking a key question: When did those behaviors begin? The early life of harassers and abusers hasn't been studied, and although workplace education is important, she said, "the effectiveness of any earnest educational efforts on adults with fully established, lifelong behavior patterns and practices of abuse remains nebulous."

As a result of her research, Kathleen is developing a program for conduct education and learning-based tools for children in grades K through 12. She contends that it's the only way adults in the workplace will positively contribute to building fair, equitable, hostility-free, and respectful environments—to "get them early," as she puts it. Her training is designed to show kids what is, and is not, socially acceptable behavior.

Kathleen's work got me thinking about all the cultural messages boys receive, in and out of sports. Consider the phrase "boys will be boys." It's almost always used to excuse negative or antisocial behaviors, including physical violence. You don't hear people saying, "Boys will be boys" to justify their sons being kind to animals or doing a good deed.

"Boys will be boys" doesn't only create a stereotype that leads to harassment of girls and women. It hurts boys, too, trapping them in a narrow definition of what it means to be a boy. This attitude also leads even those who are more sensitive to prove their "manhood" by behaving aggressively. It doesn't give them a chance to figure out who they really are. Boys deserve to have parents and other adults challenge them to be their best selves. They deserve to be taught that they can control themselves, that they can master their impulses, and that they can be kind and generous.

The Good Men Project recently published "A Manifesto: Relational Intelligence for Our Children" by Mark Greene. His manifesto reads: "We must commit to granting our children their birthright. Their birthright is their inherent capacity to form authentic, emotionally vibrant relationships. All we need do is stop training them out of these capacities, either by action or inaction. Through helping them grow their relational intelligence, we can ensure they become what they are born to be: emotionally connected, joyful and thriving human beings."

Greene points out that teaching boys to be strong and self-reliant is a good thing, but when "true manhood" is reduced to these values at the expense of relational skills (which are associated with females), this narrow definition does a disservice to both boys and girls.

THE BULLY CULTURE

While researching this book, I found that negative stereotypes thrive in an atmosphere where bullying occurs. There is a striking correlation between the bullying and cyberbullying that have grown more commonplace among middle and high school students, and the broader arena of sexual harassment and response that plays out in adulthood.

A no-tolerance policy against bullying in schools, whether it is on the Internet or the "regular" kind, is the absolute minimum starting point in eliminating harassment. But parents have a critical role to play. We need to model behaviors for our sons and daughters. We need to teach them what is and is not acceptable. And most of all, we need to believe them and support them if they say they are being bullied or harassed. When we teach our kids to stand up for themselves early on, they retain that skill for the rest of their lives.

Schools need to start talking about bullying, and teaching kids about acceptable and unacceptable behaviors in *elementary* school. Starting in high school is too late. School administrators need to admit that this is an issue. They might not want to address bullying, maybe because they think it can't happen in their school, but we have to reach kids early on. The issue of bullying comes down to self-confidence—a lack of it for those who bully, and the courage to stand up for those who are bullied. But it's wrong to pretend it isn't happening because we don't want to talk about it.

According to extensive surveys by the Cyberbullying Research Center, 28 percent of students say they have been cyberbullied, and 16 percent admitted they had cyberbullied others.

The bystander effect is a big factor in cyberspace. Scrolling down those long, abusive threads, kids are frozen in place. Even if they feel inclined to defend their friends, many just don't know what to say.

Monica Lewinsky, whom I mentioned earlier in this book, has an answer for that. She created the #BeStrong emoji keyboard app, which displays a symbol of love and support that friends can use to be there for someone who is being bullied online. It seems like a small thing, but that peer support counts for a lot. Studies show that students who are bullied find that what helps the most is supportive actions from their peers.

Having that support also encourages them to stand up for themselves. According to NoBullying.com, the most effective way to stop bullying is for students to discover their power. Empowering our kids to stand up for themselves and to support their friends who are experiencing abuse is the best way to embolden them in their own lives, while teaching compassion and supportive behavior. I believe that kids who are in the habit of speaking out when they see something wrong will not so readily become bystanders when they see abuse in the workplace.

But we can't expect our kids to go it alone. Addressing bullying is something each parent should expect to do, and be ready to do, whether his or her child is the one being bullied, is the bully, or the bystander. Here are some basic guidelines:

Talk about it before it happens: Have frank discussions with your children about bullying and cyberbullying, and let them know you're open to having a nonjudgmental, confidential conversation if they encounter it. Take opportunities to discuss bullying when it comes up on TV programs or in the media.

Stay vigilant: Don't expect your child to necessarily tell you if there is a problem. Watch for signs that your child might be upset or not interested in doing activities that he or she usually enjoys.

Offer practical tools: If your child is being bullied, talk specifically about what he or she can do. Role-play different scenarios. If the matter is serious, enlist the cooperation of school officials and teachers.

If your child is the bully: We often talk about what to do if our children are being bullied, but we less often address what to do if our child is doing the bullying. I know that nobody wants to admit it. It's hard to face the fact that your child is bullying others. But it's our job as parents to teach personal responsibility—to not let kids off the hook, or allow them to blame others for their actions. Kids inherently want to blame other people, or make excuses—"I didn't do it"; "I didn't mean it"; "He started it"—but we can't let them.

Encourage your school: Parents can advocate for their children by encouraging their schools to institute antibullying curricula, starting in first grade. There are many good resources to help parents, teachers, and children fight bullying (see the resources chapter at the back of this book). And according to StopBullying.gov, we should also avoid strategies that don't work or may have negative consequences. For example, research shows that suspending or expelling bullies does not reduce bullying, and, in fact, makes it less likely that students will speak out because they're worried that the consequences are so grave it might lead to retaliation.

It is up to us to be smart, observant, and educated about how to help our children stand up for themselves.

LIFE LESSONS FOR OUR KIDS

The values that our kids learn at home will stick with them, in spite of the onslaught they face out in the world. For me, these values include openness, aspiration, responsibility, and self-esteem.

Reject Rigid Gender Roles

In my family growing up, the stereotypical gender roles were sometimes reversed. My dad could be sentimental and my mom could be tough. Dad and I used to sit on the couch together and both cry over emotional TV shows. I never thought anything of it, and that was a good thing. It helped me see people for who they really are, without rigid role distinctions. It's the same with my kids. I always enjoyed the way my son loved to play with the Easy Bake Oven as much as my daughter did. To this day, he'll say to me, "Mom, do you need any brownies today?" (He's more interested in baking than *I* am, I can assure you.) He gets a kick out of it, and it doesn't take away from his masculinity. I used to talk about it on the show. I said, "We have a pink Easy Bake Oven, and he loves it." I celebrated it, just as I celebrate my daughter working with science projects and playing soccer. And both of my children play the piano.

These are minor examples. The daily task is to honor our children as individuals, no matter how they express it. I imagine my son will hear the challenge to "man up" in his life, but I try not to let him hear it at home. I think it's good when he expresses his emotions, and we teach him that he can be both sensitive and strong. They aren't mutually exclusive.

I always strive to see my children as individuals, and to resist gender biases. I am blessed to have grown up playing music in an environment where boys and girls alike were acknowledged for the music they created, not for their gender. When I was sixteen, I participated in a competition in which they put us behind screens to play so the judges could only hear us, but not see us. At the time, I was annoyed. I was a performer—I wanted to see the audience, and I wanted the judges to see me. But later I understood that they were trying to strip away all the unconscious biases people have.

There's a lot of talk these days about raising kids in a gender-neutral environment. I'm not sure that's possible, but there are things we can do to help our kids develop as individuals. In 2015, Target announced that it was doing away with gender-specific toys and labels on products such as bedding. That's a good start. Let kids choose. Don't tell them what to prefer or how they're supposed to act as boys or girls. Give them room to explore and discover their own way.

Help Kids Build Self-Esteem from the Inside Out

In every era, but especially this one of judgmental social media and unrealistic expectations, it's important to help kids build self-esteem from the inside out. This has been a matter of primary importance for me, and it's a topic I often return to when I am speaking publicly.

I know something about this because I was a chubby kid, but I didn't let it define me. I built my self-esteem from the inside. But as I reached my teens, my weight did start to bother me. It prevented me from getting picked for cherished roles in school plays. I was beginning to be interested in boys, and was crushed when I overheard a boy I liked say, "Gretchen has a great personality, but she's too fat to date." I had to fight these battles on my own, figure out a healthy way to be, love myself for who I was, and learn not to rely on the judgments of others to define me. When I did lose weight, it was for *me*, not for others. In my home now, I'm sensitive to not focusing on my own weight or that of my children, but rather the importance of healthy eating, and building self-esteem in other ways.

Weight is just one example. There are countless external judgments our kids face every day. Sometimes it seems like an impossible battle.

The comedian Pete Dominick, whom I wrote about earlier, is a father to two daughters. He observed to me that people always tell little girls, "You're so pretty," or comment on their beautiful eyes and hair. When it happens with his daughters, he always replies, "That's not her best quality," and goes on to list others: "She's hilarious, brave, intelligent, kindhearted, a great dancer." His daughters don't always appreciate it— "Daddy, can you stop telling people not to say we're beautiful?"—but he tells them, "Your face might get you in a room, but it won't keep you there." He teaches them that they have to develop skills, character, passion, and intelligence to get where they want to go in life.

Kaia gave me a moving example of building self-esteem from the inside when she wrote a piece in 2017 for a school assignment about the origin of her name. I was blown away by her insight and quiet strength, and I think every parent would be proud to read such a thoughtful piece by his or her daughter—written at the age of fourteen:

Kaia means "wise woman." My mother knew it was the name that would fit me and describe my personality, because Kaia means more than just "wise woman." Wiseness does not only define as 'knowledgeable' but can also describe braveness, courage, and strength. Wiseness can pass through generation by generation. By giving this name to me, my mother passed on the strength throughout our family. My grandmother is powerful and forceful and doesn't let anything get past her. My mother is the most courageous woman I know and is not afraid of any challenge in her way. Kaia, "wise woman." Even if I do not live up to being 'Kaia,' the name itself can take my place and pass on the wiseness to the next generation of our family.

Help Kids Choose Role Models

Thanks to the Internet and reality TV, many of the role models our children see promote values that include selfishness, aggressiveness, self-absorption, and meanness—when we want them to learn kindness, compassion, and personal responsibility. What to do? First, talk about it. Ask them what they think about the behavior of a favorite star, and have a family discussion about it: "Why do you think she said that?" "Do you agree with what he did?"

Introduce positive role models by calling their attention to people who've done amazing things, both kids and adults. Talk about why you're impressed, and ask them to tell you what they think.

Recently I had lunch with a woman who was looking for investors for her new media company. Her ambition was to produce a new model of reality shows, to contrast the current model, in which women are portrayed as constantly fighting and being mean to each other. (I'm talking about the *Real Housewives* model.) The show this young woman was pitching was designed to reprogram the messaging our girls and boys are receiving, and to introduce good female role models that will counterbalance the current swamp, which elevates bad behavior as a road to stardom. This is important because, as Paul Feig pointed out to me, a large proportion of movies and TV shows are marketed to teenagers. We need to decide to be in charge of what our children see and hear.

And we need to be role models for them. I was extremely fortunate to be raised in a family where I was told every single day that I could be anything I wanted to if I put my mind to it, worked hard, had courage, and believed in myself. This constant encouragement provided me the foundation to go out into the world and realize my dreams, as well as giving me the confidence and bravery to always speak up and stand up for myself. I truly believe that this kind of encouragement, combined with important lessons about the power of community and helping others when they need a hand, are the best gifts we can give our children. I have always been a supporter of organizations that empower girls, but after my story broke, I realized I needed and wanted to give back in an even bigger way.

It's why I recently created the Gift of Courage Fund, with the primary focus being to help girls and young women recognize their full potential and the bright future that awaits them, as well as helping women speak up and demand a safe and nurturing place in the workforce. Through the fund, I give financial support to organizations doing good work, such as RAINN (Rape, Abuse, and Incest National Network) and the Center for Sexual Assault Crisis Counseling and Education. I also help fund the New Agenda, All In Together, TIA Girl Club, Girls Leadership, the March of Dimes Foundation, and the Miss You Can Do It Pageant, which celebrates girls with disabilities. Emceeing the pageant last year, and having my daughter in attendance with me to help hand out the awards, was a life-changing experience for both of us. And in financially supporting the organization, we have learned what real inner beauty is all about.

I'm also passionate about the Catherine Violet Hubbard Animal Sanctuary in Newtown, Connecticut. Catherine was one of the six-year-olds killed in the Sandy Hook Elementary School shootings in December 2012. My daughter, Kaia, performed a piano recital the next year to benefit the sanctuary that Catherine's parents vowed to build in her honor, and now Kaia is on the children's advisory board, and I have joined the adult board. In December 2017, the sanctuary will hold its first-ever fund-raiser, on the five-year anniversary of Catherine's death, to help raise money to start building on a beautiful piece of land in Newtown. I will emcee, and Kaia will again perform on the piano.

What's beautiful about giving back is seeing what can happen when you do. Kaia has experienced firsthand how meaningful it is to be a part of something greater than herself. And we've all witnessed the incredible courage of parents working through unimaginable grief to carry on the memory of their children and find purpose. Through the Gift of Courage Fund, I am able to help organizations like this advance their mission, and in the process, teach my children values that will last a lifetime.

Teach Kids Personal Accountability

We need to teach kids at a young age to be accountable for their actions. I don't let my kids off the hook. I tell them, "If you did it, you own it." But to help them be responsible, we can give them practical strategies for how to succeed. In our home, that might mean telling my son that if he practices the piano for ten minutes every day, he might learn the piece by the end of the week. That's how you boost self-confidence; by giving children the tools to accomplish tangible goals. Kids learn from an early age that when they put time into something, whether it's music or school or sports, they get better at it. And it's through this disciplined approach that they build the right kind of confidence and self-esteem. They learn to feel proud of themselves for their own accomplishments, and that's a trait they will carry with them for the rest of their lives.

Give Kids Problem-Solving Tools

The job of a parent isn't to solve our kids' problems—not that we always can, anyway. Rather, we can encourage children to develop the skills to solve problems themselves. These are skills that will help them all their lives. There is nothing more empowering than being able to solve a problem. So, if our children come to us with complaints—someone is mad at them, kids aren't talking to them, someone said something unfair—instead of reacting, we can make it a teachable moment: "Why do you think he said that?" "What can you say back?" "What can you do?" "What do you think will happen if you do that?" And so on. We all have the impulse to shower our kids with sympathy when they're hurt, but if we want them to really feel better, we can empower them to handle their everyday battles on their own. These are essential life skills. Our kids can learn how to cope with people who bully or bug them, how to move past their anxiety and become equipped to handle stressful situations later in life.

Many of the difficulties that we encounter in the adult workplace, such as when people lash out or act out of revenge or speak disrespectfully, have their roots in childhood, when we were not taught effective ways of handling our problems.

INSPIRE KIDS TO REACH FOR THE STARS

I've always believed that the best thing my parents did for me was to inspire me to follow my dreams. That belief in myself, embedded in my earliest years, gave me the confidence to work so hard and achieve my goals. The word "impossible" was never used. I always thought I was special and capable. In my mind, that's the best gift we can give our children.

On Wednesday, March 8, 2017, International Women's Day, I went to see my daughter perform the role of JoJo in the musical *Seussical* at her school. How apropos that her role included singing the song "It's Possible." The lyrics repeat that anything's possible. It was a great moment for me to see that—because I have always believed *anything* is possible.

LET'S MAKE A PLEDGE

When we make a pledge, we formalize a promise. I ask all parents to join me in pledging a commitment to raising our children with values, leadership, compassion, and openness. It is in our hands to help the next generation become leaders in creating equality for all.

The Parent's Pledge

As a parent, I pledge my commitment to raise my daughters and sons to be full, happy, healthy human beings, who can achieve anything they set out to do.

- I will treat my sons and daughters as individuals, and resist stereotypes that box them into rigid gender roles.
- I will teach my sons to respect girls and women, and my daughters to expect and demand respect, and to be respectful in return.
- I will talk to my children often about the importance of treating others the way they want to be treated, and help them problem-solve how to do that.
- I will be an active role model for demonstrating kindness, listening, and regard for others in my interactions with family, friends, colleagues, and other parents. I will not use derogatory comments or slurs in front of my children.
- I will help my children develop self-esteem, be fearless, and treat failure as a lesson for success.
- I will talk openly about the existence of bias, whether it involves race, gender, or sexual orientation, and encourage my children to be open to people's differences.
- I will encourage my children to be involved in the world around them, and will promote the idea of giving back as a key quality for a successful person.
- I will tell my children that the world is theirs to create, as a better place for all people.

This is my pledge.

_____

[Signed and dated]

TEN

Be Fierce

As 2016 began, my fiftieth birthday was looming. And like so many other women, I had been conditioned to view it as a scary rite of passage. So I decided to make my half-century mark empowering instead. I wanted to challenge myself and tackle new goals, to make it a positive experience and celebrate it. I was taking stock, one step at a time. First, I wanted to feel good about myself, so I decided to go carb-free. I also decided it was time to leave some boards on which I had served for many years, and join new ones.

My family gathered to celebrate my birthday in a special way. I was overwhelmed with emotion by lyrics that my husband and dad rewrote to the tune of the well-known song "7 Years" by Lukas Graham, performed by my son Christian. One refrain they rewrote went:

Now that I'm fifty years old,
Will I live a life so bold?
Will I follow bolder dreams that inspire me?
Now that I'm fifty years old.

Ever sweet and loving, Kaia gave me a book of inspirations and personal reflections, her top fifty things about mom. My favorite: "If you wanted to, you could easily become the first woman president of the United States." I don't know about *easily*, but I loved that I've raised my daughter to think big and know that anything is possible.

As my family and friends celebrated my life that day, I could not have anticipated that my small, immediate goals would be overwhelmed by a tsunami of change that threatened to sweep me off my feet.

I've always been a thinker and planner, whether preparing myself for a violin competition or a job I really wanted. But I've also been motivated by other people's accomplishments, as reflected by such simple things as a few inspirational words. Over the past few years, I'd made it a habit to post a motivational quote each day on Instagram as a way of lifting myself up while trying to inspire those who follow me.

But in the spring of 2016, I started posting with more intensity:

Never forget three types of people in your life. #1: Who helped you in your difficult times. #2: Who left you in your difficult times. #3: Who put you in difficult times.

And this one:

The strongest people are not those who show strength in front of us, but those who win battles we know nothing about.

I was trying not only to motivate others, but also to infuse myself with the courage to face what might lie ahead.

And though she be but little, she is FIERCE.

This was me. I had decided to *Be Fierce.*

And so I did it. I decided to jump off a cliff, all by myself, with no safety net and no way of knowing what would lie below. I never, ever expected to be the face of sexual harassment, but here I am. Sometimes you can't choose your life's direction. My life has been proof of that, always working in mysterious ways. There have been many twists and turns, from concert violinist to Miss America to twenty-five years in TV, but I've always had one constant as my foundation: when faced with a challenge, no matter how big or small, I never give up, and I always give it my all.

In August 2016, Casey and I went on one of the most magnificent trips we've ever done. I'd always wanted to see Croatia, and it lived up to every expectation. It was an incredibly adventurous trip, which was fun for me after being locked down in my house and, of course, not working. One of the more daring tours was a zip line across the Cetina Canyon and River—eight wires running a total of nearly seven thousand feet. But it was the drop below that really mattered. I'd never seen anything like it. If you're looking for a serious adrenaline rush, imagine zipping your way across a gorge five hundred feet above a canyon suspended by just a wire!

For the record, I may be a badass, but I've never been fond of roller coasters or heights, so the zip line was going to be a huge challenge for me. I'd signed up to do it not knowing the full details, and when I saw it, I was ready to bail. I was literally having a mini panic attack. My heart was racing beyond control, and I started getting that feeling you get before you pass out. I was weak in the knees as I watched other brave souls jump into oblivion. But with my helmet and protective belts all attached, waiting for my turn, I decided to say "Screw it." I'd already jumped off a cliff earlier that summer. How could this be any worse?

So I did it. There was no turning back. And with every jump it became easier and easier, even as the gorges below became deeper and deeper. Confronting challenges that you've never had the guts to face before feels great. I empowered myself to say "I can do this"—and that's my message for others.

While I was going through this transition in my life, I received a very moving email from a male friend. He wrote about his wife, who had recently passed away, and a vivid dream he'd had in which she was standing in front of him speaking. He said he also saw me in the dream, and he thought his wife was telling him to reach out to me. So he did. What he said *really* made an impression. He wrote, "What you have gone through in the last month or so is what I call a 'pivot point.' We all have them. My wife dying was the biggest pivot point of my life. When you face pivot points, you have two options: stay the course, or pivot and change the direction of your life. I chose to pivot at age forty-nine. I think the same opportunity presents itself to you now."

It felt so poignant and true to me, I'm so thankful he made the effort to send his message along. It's amazing what small gestures or notes can do to affect peoples' lives. After reading his email, I printed it and looked at it frequently. And I finally decided to accept the challenge and pivot, starting with this book. I chose the title *Be Fierce* because it is a call to action. It means being powerful, strong, brave, and having integrity—and it evoked those aspirations. "Be fierce" was definitely a rallying cry that we could all believe in. But on a deeper level, the call to be fierce spoke to what was in my heart.

Let me tell you more about what being fierce means to me.

TO BE FIERCE IS TO STAND TALL

Even when you're small, being fierce means standing tall. Like many people, I was delighted by the unexpected appearance on March 7, 2017, of a bronze statue named *Fearless Girl*, which appeared suddenly across from the *Charging Bull* sculpture on Wall Street. Hands on her hips, the girl looked as if she was challenging the mighty bull. "Know the power of women in leadership," the plaque at her feet read. "SHE makes a difference."

The statue was part of a campaign by the asset managers State Street Global Advisors, and was created by sculptor Kristen Visbal. McCann North America, the advertising agency for the project, designed the girl to appeal to the largest audience. For this reason, they made her Latina, so, in the words of Devika Bulchandani, the president of McCann XBC and the managing director of McCann New York, she could feel universal and "be an inspiration for everybody— fathers who have little girls and husbands who have wives . . . white, black, Indian—it should speak to the broadest audience."

The statue has inspired a lively public conversation, which I've enjoyed. The juxtaposition of traditional male power with female ferocity thrilled many women and girls, and infuriated others, including the bull's sculptor, Arturo Di Modica, who complained it was just a gender-oriented publicity stunt. "My bull is a symbol for America," Di Modica told the press. "My bull is a symbol of prosperity and for strength." And the girl was not? Perhaps his statement was an inadvertent expression of the attitudes that have defined Wall Street and many corporate environments for too long.

Being fierce is controversial, as this statue has been. But the statue has also been celebrated. It has become a common sight to see young girls posing beside the statue or taking selfies with their arms wrapped around her. The placement of *Fearless Girl*, which was originally given a thirty-day permit, was extended for a year. But petitions are under way to make it permanent. I, for one, hope she sticks around. But we can't afford to be naive about how hard this fight is. In May 2017, another New York City artist placed a statue of a peeing dog, titled *Pissing Pug*, aimed at Fearless Girl. Yes, it's all free speech, but I think it just makes her look stronger.

To be fierce means to stand up and show our faces. Be bold. A man wrote to me, "Please do not look in the mirror, because we have enough broken mirrors in the world already!" Ha! I will not look away at the behest of a crude commenter. I will engage, not retreat.

Even women who are defined by their boldness have moments when they are faced with a painful choice about standing up for themselves. That was the case for Lady Gaga, one of the most talented and flamboyant performers, who realized that the story of her rape, many years earlier, needed to be shared. In a 2015 TimesTalk, Gaga described how she didn't tell anyone for many years about her rape by a man twenty years her senior. "I didn't know how not to blame myself or think it was my fault," she said. She thought her provocative style, as a woman and a performer, had "brought it on myself." But she felt compelled to stand up and speak out, for the good of others. "I'm here because when I look out onto the sea of beautiful young faces that I get to sing and dance for, I see a lot of people who have secrets that are killing them," Gaga said. "We don't want you to keep your pain inside and let it rot like an old apple on your counter, you know? It's like, just get rid of all that trash. Let's get rid of it together."

The many women who spoke to me for this book are standing tall. Even though they were unable to advocate for themselves in the moments when they were suffering, they are doing it now. Time and again, women told me they were setting aside their pain, their shame, and their desire to lock their experiences away, in order to be part of the change. And many of them said they were surprised how, in finally speaking openly and frankly, they were released from the self-critical thoughts that had haunted them. Sometimes all it takes is for someone else to say:

You were assaulted.
You were harassed.
You were bullied.
You were wronged.
It's not your fault.
You deserve to be whole.

"It's not bigger than you," wrote a woman who was driven out of her job by sexual harassment, but who now works as a resilience coach. She didn't always have the strength to see that. Describing her frame of mind when she left her job, she wrote, "The violation hurt me to the depth of how I defined myself. I had done nothing wrong, but I felt shame. I felt low self-worth. I was resentful because I had done everything right. Everything I had always believed about myself was shattered. My career just blew up. Now I channel my compassion to give women the gift of what I didn't have."

These kinds of statements make me sad. There is so much pain out there. One woman, who had been retaliated against and fired after reporting sexual harassment, told me that sometimes she couldn't get out of bed in the morning. She referenced the "Index of Dread," which she'd read about in Oprah Winfrey's *O* magazine, saying, "My dread level right now is off the charts." Yet even in such great pain, she said, "They robbed me, but I am going to take it back."

It's important for us all to agree that there's another big step we have to take, beyond the personal. We all must not only be advocates for ourselves, but for each other, and for the future we want to create for our children. That means getting involved in advocacy programs to fight sexual harassment and assault. It means fighting public policies that diminish women's worth in these situations. It means calling your congressperson, state and local representatives, and governor's office to lobby for bills that protect women and fight laws such as forced arbitration. It means refusing to support companies with bad sexual harassment records. It means always, always voting, whether it's for the local school board or the president of the United States.

This fight is bigger than any individual. Lisa Bloom's advice: "Toughen up. We have rights that other generations fought for. We have to defend them."

TO BE FIERCE IS TO STICK TO YOUR VALUES

Hypocrisy is killing any attempt for bipartisan action. And sometimes you just have to stick to your values, even when your position is unpopular. On June 12, 2016, mere weeks before my job ended, a twenty-nine-year-old security guard burst into an Orlando nightclub with a military-style assault weapon, killing forty-nine and wounding fifty-three more. It was the worst terrorist attack on American soil since 9/11. The victims were mostly young people. I was heartsick and also outraged at the senseless nature of the crime, and because the perpetrator would not have been able to randomly slaughter so many people so quickly if he hadn't been able to buy an assault weapon. I decided to state publicly my feelings about reinstating the military assault weapon ban.

And the criticism was rampant. To me, this is an issue that seems like common sense, but if you even hint at creating any restrictions in the gun laws, the response is immediate and vicious. The f-bombs were flying. I was called a "libby," a "moron," and "brain dead." I was accused of being a traitor. People wrote, "It's bimbos like her that hurt good people." I'd never seen anything like it. So the next day I decided to come out again, stronger than ever. In my mind, the assault weapons ban was the right thing to do. I wasn't saying to get rid of the Second Amendment. Far from it.

I tell this story because we all have moments in our lives when we are faced with a choice to speak out about what's right or remain silent. Acts of bravery can be small and large. They don't have to occur before audiences of millions to make an impact. Writing this book, I've had the honor to meet many women and men who perform acts of courage in their own workplaces and communities on behalf of women, and suffer the consequences. They know this is a moment in history when they must stick to their values and be fierce. And they might suffer for it, but in the long run they are creating a change that will mean a better society for future generations.

It's been gratifying to me that the world is finally paying attention too. Recently I was honored at the *Variety* Power of Women Luncheon. I felt like I was having an out-of-body experience in front of two thousand people as they spoke about how proud they were of me for standing up and speaking out. It demonstrated that a single decision you make can be a huge, defining moment. It made me realize once again that I will not tolerate hypocrisy in our national discussion of life-and-death issues. If we're going to combat the evils in our society—and they include the way women are objectified, harassed, bullied, and abused—we have to open our minds and hearts, and confront truths that might be uncomfortable. We must then do the right thing, whether or not it fits neatly into our chosen political box.

TO BE FIERCE IS TO STAND TOGETHER

I've often referred to a quote, attributed to various people, that has come to mean a great deal to me: "One woman can make a difference, but together we can rock the world." I believe this is demonstrably true. But I also believe that *together* means all of us.

We've talked a lot about how the passivity of bystanders contributes directly to a harassment culture. Don't be a bystander. That directive is for both women and men. I was quite struck to hear the thoughtful and honest reflections of one woman who acknowledged that early in her career in a male-dominated field, she too participated in the environment of disrespecting women. Relieved that she was accepted by the men as one of the "guys," she wanted very much to hold on to that status. On occasion, she participated when they joked about other women in the company, and she shared their judgmental opinions. Only later, when she encountered serious harassment herself, did she recognize that by failing to support other women, she had inadvertently been part of the problem.

It has been sad for me to receive many negative and hurtful messages from women, who clearly do not understand the damage created by sexual harassment. Like this one: "I'm disappointed in what you and now every woman is crying about. So a man makes a rude comment, so a man looks at you inappropriately, so you don't get a promotion you were promised. Were you violently attacked? No! Walk out! Be lucky you have what you have, keep your mouth shut, and move on."

I have resisted responding directly to these emails and tweets. I realize that changing the old biases and stereotypes in the culture is a big job. Instead of tearing each other down, we have to find ways to support more enlightened work policies that will benefit all of us.

On a personal level, I know a lot about standing together, because over the last year I have been the recipient of such a wonderful outpouring of support and encouragement. One thing I've learned is that it's always meaningful to reach out. Sometimes people hold back because they're not sure their words will be welcome. It's the same thing that often happens when people have a death in the family or are going through a difficult time. They have no idea how much their words mean. Recently, I ran into an acquaintance who said, "I feel bad. When your story happened, I put together all these [Bible] verses for you, and then I just didn't send them. I don't know why." She confessed, "It's unlike me to not follow through, and

I feel that on my heart. I guess I didn't want to presume you wanted to hear from me."

I assured her that I'd heard the same thing from others. "People didn't know what to say to me. But I was by myself, and would have loved to have received them." So I said, "Send them to me now." And she did. They were beautiful and meaningful, and I cherish them. The first one she chose was Psalm 37: "Do not fret because of those who are evil, or be envious of those who do wrong, for like the grass they will soon wither . . . Trust in the Lord and do good; dwell in the land and enjoy safe pasture."

TO BE FIERCE IS TO BELIEVE

We have to act as if we truly believe that anything is possible for women—to refuse to be defeated in achieving our goals.

When I was growing up, people were still saying, "Any young boy can be president." It was an aspiration encouraged for boys alone. Times have changed, but not as much as we'd like to think. A study by Jennifer L. Lawless of American University and Richard L. Fox of Loyola Marymount University, shows that male college students are twice as likely as women college students to consider running for office one day.

The reality on the ground is stagnant in terms of women's political presence. For example, women gained no additional seats in the US Congress in the 2016 election. Some of the faces changed, but the numbers in the House and Senate remained unchanged at 104—only about 19 percent.

There are a number of reasons that women don't run for office in anywhere approaching equal numbers with men. Studies have shown that there's no ability gap. There isn't even a credibility gap—women who run are as likely as men to be elected. There are other, more subtle reasons for the stagnation in women's public presence, including fewer sponsorships and less encouragement for young women to consider political careers. But the primary reason might be that women suffer from a confidence gap—they don't believe in themselves.

We're all familiar with the term "imposter syndrome," which has been around since the 1970s. It is often used to refer to high-achieving women who are plagued by self-doubt. Studies show that women are less likely than men to be self-promotional, to boast about their accomplishments, and to lobby for themselves. There seems to be a direct correlation between that confidence gap and the gap in women running for public office, one of the most self-promotional endeavors there is.

But something broke loose in the 2016 election, and that new resolve and energy were abundantly visible in the Women's March on January 21, 2017. Many people who witnessed and participated in the march wondered if it would be (like so many other marches) a one-off that didn't lead to a real movement. But so far, the signs are convincing that the movement is not going away. For example, some groups across the country—such as She Should Run and Run for Something—are seeing a surge in young women planning to run for office since the 2016 election.

We must believe—and teach our daughters—that the highest office in the land, or the highest office in a corporation, is our birthright too. And then decide to be the ones who make that happen.

TO BE FIERCE IS TO BE A WARRIOR

When W. Brad Johnson and David Smith wrote their book *Athena Rising,* they chose the goddess Athena as a model that perfectly reflected the character, wisdom, courage, and promise of the female midshipmen they train at the military academy, whom they call "everyday Athenas." They point out, "It's not just Athena's status as a fierce warrior, but other qualities as well, particularly her role as diplomat, mediator and wise counselor." What defined her as a warrior was more than physical prowess. It was a full range of qualities. Women in the workplace, they propose, shouldn't just be seen as women, but as rising Athenas. It's a powerful image.

I have been underestimated all my life. But the single reason I prevailed when others thought I couldn't was because I never gave up.

I just kept going and going. If it meant working harder than everyone else, I did it. If it meant trying things that seemed over my head, I kept striving. Even at my lowest points, my mind was working on my next step.

What inspires me to keep going is the army of women who stand behind me. They tell me, "Thanks to you, I can speak out." They write, "Your story gives me the courage to do it, too." It's exhilarating and also humbling to see how our individual acts can have a vast impact. It's profound for me to realize that so many of these women say they have experienced a sense of victory through me.

When women are facing their own struggles, it helps to know that life has a way of changing, sometimes overnight, and we have to be ready to seize the opportunities that come to us. It can be difficult, even agonizing, to be the lone woman in a male-dominated environment. Or to listen time and again to people challenging your right to be there, or your right to stand up for yourself.

"I buried it in order to move on," a woman said to me of her sexual assault. This was a common sentiment. But I want to say to that woman, and others, that we don't have to bury our pasts in order to be fulfilled in our futures. We can take our failures and our pain, and use them as armor to become more fearless and fierce.

As a young girl, playing the violin competitively, I can remember how my heart was in my throat as I stood on the stage and faced large audiences. There was some fear, of course, but my greatest feelings were of exhilaration and anticipation. Today, my heart is in my throat again, but the notes I am playing are global in reach. And I hope the world is listening. In a *New York Times* op-ed I wrote in the fall of 2016, I posed the question that is still constantly on my mind: "When I lie awake at night, I ask myself this question: Will our girls finally be the ones to have workplaces, streets, and campuses free from sexual harassment?" That is my prayer and my mission. I believe we can do it if we have the will.

Together, we can stand as warriors and show the world we're a force that cannot be beaten. We can do this in big ways and small.

As Maya Angelou said, "Each time a woman stands up for herself, without knowing it possibly, without claiming it, she stands up for all women."

We will speak openly, without hesitation and with great strength, and be the women we were meant to be. And in doing so, we will keep this saying in the back of our minds: "The Devil whispered in my ear, 'You are not strong enough to withstand the storm.' Today, I whispered in the Devil's ear, 'I am the storm.'"

We will *Be Fierce*.

Join Me

Before you close this book, take a moment to consider what you can do to be part of a movement for change.

What are the next steps you will take in your own life? How will you be a stronger advocate for others? What conversations will you have—starting now? What organizations will you join—or start? What blog will you pen? How will you make your voice heard?

When I started out, I knew I was not just going to write an "issue book." This is a *movement*. Won't you join me?

Let me hear from you at www.gretchencarlson.com. Together, we can rock the world!

Gretchen

Selected Resources

FIGHTING SEXUAL HARASSMENT AND ABUSE

HOLLABACK! (ihollaback.org) is a global movement to end harassment, powered by a network of grassroots activists. It encourages people to work together to understand harassment, ignite public conversations, and develop innovative strategies to ensure equal access to public spaces.

JOYFUL HEART FOUNDATION (joyfulheartfoundation.org) is organized to transform society's response to sexual assault, domestic violence, and child abuse, support survivors' healing, and end violence.

KNOW YOUR IX (knowyourix.org) is a survivor and youth-led organization that aims to empower students, specifically focused on sexual violence, harassment, and abuse on US college and university campuses and in high schools.

NATIONAL SEXUAL VIOLENCE RESOURCE CENTER (nsvrc.org) provides leadership in preventing and responding to sexual violence through collaboration, sharing, creating resources, and promoting research.

PROTECT OUR DEFENDERS (protectourdefenders.com) is a national organization dedicated to ending the epidemic of rape and sexual assault in the military, and combating a culture of pervasive misogyny, sexual harassment, and retribution against victims.

RAINN (Rape, Abuse, and Incest National Network; rainn.org) is the nation's largest anti–sexual violence organization. RAINN created and operates the National Sexual Assault Hotline in partnership with more than one thousand local sexual assault service providers across the country, and operates the DoD Safe Helpline for the Department of Defense.

RAINN also carries out programs to prevent sexual violence, help victims, and ensure that perpetrators are brought to justice.

THE RAPE FOUNDATION (therapefoundation.org) provides expert care and treatment for sexual assault victims, both children and adults; prevention-education programs to reduce the prevalence of sexual violence; training for police, prosecutors, school personnel, and other service providers to enhance the treatment victims receive wherever they turn for help; and policy reforms and other initiatives that increase public understanding about rape, encourage victims to report these crimes, and foster justice and healing.

STOP STREET HARASSMENT (stopstreetharssment.org) is a nonprofit organization dedicated to documenting and ending gender-based street harassment worldwide.

STUDENT COALITION AGAINST RAPE (studentcoalitionagainstrape. wordpress.com) educates high school and college students about their rights under the law, tracks problematic police departments and school administrations, and supplements high school health education with up-to-date information on gendered and student-on-student violence.

IT'S ON US (itsonus.org) is a movement started by President Barack Obama and the White House Council on Women and Girls that encourages people to stand up and be a part of stopping sexual assault on campus, through campaigns and events at hundreds of schools and extensive social media messaging.

FIGHTING BULLYING

CYBERBULLYING RESEARCH CENTER (cyberbullying.org) is dedicated to providing up-to-date information about the nature, extent, causes, and consequences of cyberbullying among adolescents.

END TO CYBER BULLYING (endcyberbullying.org) is working to create a global social networking arena where all users can feel safe and positive.

KIND CAMPAIGN (kindcampaign.com) is a nonprofit organization devoted to overcoming the negative and lasting effects of girl-against-girl bullying through a global movement, documentaries, and educational programs for schools.

NOBULLYING.COM is an online forum aimed at educating, advising, counseling, and helping to stop bullying; in particular, cyberbullying.

STOMPOUTBULLYING.ORG focuses on reducing and preventing bullying, cyberbullying, sexting, and other forms of digital abuse; educating against homophobia, racism, and hatred; and deterring violence in schools, online, and in communities across the country.

STOPBULLYING.GOV is a government resource to provide information, education, and support about recognizing, addressing, and preventing bullying and cyberbullying.

WOMEN'S EMPOWERMENT AND RIGHTS

THE AMERICAN ASSOCIATION OF UNIVERSITY WOMEN (aauw.org) is the nation's leading voice promoting equity and education for women and girls. Since the group's founding in 1881, AAUW members have examined and taken positions on the fundamental issues of the day—educational, social, economic, and political.

INSTITUTE FOR WOMEN'S LEADERSHIP (womensleadership.com) focuses on gender partnership as a key component to growing women leaders.

LEAN IN (leanin.org) is an organization dedicated to empowering women to achieve their ambitions. This organization grew out of the groundswell of response to Sheryl Sandberg's book *Lean In*.

NATIONAL WOMEN'S LAW CENTER (nwlc.org) champions policies and laws that help women and girls achieve their potential throughout their lives, at school, at work, at home, and in their communities.

9TO5 (9to5.org) is one of the largest national membership organizations of working women in the United States, dedicated to putting working women's issues on the public agenda.

SERVICE WOMEN'S ACTION NETWORK (servicewomen.org) advocates for all servicewomen, past, present, and future. Its mission is to be the nation's most influential and effective network of servicewomen, acting as their champion, advocate, and best information resource.

STEM WOMEN (stemwomen.net) promotes careers for women in STEM fields, highlights issues of gender inequality, and strives to give STEM women a full voice.

WOMEN IN STEM (womeninstem.com) is dedicated to growing awareness of STEM as a viable option for girls, women, and their institutions, and to inspire a global shift in the attitude toward women in STEM.

WOMEN UNLIMITED (women-unlimited.com) focuses on developing women leaders in major corporations by pinpointing, developing, and retaining diverse, high-potential leadership talent.

WORKPLACE FAIRNESS (workplacefairness.org) provides links to information in Q&A format on the following topics: sexual harassment, legal rights, racial harassment, bullying bosses, intentional infliction of emotional distress, filing a harassment claim, employer policies, fraud, defamation, false imprisonment, assault and battery, negligence, and domestic violence and the workplace.

MALE ENGAGEMENT AND SUPPORT FOR WOMEN

BETTER MAN CONFERENCE (bettermanconference.com) seeks to create a unique space to educate, activate, and mobilize men as inclusionary leaders. It enables men to leverage their position and privilege to support and empower women and minorities.

A CALL TO MEN (acalltomen.org) educates men all over the world on healthy, respectful manhood, with the understanding that embracing and promoting a healthy, respectful manhood prevents violence against women, sexual assault and harassment, bullying, and many other social ills.

THE GOOD MEN PROJECT (goodmenproject.com) explores what it means to be a good man in the twenty-first century, tackling issues from family and fatherhood to gender, sex, and ethics.

THE NATIONAL ORGANIZATION FOR MEN AGAINST SEXISM (nomas.org) is an activist organization of men and women supporting positive changes for men. NOMAS advocates a perspective that is profeminist, gay affirmative, and antiracist, dedicated to enhancing men's lives, and committed to justice on a broad range of social issues, including class, age, religion, and physical abilities.

YWOMEN (ywomen.com) is the website of the gender strategist Jeffery Tobias Halter, which includes resources, research, and special initiatives, such as the Father of a Daughter Initiative.

RAISING EMPOWERED GIRLS AND BOYS

FEARLESSLYGIRL (fearlesslygirl.com) is an internationally recognized leadership and empowerment organization dedicated to empowering a generation of young women to be bold, authentic leaders in their lives, schools, and communities. It's a movement of real girls redefining what is beautiful, valuable, and possible.

GIRLS CAN'T WHAT? (girlscantwhat.com) challenges girls and women to break through stereotypes, whether in careers, dress, play, sports, or dreams.

GIRLS INC. (girlsinc.org) is a nonprofit organization that inspires all girls to be strong, smart, and bold. Through research-based programs and education, Girls Inc. empowers girls to understand, value, and assert their rights.

GIRLS LEADERSHIP (girlsleadership.org) works with girls, their parents, teachers and others to help girls exercise the power of their voice. Programs include workshops, camps, parent education and community partners, which emphasize the core values of authentic communication, courageous growth, equity, and play.

GIRLS ON THE RUN (girlsontherun.org) fosters positive emotional, social, mental, spiritual, and physical development in girls ages eight to thirteen through running programs and workouts. The goal is to prevent girls from engaging in at-risk activities as they mature.

THE RAP PROJECT (therapproject.co.uk) aims to raise awareness about personal safety and prevention for teenagers, and openly discuss how pornography and social media influence attitudes and expectations.

TIA GIRL CLUB (tiagirlclub.com) provides a supportive and encouraging environment that helps girls discover who they authentically are, and find motivation and inspiration. TIA stands for Today I Am, used for mantras, such as "Today I Am Fearless," and "Today I Am Happy."

COMMUNITY AND POLITICAL ENGAGEMENT

ALL IN TOGETHER (aitogether.org) is the only non-partisan women's organization dedicated to advancing the progress of women's political, civic, and professional leadership in the U.S. They collaborate with both political parties, corporations, women's organizations and policy makers on both sides of the aisle to ensure that women from all backgrounds are fully represented at the nation's leadership tables.

GIFT OF COURAGE FUND (gretchencarlson.com/philanthropy) is my fund to help girls and young women recognize their full potential and the bright future that awaits them, help women realize a safe and nurturing place in the workforce, and promote community commitment and volunteerism.

OFF THE SIDELINES (offthesidelines.org) is Senator Kirsten Gillibrand's call to action for women to make their voices heard on the issues they care about. Women have the power to shape the future—it's just a matter of getting off the sidelines and getting involved.

RUN FOR SOMETHING (runforsomething.net) empowers and supports young people to run for offices like state legislatures, mayorships, and city council seats.

RUNNING START (runningstartonline.org) is a nonpartisan organization aimed at bringing young women into politics through education, advocacy, and support.

SHE SHOULD RUN (sheshouldrun.org) aims to get more women into elected leadership roles, by educating, empowering and recruiting them to run for office.

WOMEN IN THE WORLD (@WomenintheWorld; #witw) was inspired by Tina Brown to give a platform to global women on the front lines—activists, artists, CEOs, peacemakers, entrepreneurs, and firebrand dissidents who have saved or enriched lives and shattered glass ceilings in every sector.

RESISTBOT (resistbot.io) is an app that finds out who represents you in Congress, and delivers your message to him or her in under two minutes.

READING LIST

Athena Rising: How and Why Men Should Mentor Women, by W. Brad Johnson and David Smith. Routledge, 2016.

Because of Sex: One Law, Ten Cases, and Fifty Years That Changed American Women's Lives at Work, by Gillian Thomas. St. Martin's Press, 2016.

Bullying Hurts: Teaching Kindness Through Read Alouds and Guided Conversations, by Lester Laminack. Heinemann, 2012.

Cybersafe: Protecting and Empowering Kids in the Digital World of Texting, Gaming, and Social Media, by Gwen Schurgin O'Keefe. American Academy of Pediatrics, 2010.

Feminist Fight Club: An Office Survival Manual for a Sexist Workplace, by Jessica Bennett. Harper Wave, 2016.

Lean In: Women, Work, and the Will to Lead, by Sheryl Sandberg. Knopf, 2013.

The New Soft War on Women: How the Myth of Female Ascendance is Hurting Women, Men, and Our Economy, by Rosalind Barnett and Caryl Rivers. TarcherPerigee, 2013.

Off the Sidelines: Speak Up, Be Fearless, and Change Your World, by Kirsten Gillibrand. Ballantine Books, 2014.

Plenty Ladylike: A Memoir, by Claire McCaskill. Simon & Schuster, 2015.

Raising Girls: How to Help Your Daughter Grow Up Happy, Healthy and Strong, by Steve Biddulph. Ten Speed Press, 2014.

Raising Boys: Why Boys Are Different—and How to Help Them Become Happy and Well-Balanced Men, by Steve Biddulph. Ten Speed Press, 2014.

Sexual Harassment and Bullying: A Guide to Keeping Kids Safe and Holding Schools Accountable, by Susan Strauss. Rowan & Littlefield, 2011.

Sexual Harassment in Education and Work Settings: Current Research and Best Practices for Prevention, edited by Michele Paludi, Jennifer Martin, James Gruber, and Susan Fineran. Praeger, 2015.

We Believe You: Survivors of Campus Sexual Assault Speak Out, by Annie E. Clark and Andrea L. Pino. Holt, 2016.

Why Women: The Leadership Imperative to Advancing Women and Engaging Men, by Jeffery Tobias Halter. Fushian, 2015.

Notes

Introduction: Are You Done Taking Sh*t?

5: *Such as Carmen*: Author interview, March 3, 2017.

6: *A 2016 study*: Stefanie K. Johnson, Jessica Kirk, Ksenia Keplinger, "Why We Fail to Report Sexual Harassment," *Harvard Business Review*, October 4, 2016.

7: *The attorney Lisa Bloom*: Author interview, February 10, 2017.

7: *I was interviewed*: ABC, *20/20*, November 18, 2016. abc.go.com.

8: *Statistics support*: EEOC Select Task Force on the Study of Harassment in the Workplace, Executive Summary and Recommendations, June 2016, https://www.eeoc.gov/eeoc/task_force/harassment/report_summary.cfm.

8: *You cannot experience*: Giana Ciapponi, "Study Reveals Sexual Harassment Leads to 'Insidious Trauma,'" Ravishly.com, December 16, 2014.

10: *In an interview*: Brie Larson, "Jane Fonda Talks Feminism with Brie Larson, *The Edit*, March 2, 2017, www.net-a-porter.com/magazine/391/17.

Chapter 1: Speaking the Unspeakable

16: *The first real*: Paulette L. Barnes, Appellant, v. Douglas M. Costle, Administrator of the Environmental Protection Agency, 561 F.2d 983 (DC Cir. 1977).

16: *forbidden under Title VII*: www.justice.gov/crt/laws-enforced-employment-litigation-section.

17: *"Sexual harassment" first*: Enid Nemy, "Women Begin to Speak Out Against Sexual Harassment," *New York Times*, August 19, 1975.

17: *"is sufficiently pervasive"*: Catharine McKinnon, *Sexual Harassment of Working Women: A Case of Sexual Discrimination* (New Haven, CT: Yale University Press, 1979).

17: *In January and April*: Hearings before the Committee on Labor and Human Resources, United States Senate, Ninety-seventh Congress, first session, an examination on issues affecting women in our nation's labor force, January 28 and April 21, 1981, by United States Congress.

17: *One loud voice*: Ibid.

18: *As the legal*: Debra A. Profio, "Ellison v. Brady: Finally, a Woman's Perspective," *Women's Law Journal*, 1992.

18: *Madeline, a TV broadcaster*: Author interview, March 16, 2017.

19: *A recent study*: Jonathan Woetzel, Ann Madgavkar, Kweilin Ellingrud, Eric Labaye, Sandrine Devillard, Eric Kutcher, James Manyika, Richard Dobbs, and Mekala Krishman, *How Advancing Women's Equality Can Add $12 Trillion to Global Growth* (McKinsey Global Institute, 2015).

19: *In January 2015*: EEOC Select Task Force on the Study of Harassment in the Workplace, Report of Co-Chairs Chai R. Feldblum and Victoria A. Lipnic, June 2016, www.eeoc.gov.

20: *Women can experience*: "Key Findings from a Survey of Women Fast Food Workers," Hart Research Associates, October 5, 2016.

23: *The EEOC defines*: "Facts about Sexual Harassment," EEOC. https://www.eeoc.gov/eeoc/publications/fs-sex.cfm.

24: *For fifteen years*: Author interview, February 27, 2017.

26: *Susan, who spent*: Author interview, March 6, 2017.

28: *It took Karla Amezola*: Veronica Villafane, "Estrella TV Fires Anchor Karla Amezola, Who Sued Her Boss for Sexual Harassment," *Forbes*, March 2, 2017; author interview with Karla Amezola, April 14, 2017.

31: *"HR is the KGB"*: Author interview with Nancy Erika Smith, March 30, 2017.

32: *Susan Fowler, an engineer*: Susan Fowler, "Reflecting on One Very, Very Strange Year at Uber," Susanfowler.com, February 19, 2017; also Subrat Patnalk, "Uber Hires Ex–U.S. Attorney General Holder to Probe Sexual Harassment," Reuters, February 21, 2017.

32: *Holder's report*: "Uber's Report: Eric Holder's Recommendations for Change," *New York Times*, June 13, 2017.

33: *As one example*: Katie Benner, "Women in tech speak frankly on culture of harassment, *New York Times*, June 30, 2017.

Chapter 2: You Can't Break a Badass

43: *In her quiet*: "Thomas Second Hearing Day 1, Part 2." C-Span, October 11, 1991, https://www.c-span.org/video/?22214-1/senator-specter-anita-hill-testimony.

45: *"a little bit nutty"*: David Brock, *Blinded by the Right: The Conscience of an Ex-Conservative* (New York: Crown, 2002).

47: *Tailhook is an*: Michael R. Gordon, "Pentagon Report Tells of Aviators' Debauchery," *New York Times*, April 24, 1993.

48: *Missouri senator*: Author interview with Senator Claire McCaskill, March 7, 2017.

48: *The sweeping reforms*: Ed O'Keefe, "Senate Easily Passes McCaskill's Military Sexual Assault Bill," *Washington Post*, March 10, 2014.

49: *"My concern is"*: Author interview with Senator Kirsten Gillibrand, March 7, 2017; also Kirsten Gillibrand, "The Pentagon Deliberately Misled Congress on Sex Assault Cases. Do Lawmakers Care?," *Washington Post*, May 26, 2016.

49: *Sandra, who was*: Author interview, March 3, 2017.

50: *Still, assault and rape*: Andrew R. Morral, Kristie L. Gore, Terry Schell, eds., *Sexual Assault and Sexual Harassment in the U.S. Military*, vol. 1, Design of the 2014 RAND Military Workplace Study (RAND Corporation, 2014).

50: *According to Lyndsay Ayer*: "Rate of Suicide Among Female Veterans Climbs, VA Says," NPR Morning Edition, April 25, 2017.

51: *When I spoke with Elizabeth*: Author interview, March 1, 2017.

53: *As I learned*: Author interviews with Senators Claire McCaskill and Kirsten Gillibrand, March 7, 2017.

53: *In her 2014 book*: Kirsten Gillibrand, *Off the Sidelines: Speak Up, Be Fearless, and Change Your World* (New York: Ballantine Books, 2014).

Chapter 3: Don't Rob My Dream!

57: *"If this hadn't"*: Author interview, April 16, 2017.

58: *Sophia's collapsing*: Jason N. Houle, Jeremy Staff, Jeylan T. Mortimer, Christopher Uggen, and Amy Blackstone, "The Impact of Sexual Harassment on Depressive Symptoms During the Early Occupational Career," *Society and Mental Health Journal*, August 31, 2011.

59: *Donald Trump commented*: Kristen Powers, "Trump Says He Hopes Ivanka Would Quit If She Got Harassed," *USA Today*, August 1, 2016; also, Nick Gass, "Eric Trump: Ivanka wouldn't allow herself to be subjected to sexual harassment," *Politico*, August 2, 2016.

60: *One of the strong*: Author interview, March 2, 2017.

60: *But discouragingly*: Joan C. Williams and Kate Massinger, "How Women Are Harassed Out of Science," *The Atlantic*, July 25, 2016.

60: *One of those women*: "Ex-USC Employee Says She Was Fired Over Sexual Harassment Complaint," LosAngeles.cbslocal.com, October 5, 2016; author interview with Nathalie Gosset, March 13, 2017.

63: *The National Bureau*: David Neumark, Ian Burn, and Patrick Button, "Is It Harder for Older Workers to Find Jobs? New and Improved Evidence from a Field Experiment," National Bureau of Economic Research, October 2015; also Margaret Kane, "Say What? 'Young People Just Smarter,'" Cnet.com, March 28, 2007.

63: *That's what Claudia*: Author interview, March 13, 2017.

64: *According to a PBS*: "55, Unemployed and Faking Normal: One Woman's Story of Barely Scraping By," *PBS NewsHour*, January 19, 2017.

64: *Keep in mind that age*: Anna MacSwain, "US Ranks Lower than Kazakhstan and Algeria on Gender Equality," *Guardian*, October 11, 2016.

65: *Juliana, now in*: Author interview, June 15, 2017.

67: *A large study*: "Sexual Violence on College Campuses," US Department of Justice, justice.gov.; also Kirsten Gillibrand, "Key to Ending Campus Sexual Assaults Is Transparency," *Roll Call*, April 11, 2016.

71: *Research by Cornell's*: "ILR and Hollaback! Release Largest Analysis of Street Harassment to Date," ILR School, Cornell University, June 1, 2015.

72: *series of short films produced by David Schwimmer*: Peggy Truang, "David Schwimmer Launches New Campaign to Fight Sexual Harassment," *Cosmopolitan*, April 3, 2017.

74: *That's exactly what happened*: Alanna Vagianos, "Read the Powerful Letter Harvard Soccer Players Wrote to Their Sexist Classmates," *Huffington Post*, October 31, 2016.

Chapter 4: You Have the Right

79: *In one 2014 case*: Aaron Taube, "Some States Are Finally Making It Illegal to Sexually Harass Unpaid Interns," *Business Insider*, October 6, 2014.

80: *"Document, document"*: Author interview with Lisa Bloom, February 10, 2017.

82: *Brianna, who is*: Author interview, April 4, 2017.

83: *A Pew Research*: Maeve Duggan, "Online Harassment," Pew Research Center, October 22, 2014.

84: *I admire Martha Langelan's book*: Martha Langelan, *Back Off! How to Confront and Stop Sexual Harassment and Harassers* (New York: Fireside, 1993).

86: *Sterling Jewelers . . . is a case*: Susan Antilla, "Sterling Jewelers Suit Casts Light on Wider Policies Hurting Women," *New York*

Times, March 6, 2017; Drew Harwell, "Sterling Discrimination Case Highlights Differences Between Arbitration, Litigation," *Washington Post*, March 1, 2017.

88: *Naomi had been*: Author interview, February 28, 2017.

93: *After the principal*: Author interview, February 28, 2017.

94: *Zoe was a*: Author interview, April 5, 2017.

95: *"We scheduled a"*: Author interview, March 3, 2017.

95: *"I am still crying"*: Author interview, March 6, 2017.

97: *Jada's boss was*: Author interview, March 16, 2017.

97: *"Powerful people say"*: Author interview with Lisa Bloom, February 10, 2017.

99: *study of fifty harassment settlements* : Mina Kotkin, "Outing Outcomes: An Empirical Study of Confidential Employment Discrimination Settlements," law2.wlu.edu/deptimages/Law%20 Review/64-1%20Kotkin%20Article.pdf.

100: *Rebecca, who filed*: Author interview, March 2, 2017.

102: *The EEOC's 2016*: EEOC Select Task Force on the Study of Harassment in the Workplace, Executive Summary and Recommendations, June 2016, www.eeoc.gov/eeoc/task_force/ harassment/report_summary.cfm.

103: *"Mandatory sexual harassment"*: Author interview with Cliff Palefsky, April 4, 2017.

103: *"It boils down"*: Author interview with Jeffery Tobias Halter, May 1, 2017.

Chapter 5: "Asking for It"

107: *Until I wrote*: Gretchen Carlson, *Getting Real* (New York: Viking, 2015).

109: *The truth is, a modern woman*: Marge Piercy, *What Are Big Girls Made Of? Poems* (New York: Knopf, 2007).

109: *On October 7, 2016*: David A. Fahrenthold, "Trump Recorded Having Extremely Lewd Conversation about Women in 2005," *Washington Post*, October 8, 2016.

110: *Those who believe*: Author interview with Natasha Stoynoff, March 28, 2017.

111: *The* People *feature*: *People*, September 18, 2005.

112: *In her October 2016*: Natasha Stoynoff, "Physically Attacked by Donald Trump: A *People* Writer's Own Harrowing Story," *People*, October 12, 2016.

113: *Heather McDonald is*: Teresa Watanabe, "UC Regent Apologizes for 'Inappropriate' Comments about Women's Breasts," *Los Angeles Times*, November 2, 2016; author interview with Heather McDonald, March 6, 2017.

116: *Tamra was a*: Author interview, March 6, 2017.

117: *But the high-profile*: Michael S. Schmidt and Maria Newman, "Jury Awards $11.6 Million to Former Knicks Executive," *New York Times*, October 7, 2007.

118: *The "he said, she said"*: D. Lisak, L. Gardinier, S. C. Nicksa, and A. M. Cote, "False Allegations of Sexual Assault: An Analysis of Ten Years of Reported Cases," Sage Journals, December 16, 2010; Dara Lind, "What We Know about False Rape Allegations," *Vox*, June 1, 2015.

120: *Nancy French, a bestselling*: Nancy French, "What It's Like to Experience the 2016 Election as Both a Conservative and a Sex Abuse Survivor," *Washington Post*, October 21, 2016.

120: *When I spoke with Nancy*: Author interview with Nancy French, April 12, 2017.

Chapter 6: Forced into Silence

124: *The purpose of Franken's*: The Arbitration Fairness Act of 2017, www.franken.senate.gov/files/documents/170307_Arbitration FairnessAct.pdf; "Taking 'Forced' Out of Arbitration," The Employees Rights Advocacy Institute for Law and Policy, Employeerightsadvocacy.org.

125: *Ask Jennifer Fultz*: Bill Lueders, "Companies Bar Workers and Consumers from the Courts," *The Progressive*, December 7, 2016.

126: *"The idea is"*: Author interview with Nancy Erika Smith, March 30, 2017.

128: *"Think about it"*: Author interview with Cliff Palefsky, April 10, 2017.

129: *"The plaintiff has"*: Ibid.

129: *According to a 2011*: Alexander Colvin, *An Empirical Study of Employment Arbitration: Case Outcomes and Processes*, ILR School, Cornell University, 2011; also Elizabeth Dias and Eliana Dockterman, "The Teeny, Tiny Fine Print That Can Allow Sexual Harassment Claims to Go Unheard," Time.com, October 21, 2016.

130: *"Today there is a false"*: Author interview with Nancy Erika Smith, March 30, 2017.

131: *We can find some good news*: Kate Samuelson, "Hundreds Allege Sexual Harassment at the Parent Company of Kay Jewelers," *Fortune*, February 28, 2017; also Theresa Avila, "Class-Action Lawsuit against Kay and Jared Jewelry Company Alleges Widespread Sexual Harassment," *New York*, February 27, 2017.

132: *But during his first*: Mary Emily O'Hara, "Trump Pulls Back Obama-Era Protection for Women Workers," NBC News, April 13, 2007.

Chapter 7: Men Who Defend

135: *"I don't see these"*: Jackson Katz, "Violence against Women: It's a Men's Issue," TED, November 2012, www.ted.com/talks/jackson_katz_violence_against_women_it_s_a_men_s_issue.

136: *I was struck*: Jessica Bennett, "A Master's Degree in . . . Masculinity?," *New York Times*, August 8, 2015.

136: *"I may be a little grayer"*: Remarks of President Obama at the United States of Women Summit, June 14, 2016, Obamawhitehouse. archives.gov.

137: *Jake Tapper credits*: Author interview with Jake Tapper, April 7, 2017.

137: *His interview on* State of the Union: "CNN's Jake Tapper Destroys Rudy Giuliani's Argument that Trump's Sexual Assault Comments are Normal," Media Matters, October 9, 2016.

139: *"A huge part"*: Author interview with Paul Feig, April 7, 2017.

140: *A few years*: Yashar Ali, "A Message to Women from a Man: You Are Not 'Crazy,'" *The Current Conscience*, June 9, 2012.

141: *"I wanted to rebrand"*: Author interview with Yashar Ali, April 7, 2017.

142: *Matthew Dowd grew up*: Author interview with Matthew Dowd, April 11, 2017.

143: *Larry Wilmore stands*: Author interview with Larry Wilmore, April 17, 2017.

143: *On one segment*: Lisa de Moraes, "Larry Wilmore Defines 'Rapist' for Bill Cosby," *Deadline Hollywood*, July 28, 2015.

144: *Another prowoman*: *Stand Up! with Pete Dominick*, Sirius radio, April 4, 2017.

145: *Later, I sat*: Author interview with Pete Dominick, May 4, 2017.

146: *W. Brad Johnson, PhD*: W. Brad Johnson and David Smith, *Athena Rising: How and Why Men Should Mentor Women* (New York: Bibliomotion, 2016).

146: *"The nature of"*: Author interview with W. Brad Johnson and David Smith, May 4, 2017.

147: *Kathleen Neville, a leader*: Author interview with Kathleen Neville, April 19, 2017.

148: *Vincent believes that men*: Troy Vincent, "Standing Together with One Voice Against Domestic Violence," NBC News, March 6, 2017.

149: *John Shouldis's New Jersey case*: John Appezzato, "Former Teaneck Cop Awarded $4.1 Million in Harassment Suit," *Star-Ledger*, December 19, 2008.

149: *"A lot of us"*: Author interview, March 21, 2017.

152: *"cool fierceness"*: Author interview with Bob Thurman, May 12, 2017.

152: *Jeffery Tobias Halter*: Author interview with Jeffery Tobias Halter, May 1, 2017.

Chapter 8: Enough Already!

156: *Patricia's case illustrates*: Author interview, April 6, 2017.

157: *It's choppier, as*: President Barack Obama's statement in the Rose Garden, November 9, 2016.

157: *Yet according to*: Rape, Abuse, and Incest National Network (RAINN), www.RAINN.org.

159: *According to a 2016 report*: Francine D. Blau and Lawrence M. Kahn, "The Gender Wage Gap: Extent, Trends, and Explanations," National Bureau of Economic Research, January 2016.

159: *"My husband was"*: Author interview, March 14, 2017.

160: *In their book*: Rosalind Barnett and Caryl Rivers, *The New Soft War on Women: How the Myth of Female Ascendance Is Hurting Women, Men, and Our Economy* (New York: TarcherPerigee, 2013).

161: *William Goldman, the famous*: William Goldman, *Hype and Glory* (New York: Random House, 1990).

161: *"I asked the CEO"*: Author interview, March 14, 2017.

162: *In 2016, the Kellogg*: WITW staff, "Survey Reveals the Names and Words Women Most Hate Being Called," *New York Times*/Women in the World, September 28, 2016.

162: *A New Zealand man*: Molly McArdle, "This Google Chrome

Extension Replaces 'Political Correctness' with Something More Accurate," *Huffington Post*, August 10, 2015.

162: *The whistleblower wore*: Manuel Roig-Franzia, "She Says She Was Harassed by Superiors. Now She Protests Outside the TSA for Hours," *Washington Post*, November 30, 2016; also, author interview with Alyssa Bermudez, March 1, 2017.

163: *Have you seen Ashley Judd's*: Ashley Judd, "How Online Abuse of Women Has Spiraled out of Control," TED, January 2017.

163: *Another famous woman*: Monica Lewinsky, "Shame and Survival," *Vanity Fair*, June 2016.

165: *It's an easy out*: Stephanie Pappas, "Men Who Blame Victim for Sexual Harassment Are Often Harassers," *LifeScience*, April 11, 2011.

166: *In fact, according*: Candace Kruttschnitt, William D. Kalsbeck, and Carol C. House, *Estimating the Incidence of Rape and Sexual Assault* (Washington, DC: National Research Council, 2014).

169: *"This was something I dreamed"*: Author interview, April 4, 2017.

170: *Robin Wright, known for her role*: Laura Bradley, "Robin Wright Fought for Pay Equity on *House of Cards*," *Vanity Fair*, May 18, 2016.

170: *Debra Messing is another*: Sara Boboltz, "Debra Messing Recalls Sexual Harassment 'Power Play' on Set with Director Alfonso Arau," *Huffington Post*, February 9, 2017.

Chapter 9: Our Children Are Watching

174: *Jodi Norgaard is the founder*: Gogosportsgirls.com; author interview with Jodi Norgaard, April 26, 2017.

176: *A couple of years*: Roo Ciambriello, "'Like a Girl' Is No Longer an Insult in Inspiring Ad from P&G's Always," *Ad Week*, June 26, 2014; also #LikeAGirl.

177: *Recently, I read*: Maggie Hendricks, "Jameis Winston Gets the Message Wrong When He Tells Fifth-Grade Girls to 'Sit Down,'" *USA Today*, February 23, 2017.

178: *A study by the German psychologist*: Marina A. Pavlova, Susanna Weber, Elisabeth Simoes, and Alexander M. Sokolor, "Gender Stereotype Susceptibility," University of Tubingen, December 17, 2014.

178: *The roots of negative*: Andrei Cimpian and Lin Bian, "Stereotypes about 'Brilliance' Affect Girls' Interests as Early as Age 6, New Study Finds," New York University, January 26, 2017.

179: *"The genie is"*: Author interview with Allison Havey, May 12, 2017.

181: *Title IX statistics show*: Titleix.info.

181: *"Waiting to educate"*: Kathleen Neville, "Addressing Social Misconduct in Schools, Sports and the Workplace: Bullying, Harassment, Discrimination and Harmful Interpersonal Behavior"; Exploring Innovative and Effective Solutions for Youth Awareness and Education, IDS 600 and 601 capstone project, Dr. Mustafa Gokcek, April 20, 2015.

182: *The Good Men Project recently*: Mark Greene, "A Manifesto: Relational Intelligence for Our Children," Good Men Project, April 20, 2017; also Elizabeth J. Meyer, "The Danger of 'Boys Will Be Boys': Why This Phrase Should Be Banned from Our Vocabulary," *Psychology Today*, March 14, 2014.

183: *According to extensive surveys*: Cyberbullying Research Center, cyberbullying.org.

184: *Monica Lewinsky, whom I mentioned*: Monica Lewinsky, "Meet the New Emoji Tool to Combat Cyberbullying," *Vanity Fair*, February 6, 2016.

185: *There are many good resources*: Stopbullying.gov; Susan Strauss, *Sexual Harassment and Bullying: A Guide to Keeping Kids Safe and Holding Schools Accountable* (Lanham, MD: Rowan & Littlefield Publishers, 2011).

186: *In 2015, Target*: Hiroko Tabuchi, "Sweeping Away Gender-Specific Toys and Labels," *New York Times*, October 27, 2015.

187: *The comedian Pete Dominick*: Author interview with Pete Dominick, May 4, 2017.

188: *This is important*: Author interview with Paul Feig, April 7, 2017.

Chapter 10: Be Fierce

196: *Like many people*: Bethany McLean, "The Backstory Behind Wall Street's 'Fearless Girl' Statue," *The Atlantic*, March 13, 2017; Lam Bourree, "Why People Are So Upset about Wall Street's 'Fearless Girl,'" *The Atlantic*, April 14, 2017; Nick Fugallo and Max Jaeger, "Pissed-Off Artist Adds Statue of Urinating Dog Next to 'Fearless Girl,'" *New York Post*, May 29, 2017.

197: *In a 2015 TimesTalk*: Lady Gaga, Diane Warren, Kirby Dick, and Amy Ziering, "The Hunting Ground," TimesTalk, December 10, 2015, timestalks.com/detail-event.php?event=the_hunting_ground.

198: *"It's not bigger"*: Author interview, March 22, 2017.

201: *I was quite*: Letter to author, April 30, 2017.

202: *A study by Jennifer L. Lawless*: Jennifer L. Lawless and Richard L. Fox, "Girls Just Wanna Not Run: The Gender Gap in Young Americans' Political Ambition," Women & Politics Institute, March 2013.

202: *For example, women gained*: www.emergeamerica.org; www.runforsomething.net.

203: *When W. Brad Johnson*: W. Brad Johnson and David Smith, *Athena Rising: How and Why Men Should Mentor Women* (New York: Routledge, 2016).

Acknowledgments

Movements start when people come together, dedicated to a common purpose. And that's what happened with this book. So many people took on the *Be Fierce* cause, and their contributions have made it all possible.

When I was first thinking about writing the book, I was lucky to meet Jan Miller and Lacy Lalene Lynch, my literary agents at Dupree/Miller, whose vision and passion matched my own. Their excitement about the project and their sharp, knowledgeable insights made it a reality. Thanks to their efforts, we found a home at Hachette under the leadership of Rolf Zettersten, senior vice president and publisher of Hachette Nashville, and Kate Hartson, Center Street executive editor. We also found a wonderful seasoned freelance editor in Leslie Wells. Thank you for your enthusiasm for this book! A book needs promotion, and I couldn't have done it without the team of Sarah Falter and Patsy Jones with Hachette marketing.

A special shout-out to my collaborator and friend Catherine Whitney, who knows me so well and was always by my side every step of the way. We did it!

My brilliant lawyers Nancy Erika Smith, Martin Hyman, Neil Mullin, and Robin Silverman have been invaluable in this process, gladly lending their knowledge and expertise on the often-tricky legal complexities of sexual harassment law. Thanks to Matt Daly, whose research and writing proved to be invaluable. The renowned lawyers Lisa Bloom and Cliff Palefsky also generously shared their insights.

A special thank-you to the team of people who helped rebrand me after my ordeal and move me into the next phase of my life: Cindi

Berger, chairman and CEO of PMK-BNC; and Jodie Magid Oriol, vice president of entertainment at PMK-BNC. Also, Stephanie Gabriel and Soham Joglekar for organizing my schedule over the last year plus. It's been a lot to keep track of, so thank you!

I am most grateful to the many courageous women who were willing to tell me their stories. In some cases, it was the first time they had shared with anyone what happened to them. By being brave, they told me they felt like I was a voice for the voiceless. More than anything, they wanted to play a part in helping other women come forward and in changing the laws and culture for future generations. We will be fierce together!

I am equally grateful to a number of women whose stories have been in the media, and who were open to speaking to me personally about what they experienced, including Natasha Stoynoff, Heather McDonald, Karla Amezola, Nancy French, Nathalie Gosset, and Patricia Tomasello.

Many experts who work in the areas of antidiscrimination, sexual harassment and assault prevention, antibullying, and empowerment for young women and girls gave me their time as well. I am very appreciative for the work and insights of Kathleen Neville, Jodi Norgaard, and Allison Havey of the RAP Project.

I especially appreciate the efforts of Senator Kirsten Gillibrand, Senator Claire McCaskill, and Senator Al Franken, who have placed themselves on the front lines of this issue, fighting against the odds to bring legislation to the floor that can combat sexual harassment, sexual assault in the military, and the scourge of forced arbitration. These senators gave their time to help make sure that these important issues were represented in this book.

One of my strongest beliefs is that sexual harassment is not just an issue for women—we need men, too. And many of them stepped up to the plate to talk about their support and their personal willingness to make this issue their own. Many thanks to Yashar Ali, Ray Arata, Pete Dominick, Matthew Dowd, Paul Feig, Jeffery Tobias Halter, W. Brad Johnson, David Smith, Jake Tapper, Bob Thurman, and Larry Wilmore for taking time to share their thoughts and experiences with me.

During my ordeal, I have said that you find out who your friends are! It's so true, and that's why I am thankful and indebted to those of you who stood by me during the toughest times. You know who you are. Thank you. You have no idea how even just a few words from close or afar meant the world to me.

Thanks to my parents, whose steadfast support has always been the rock and foundation of my life. You always told me I could be whatever I wanted to be, and provided me with the love and support to achieve my goals. But most important, you taught me how to be a good person, and life's greatest lesson: to give back. I am working hard to pass along these lessons to our children.

Finally, to my husband, Casey, who has always been supportive of my ambitions and proud of my achievements—and who models every day for our children what it means to be a good man.

INDEX

Access Hollywood tape, 109, 112, 113, 137–138, 140, 144
accountability, teaching kids, 190
age discrimination, 63–66
airline mechanic's story (Cheryl), 169–170
Ali, Yashar, 140–142
aloneness. See loneliness and isolation
Amezola, Karla, 28–30
Angelou, Maya, 205
Angulo, Andrés, 29–30
arbitration, forced, 123–132
    Arbitration Fairness Act of 2017 and, 124
    company benefitting from, 124–125, 129–130
    compared to court proceeding, 128–129
    constitutional rights and, 124, 125, 126, 131
    defined, 123
    denying justice, 125
    EEOC and, 132
    efforts to rescind, 132
    federal contractors' requirement for, 132
    in fine print of contract, 128–129
    Jennifer Fultz's story (call center employee), 125–126
    lack of discovery and access to documents, 129
    lack of transparence with, 127–128
    lawyer Cliff Palefsky on, 128, 129, 131
    lawyer Nancy Erika Smith on, 126–128, 130–131
    misconceptions of, 125–131
    original intent vs. reality today, 130–131
    paying fees for, 130
    as a "preferred system," 130–131
    reality of, 123, 125–131
    retaliation and, 128–129
    selecting arbitrators for, 130
    shrouding harassment in secrecy, 123, 127–128, 129
    Sterling Jewelers case, 131–132
    as "voluntary," 125–127, 128
"asking for it," 105–121
    Anucha Browne Sanders' story, 117–118
    Christianity, Christian women and, 119–121
    credibility questions and, 105–106, 115–119
    Gretchen as Miss America and, 105, 106–109
    Heather McDonald's story, 113–115
    idealization, disempowerment of women and, 106
    "pleasing syndrome," perfectionism and, 41–42
    Tamra's story (assistant creative director), 116–117
    Trump accusers and. See Trump, Donald
Aspen Music Festival, 39, 66
assault weapon ban, 199–200
Athena Rising (Johnson and Smith), 146–147, 203
attorney, hiring. See legal action
Avin, Sigal, 72
Ayer, Lyndsay, 50

Backlash from other employees, 59, 61, 97, 116. See also frozen out/treated as leper
badass mentality. See also being fierce; fighting back; movement for change; standing up for yourself
    anger and, 37, 42
    of Anita Hill, 43–45
    Anne Lamott on, 37
    bringing to the surface, 37–38
    Elizabeth's story (army lieutenant), 51–53
    fearlessness and, 38
    gearing up for the fight, 37–38
    Gretchen's background and, 37, 38–43
    "pleasing syndrome," perfectionism and, 41–42
    pure self-confidence and, 38
    worrying about offending offender vs., 41–42
Barnes, Paulette, 16–17
Barnett, Rosalind, 160
being fierce, 193–205
    being a warrior and, 203–205
    believing and, 202–203
    boldness and, 197–198
    controversial nature of, 197
    "cool" fierceness and, 152
    Croatia trip, zip line adventure and, 195
    defined, 197
    Fearless Girl sculpture and, 196–197
    Gretchen's 50th birthday and, 193–194
    Gretchen's decision for, 194–195
    inspirational quotes, 194
    joining/contacting Gretchen, 207

Lady Gaga's story, 197–198
 pivot point of Gretchen and, 196
 standing tall and, 196–199
 standing together and, 200–202
 sticking to your values and, 199–200
believing, being fierce and, 202–203
Bermudez, Alyssa, 162–163
Beth's story, 10–11
Biden, Joe, 74
Bloom, Lisa, 7, 62, 80, 97, 199
Blumenthal, Sen. Richard, 124
"boys will be boys," harassment, 182
Brianna's story (restaurant manager), 82–83, 92
Bridesmaids (film), 139
Browne Sanders, Anucha, 117–118
bullying
 Ashley Judd's story, 163
 bully culture and, 183–185
 cyberbullying, 163–164, 183–184, 210, 211
 Elizabeth's story (army lieutenant), 51–53
 equal to harassment, 83
 guidelines for kids/parents, 184–185
 mean tweets and, 1, 5, 83
 Monica Lewinsky's story, 163, 184
 no-tolerance policy, 183
 Paul Feig fighting back, 139–140
 resources for fighting, 210–211
 school responses to, 183, 185
 young women and, 83
Bush, Billy, 112, 144

Career. *See also* dreams taken away; *HR department references*; male-dominated work culture
 getting to know prospective company, 78–80
 Gretchen's. *See* Carlson, Gretchen, career
 job vs. dignity and, 25–26
 leaving. *See* leaving job, sexual harassment and
 married women and need for, 159–160
 mixed messages and, 41
 thieves in workplaces, 56–59
Carlson, Casey, 2–3, 13, 159, 195
Carlson, Christian, 173, 179, 193
Carlson, Gretchen
 decision to take on harassment issue, 3–4
 joining/contacting, 207
 on New Yorkers, 133
 nothing-can-hold-you-back attitude, 14–15
 on-campus experiences, 66–67, 75
 perspective on men, 133–134
Carlson, Gretchen, career
 fighter mentality and, 55
 first job in television, 57
 nothing-can-hold-you-back attitude and, 14–15

women role models and idol, 15
Carlson, Gretchen, harassment experiences
 becoming the news, 2–3
 children (Kaia and Christian) and, 2, 173–174
 feeling helpless after, 46
 first experience, 45–46
 following Miss America reign, 106–109
 nasty responses from onlookers, 1–2
 stalker terrorizing early in career, 164
 surreality of, 3
 TV and PR exec predators, 106–107
Carlson, Gretchen, Miss America
 competition and, 52
 deeper thoughts about, 106–107
 first job in television after, 57
 idealization, disempowerment and, 106
 lewd/impolite treatment from public, 105
 objectifying insults leveled in book, 161
 overcoming obstacles, 55
 paper on what was lost during reign, 108–109
 sexual harassment incidents following, 106–109
 "too short to be," 55
Carlson, Gretchen, speaking up. *See also* being fierce; movement for change
 emotional trip after story broke, 13–14
 feeling alone, then not, 14
 men supporting, 133, 134–135
 other women opening up and, 4, 158
 outpouring of gratitude/support after, 14, 133
 reaching out to other victims, 9–10
Carlson, Kaia, 2, 173, 177, 179, 187–188, 189–190, 193
Carmen's story (flight attendant), 5, 95
Casey (Gretchen's husband), 2–3, 13, 159, 179, 193, 195
Catherine Violet Hubbard Animal Sanctuary, 189–190
change, affecting. *See* being fierce; fighting back; movement for change; speaking up
Cheryl's story (airline mechanic), 169–170
children. *See also* bullying; girls/daughters
 about: overview of setting example for, 173–174
 at college. *See* college
 discussion points on Internet and social media, 180–181
 empowerment of, 180, 184, 189, 190–191, 213–214
 fathers' role in patterning behavior, 142
 future workplace and, 66
 giving problem-solving tools, 190–191
 harassment in school, 181
 helping boys become good men, 181–183
 helping build self-esteem from inside out, 186–188

helping choose role models, 188–190
inspiring to reach for the stars, 191
life lessons for, 185–191
parents' pledge for raising, 191–192
porn, sexting and, 180
rejecting rigid gender roles, 185–186
single-sex schools for, 179
social media impact, 67, 179–181
stereotypes impacting. *See* stereotypes
teaching personal accountability, 190
Christianity and harassment, 119–121
Claudia's story, 63–64
college
challenges for kids today, 67
film series on harassment and, 72–73
Gretchen's experiences, 66–67, 75
safety advice for daughters, 69–72
sexual assault problem, 67–69
sexual harassment training for students, 71–72, 74
victim inquisition, 68–69
women's soccer team fighting back, 74–75
women, standing up for themselves, 74–75
community/political engagement resources, 214–215
confidence and self-esteem
believing and, 202–203
building from inside out, 186–188
Cheryl's story (airline mechanic), 169–170
of girls, dropping around puberty, 176–177
Gretchen as "Sparkles" and, 38–39
harassment undermining, 8, 58–59, 71, 107
having faith in yourself, 168–170
helping kids build, 38, 69, 177, 186–188, 190, 192. *See also* children
imposter syndrome and, 203
Jodi Norgaard's story, 174–176
life lessons for kids in building, 185–191
long-term impact, PTSD and, 8, 107–108, 112
to resist pressure to conform, 176
Sophia's story of losing, 58–59
"throw/run like a girl" and, 176–177
confidentiality considerations, 92–93
Constand, Andrea, 118
contracts, forced arbitration in. *See* arbitration, forced
contracts, reading carefully, 79
Cosby, Bill, 118–119, 143
Coughlin, Lt. Paula, 47–48
creative director, Tamra's story, 116–117
credibility questions, "asking for it" and, 105–106, 115–119
cyberbullying, 163–164, 183–184, 210, 211

Danforth, Sen. John, 45
daughters. *See* children; girls/daughters

David versus Goliath mentality, 36
Di Modica, Arturo, 197
disempowerment, of sexual harassment, 19, 42–43, 105–106
documenting problems, 80–81, 89–92
documenting retaliation, 95–97
Dominick, Pete, 144–145, 187
Dowd, Matthew, 142
dread, index of, 198–199
dreams
fighting for American dream, 76
finding your power for, 75–76. *See also empowerment references*
joy, happiness and, 55–56
dreams taken away. *See also* career; leaving job, sexual harassment and
age/sex discrimination and, 63–66
harassed out of science, 60–62
Juliana's story (movie business), 65–66
motivation from adversity and, 55
Nathalie Gosset's story, 60–62
Sophia's story, 58–59
taken away in workplaces, 56–59
young women, sexual harassment and, 64–65. *See also* college
Dress for Success, 168
Dunham, Lena, 115

EEOC (US Equal Employment Opportunity Commission)
Clarence Thomas, Anita Hill and, 43–44
definition of sexual harassment, 23
discouraging outcome from, 56
finding ways to prevent harassment, 19–20
forced arbitration and, 132
prerequisites for filing claim with, 23–24
reality of filings with, 100
"reasonable woman" standard, 18
Rebecca's story, 100
recommendations for companies and sexual harassment, 87–88
report on workplace harassment (2016), 102
right to sue and, 23–24, 99–100
Select Commission on the Study of Harassment in the Workplace, 19–20
selecting lawyer familiar with, 98
sexual harassment reporting statistic, 8
Elizabeth's story (army lieutenant), 51–53
employee handbook, 79
empowerment
for community/political engagement, 214–215
confidence and, 176
factors feeding, 20
finding your power, 75–76
Gretchen's experiences, 55, 56

Jodi Norgaard's story, 174–176
of kids, 180, 184, 189, 190–191, 213–214.
    See also children
nothing-can-hold-you-back attitude and,
    14–15
resources for empowered kids, 213–214
resources for women's rights and, 211–212
rights mantra for, 77–78
sexual harassment undermining, 19, 42–43,
    105–106
sharing with others, 168
support community for, 52–53
symbolizing, ritualizing, 168
tip for daughters entering college, 71
using your own experience for, 52–53, 158
visualizing power, 75–76
empowerment, twelve-point playbook,
    78–104. *See also* HR department, reporting
    harassment to
    about: rights mantra and, 77–78
    avoiding traps, 94–95
    being the change, 101–104
    documenting problems, 80–81, 89–92
    documenting retaliation, 95–97
    going legal, 97–99. *See also* legal action
    group confrontations and, 84–85
    intern precautions, 79–80
    knowing company policies, 85–86
    knowing your rights, 78–80
    making official complaint, 86–94
    remedies to ask for, 93–94
    sample complaint letter, 89–92
    securing right to sue, 99–100
    signs of harassment in companies, 102–103
    taking offense, 81–83
    taping interactions if you can, 85
    telling people you trust, 84–85
enduring effect of harassment, 5, 50. *See also*
    PTSD
equality. *See* women's equality and rights

Faith in yourself, 168–170
Fearless Girl sculpture, 196–197
Feig, Paul, 139–140, 188
fierceness. *See* being fierce
fighting back. *See also* being fierce;
    empowerment, twelve-point playbook;
    HR department, reporting harassment to;
    movement for change
    fighter mentality and, 55
    gearing up for the fight, 37–38
    Harvard women's soccer team story, 74–75
    "He got you one night. Don't let him get
        the rest of your life.," 172
    Naomi's story (manager), 88–89
    taking offense at name-calling/nicknames,
        81–83

firefighter's story (Patricia Tomasello), 155–156
flight attendant's story (Carmen), 5, 95
Fonda, Jane, 10
forced arbitration. *See* arbitration, forced
Fowler, Susan, 32–33
Franken, Sen. Al, 124
Fran's story, 34–35
Fredericka's story (law enforcement), 60
French, Nancy, 120–121
frozen out/treated as leper, experience of, 95,
    96–97, 116, 149, 169
Fultz, Jennifer, 125–126

Gaga, Lady, 197–198
gaslighting, 141
gender equality. *See also* male-dominated work
    culture; movement for change
    age/sex discrimination and, 63–66
    college and public support for, 73–74
    evolution of women's rights and, 158–159
    fathers becoming feminists and, 138
    fighting for, 64–65
    "men's issues," "women's issues" and, 135–136
    men's role in stopping harassment. *See* men
        standing up for women
    pay gap and, 11, 159, 170
    respect for women and, 159
    sexism vs., 141, 142, 158, 170
    teaching kids to reject rigid gender roles,
        185–186
    "tone" of women and, 161–162
    women's looks, objectification and,
        160–161
Getting Real (Carlson), 107
Ghostbusters (film), 139
Gift of Courage Fund, 189, 190, 214
Gillibrand, Sen. Kirsten, 48–49, 53–54, 214
girls/daughters. *See also* children being
    harassed, 4
    college-bound, safety advice, 69–72
    fathers' role in patterning behavior, 142
    self-confidence dropping around puberty,
        176–177
    single-sex schools for, 179
    stereotypes impacting, 174–177, 178–179
Giuliani, Rudy, 137–138
Good Men Project, 182, 212
Gosset, Nathalie, 60–62
Greene, Mark, 182–183
Gretchen. *See* Carlson, Gretchen references
"The Grey Flannel Sexual Harassmant Suit"
    (Piercy), 109
group confrontations, 84–85

Halter, Jeffrey Tobias, 152–153, 203
Hatch, Orrin, 17, 44
Havey, Allison, 179–180

"he said, she said," credibility and, 115–119
Hidden Figures (film), 62
Hill, Anita, 17, 43–45, 46, 87
history of sexual harassment, overview, 15–20
Holder, Eric, 32–33
Hollaback!, 71, 209
hotlines, sexual harassment, 86
HR department
    authorizing many key employees to handle
        complaints, 87–88
    disputes and, 32
    EEOC-recommended steps for, 87–88
    employee handbook, 79
    getting to know company and, 78–80
    giving offender a pass, example, 32
    lack of trust in, 86–87
    lawyer Nancy Erika Smith on, 31
    looking out for company, not necessarily
        employees, 24, 31–32, 36, 92, 169–170
    ombudsman to oversee company efforts, 87
    primary role of, 31–32
    putting onus on complainant, 34–35
    sexual harassment training and, 101–102,
        103–104
    sincerity of managers of, 35–36
    training people in civility, 88
HR department, reporting harassment to. *See
    also* empowerment, twelve-point playbook;
    reporting harassment; silence
    Brianna's story (restaurant manager),
        82–83, 92
    Cheryl's story (airline mechanic), 169–170
    confidentiality considerations, 25, 92–93
    documenting problems, 80–81, 89–92
    Fran's story, 34–35
    job vs. dignity and, 25–26
    Karla Amezola's story (TV personality),
        28–30
    lack of support from HR and, 61–62
    making decision to report, 26, 92–93
    making official complaint, 86–94
    Naomi's story (manager), 88–89
    Paula's story (park ranger), 24–25
    remedies to ask for, 93–94
    repercussions of, 25, 26, 27, 29–30, 35,
        92–93, 95–97. *See also* leaving job, sexual
        harassment and; retaliation
    Robin's story (school principal and), 93
    sample complaint letter, 89–92
    seeking guidance elsewhere before, 35
    Susan's story (cop), 26–27
    Tamra's story (assistant creative director),
        116–117
    threats resulting from, 24
    traps for complainants and, 33–34, 94–95
    why women don't report incidents, 27–28,
        34–35, 86–87

Zoe's story (teacher), 94
Hubbard, Katherine Violet, pet sanctuary
    named for, 189–190
human resources. *See* HR department
husband(s)
    finally telling harassment story to, 7
    of Gretchen (Casey), 2–3, 13, 159, 179,
        193, 195
    income of, women's careers/livelihood and,
        159–160
    keeping stories from, 7, 8, 84

Insidious trauma, 9
inspirational quotes, 194
interns, protections for, 79–80
intimidation, power and, 65, 87, 94, 97, 114,
    129. *See also* power, abuse of; retaliation
It's On Us, 74, 210

Job search. *See* empowerment, twelve-point
    playbook
Johnson, Katherine, 62
Johnson, Rep. Hank, 124
Johnson, W. Brad, 146–147, 203
journal, documenting problems, 80–81, 89–92
Joyful Heart Foundation, 209
Juliana's story (movie business), 65–66

Kalanick, Travis, 32–33
Karen's story (Wall Street trader), 42, 159–160
Katz, Jackson, 135–136
Kimmel, Michael, 136
Know Your IX, 209

Lahey, Joanna, 64
Lamott, Anne, 37
law enforcement, stories of harassment, 26–27,
    60, 149
lawyer, hiring. *See* legal action
Leahy, Sen. Patrick, 124
leaving job, sexual harassment and. *See also*
    dreams taken away
    being strong, fighting back vs., 59–60
    Fredericka's story (law enforcement), 60
    "just leave" mentality, 59–60
    Madeline's story (TV broadcaster), 18–19
    "making deal with the devil" and, 25–26
    Nathalie Gosset's story, 60–62
    staying vs. leaving, job vs. dignity, 25–26
    thieves in workplaces and, 56–59
    Trump's comment on daughter and, 59
    women in science and, 60–62
legal action, 97–99
    about: overview of, 23–24
    Anucha Browne Sanders' story, 117–118
    arbitration compared to, 128–129. *See also*
        arbitration, forced

benefits of hiring lawyer, 98
against Bill Cosby, 118–119
confidentiality considerations, 92–93
EEOC and, 23–24, 100
hiring lawyer, 97–99
knowing company policies, 85–86
Lihuan Wang's (intern) story, 79
Nathalie Gosset's story (in STEM job), 60–62
Paula's story (park ranger), 24–25
questions to ask prospective lawyer, 98
reality check of taking, 99
Rebecca's story, 100
retaining lawyer before filing complaint, 97
right to sue and, 23–24, 99–100
rules (state/local) for taking, 100
leper, treated as, 116
letter, sample of official harassment complaint, 89–92
Lewinsky, Monica, 163, 184
loneliness and isolation
Gretchen's experience, 13–14, 38
history of sexism and, 158–159
at home as well as work, 84
impacting decision to speak up, 88
job vs. dignity and, 25–26
Madeline's story (TV broadcaster), 18–19
Mark's story (standing up for coworker), 151
remembering your are not alone, 36, 38, 171
of veterans after assaults, 50

MacKinnon, Catherine, 17
Madeline's story (TV broadcaster), 18–19
male-dominated work culture. See also gender equality; men standing up for women
balancing, with more women at the top, 36
breaking the "man code," 152–153
changing, 88
circular trap for women in, 6
collegiality between sexes and, 21–22
crossing the harassment line and, 21–24
old boys' club and, 5–6, 75
ongoing misogyny, 51–54
"that guy," jerks in the office and, 21–22
women adopting behaviors of men in, 6
mandatory arbitration. See arbitration, forced
"A Manifesto: Relational Intelligence for Our Children" (Greene), 182–183
manipulation, harasser succeeding with, 66
Mark's story (standing up for coworker), 149–152
McCaskill, Sen. Claire, 48–49, 53
McDonald, Heather, 113–115
men standing up for women, 133–153
"A Message to Women from a Man: You Are Not 'Crazy'" (Ali), 140

Athena Rising: How and Why Men Should Mentor Women (Johnson and Smith), 146–147, 203
being "that guy," 146–147
breaking the "man code," 152–153
from bystanders to allies, 148–152
comedians, 143–145
cultural tracks leading to harassment and, 140
gaslighting and, 141
gender-neutrality of solving harassment issue, 135–136
"good man," "real man" and, 136, 152
for Gretchen, 133, 134–135
Gretchen's background and appreciation for, 133–134
helping boys become good men and, 181–183
importance in harassment issue, 135–136
Jackson Katz on, 135–136
Jake Tapper, 134, 137–138
John Shouldis's story (police officer), 149
Larry Willmore, 143–144
listening to women and, 144
Mark's story (standing up for coworker), 149–152
Matthew Dowd, 142
men facing retaliation too, 148–152
Paul Feig, 139–140
Pete Dominick, 144–145
President Obama on, 136–137
resources for, 212–213
as rule, not exception, 57
sports culture and, 147–148
taking action and, 145
Troy Vincent, 147–148
Yashar Ali, 140–142
"A Message to Women from a Man: You Are Not 'Crazy'" (Ali), 140
Messing, Debra, 170–171
military, 46–54
about: overview of harassment in, 46–47
being "that guy," standing up for women, 146–147
Elizabeth's harassment story, 51–53
homelessness, suicide of veterans, 50
levels of assault/harassment incidents, 49, 50
long-term impact of assault/harassment in, 50
McCaskill/Gillibrand impact on reforming, 48–49, 53–54, 214
misogyny persisting in, 51
naval academy training (Sexual Harassment and Assault Prevention and Education), 147
PTSD disability from rape in, 8

resources/support, 209
retaliations for reporting assault/
      harassment, 49
Sandra's rape story, 5, 49–50
sweeping reforms in, 48–49
Tailhook scandal and Lt. Paula Coughlin,
      47–48
Miss America. *See* Carlson, Gretchen, Miss
America
Morons and Monsters theory, 140
motivation
      adversity igniting, 55
      inspirational quotes for, 194
      joy, happiness and, 55–56
      from others' accomplishments, 194
movement for change, 155–172. *See also* being
fierce; empowerment; fighting back; gender
equality
      about: overview of, 156–157
      beginning steps, 160–172
      being brave, 170–172
      being the change, 101–104
      bully pulpit for, 162–163
      Cheryl's story (airline mechanic), 169–170
      current environment and, 156–158
      Dress for Success donations and, 168
      having faith in yourself, 168–170
      importance of speaking up, 66
      joining/contacting Gretchen, 207
      prevalence of harassment/abuse and,
            157–158
      promise for action and, 157
      reality of sexism and, 158
      rejecting the myths, 164–168
      resolve for, 157–158
      slaying the dinosaurs, 160–162
      speaking your mind, 163–164
      symbolizing and ritualizing, 168
      this book and, 11, 156
      time to stand up and shine light on
            injustices, 11
      Women in the World Summit, 155–156
      women opening up and, 158
      Women's March and, 156–157, 203
musician, Gretchen as
      Aspen Music Festival and, 39, 66
      badass music for motivation, 37
      competition and accomplishments, 39–40,
            52, 194, 204, 243
      embracing violin, 39
      overcoming fears, 204
      teachers and role models, 39, 40–41
      tenacity and commitment, 39
myths about harassment, rejecting, 164–168
      about: overview of, 164–165
      nonphysical harassment is not harmful, 167
      women bring it on, 165–166

women make it up, 166–167
women who complain want money/fame,
      167–168

Names, inappropriate, taking offense at,
      81–83
Naomi's story (manager), 88–89
NASA, women at, 62
National Sexual Violence Resource Center, 209
Neville, Kathleen, 147, 148, 181–182
The New Soft War on Women (Barnett and
      Rivers), 160
New York Knicks, Browne Sanders/Thomas
      case, 117–118
NFL, changing culture of, 147–148
Norgaard, Jodi, 174–176

Obama, Barack, 132, 136–137, 157, 210
offense, taking, 81–83
old boys' club, 5–6, 75

Palefsky, Cliff, 103, 104, 128, 129, 131
parents, ongoing importance of, 70–71
parents, raising children. *See* children; girls/
      daughters
Park ranger's story (Paula), 24–25
Pattiz, Norm, 113–115
Paula's story (park ranger), 24–25
Pavlovs, Marina, 178
pay equality. *See* gender equality
perfectionism, 41, 42
The Photographer (film), 73
Piercy, Marge, 109
"pleasing syndrome," 41
PodcastOne, Heather McDonald and, 113–115
political correctness, 162
politics
      engaging in, resources for, 214–215
      harassment positions independent of,
            157–158, 200
      Trump videotapes, Christian conservatives
            and, 119–121
      women running for office, 202
porn, kids and, 180
porn, revenge, 164
power, abuse of, 24–27. *See also* HR
department, reporting harassment to;
retaliation
      David vs. Goliath mentality and, 36
      enablers covering for harasser and, 26
      intimidation and, 65, 87, 94, 97, 114, 129
      Karla Amezola's story (TV personality),
            28–30
      manipulation as key, 66
      Morons and Monsters theory, 140
      Paula's story (park ranger), 24–25
      psychological warfare and, 65–66

Susan's story (cop), 26–27
    Trump accusers and. *See* Trump, Donald
Powers, Kirsten, 59
power, taking back. *See empowerment*
    references
preventing sexual harassment
    EEOC efforts, 19–20
    finding out what women really experience
        and, 103–104
    gender strategist on, 103–104
    getting rid of offenders, 142
    helping boys become good men and, 181–183
    other resources for. *See* resources
    RAP Project for teens, 179–180, 214
    recognizing the problem first, 145
    training for. *See* training, sexual
        harassment
    zero tolerance policy and, 103, 142
problem-solving tools, for kids, 190–191
Procter & Gamble, self-esteem video, 176
proof, written, 81. *See also* documenting
    problems
Protect Our Defenders, 209
psychological warfare, 65–66
PTSD, 8, 107–108, 112
Puccio, Diana, 179
Pulliam, Keshia Knight, 118

Race
    Brianna's diminutive nickname story,
        82–83, 92
    double standards and, 136–137
    NASA, women, segregation and, 62
RAINN, 157, 189, 209–210
RAND Corporation, 50
rape. *See* sexual assault and rape
Rape, Abuse, and Incest, National Network
    (RAINN), 157, 189, 209–210
Rape Foundation, 73, 210
Rassi, Mazdack, 72
reading list, 215–216
"reasonable person/woman" standard, 18
Rebecca's story, 100
recording harassment interactions, 85
reporting harassment. *See also* HR department,
    reporting harassment to
    Catch-22 of, 9, 86
    college assault victim inquisition, 68–69
    "forgetting," "blocking out" experiences
        instead of, 7–8
    to husband (or not reporting), 7, 8, 84
    low rate of, 8
    misgivings, reluctance and, 7–8
    "pleasing syndrome" deterring, 41
    telling people you trust, 84–85
resentment, living with, 57, 198–199

resources
    community/political engagement, 214–215
    fighting bullying, 210–211
    fighting sexual harassment and abuse,
        209–210
    joining/contacting Gretchen, 207
    male engagement/support for women,
        212–213
    raising empowered girls and boys, 213–214
    reading list, 215–216
    women's empowerment and rights,
        211–212
restaurant manager's story (Brianna), 82–83,
    92
retaliation. *See also* power, abuse of
    backlash from other employees, 59, 61, 97,
        116. *See also* frozen out/treated as leper
    being shut out by coworkers, 128–129
    bullying of kids and, 185
    direct, types of, 95–96
    documenting, 95–97
    documenting to show evidence of, 80–81,
        92, 95–97
    dreams stolen in workplace, 56–59
    environmental, 96–97
    fear of, reporting harassment and, 35
    filing EEOC complaints and, 100
    forced arbitration shortcomings and,
        128–129
    healing the effects of, 171–172, 198–199
    HR failing to protect you and, 56
    illegality of, 95–97
    "Index of Dread" after, 198–199
    intimidation and, 65, 87, 94, 97, 114, 129
    Karla Amezola's story, 29–30
    against male bystanders/allies, 148–152
    men facing same as women, 148–152
    in the military, pervasiveness of, 49
    other examples of, 24
    Patricia Tomasello's story (firefighter), 156
    Paulette Barnes' court case and, 16–17
    pervasiveness of, 6–7, 49
    pervasiveness of fear of, 166–167
    in Sterling Jewelers case, 86
    women striking back and, 156
rights to assert, delineation of/mantra for,
    77–78
Rivers, Caryl, 160
Robach, Amy, 7–8
Robin's story, school principal and, 93
role models. *See also* men standing up for
    women
    being a role model, 115, 135, 142
    fathers' role in patterning behavior, 142
    of Gretchen, 40–41
    helping boys become good men, 181–183

helping kids choose, 188–190
Obama on men standing up for women
and, 136–137
parent's pledge as, 192
Rose, Charlie, 59

Safe file, items to keep in, 81
Sandra's rape story (enlisted soldier), 5, 49–50
Schlafly, Phyllis, 17–18
school principals, harassment stories, 93, 94
Schwimmer, David, 72–73
science, women in, 60–62, 212
sculpture, *Fearless Girl*, 196–197
secrets, stress of keeping, 8. *See also* silence
self-esteem. *See* confidence and self-esteem
senators, women, facing harassment, 53–54
sexism. *See* gender equality
Sex, Lies and Social Media (Havey and Puccio),
179
sexting, kids and, 180
sexual assault and rape
Bill Cosby and, 118–119, 143
at college, 67–69
"He got you one night. Don't let him get
the rest of your life.," 172
"he said, she said" and credibility of, 118–119
Jane Fonda's story, 10
Lady Gaga's story, 197–198
in the military. *See* military
shame and, 10
woman raped by off-duty police officer,
171–172
sexual harassment
age/sex discrimination and, 63–66
clarifying definitions and examples, 21–24
cost to businesses, 102
cultural tracks leading to, 140
early perceptions of, 16
as equal-opportunity plight, 20
film series on (#ThatsHarassment), 72–73
first real legal case, 16–17
historical perspective, 15–20
impacting young women, 64–65
independence of clothing/appearance, 4–5
Morons and Monsters theory, 140
most vulnerable suffering most, 20
myths to be rejected, 164–168
of non-management and service personnel,
20
not asking for/not bringing on, 4–5
origin of term, 15–16, 17
pervasiveness of, 4, 17
situations that might be, 22–23
"that guy," jerks in the office and, 21–22
Sexual Harassment and Assault Prevention and
Education, 147

Sexual Harassment of Working Women
(MacKinnon), 17
shame
assault, rape and, 10
being *ashamed* and, 10
Beth's story, 10–11
forced arbitration, secrecy and, 127–128
Gretchen growing up without, 38–43
Gretchen's experiences, 105, 107
harassment and, 10
inhibiting reporting of harassment, 66
Jane Fonda's story, 10
misplaced, 128
Nancy French's story (Christian author),
120–121
power of, 10
social media shaming campaigns, 67
transcending, to be part of change, 198–199
shaming of Anita Hill, 44–45
shaming of Monica Lewinsky, 163
Shouldis, John, 149
silence. *See also* HR department, reporting
harassment to; reporting harassment
being nurtured, 156
feeling helpless and, 46
Gretchen's experiences, 46
Juliana's story (movie business), 65–66
"pleasing syndrome," perfectionism and,
41–42
power of, for harasser, 5
worrying about offending offender and,
41–42
silent treatment. *See* frozen out/treated as leper
Smith, David, 146–147, 203
Smith, Nancy Erika, 31, 33–34, 126–128,
130–131, 155
Snyder, RDML John, 47
soccer team (women's), standing up for
themselves, 74–75
social media, impact on kids, 67, 179–181
Sophia's story, 58–59
speaking up. *See* Carlson, Gretchen, speaking
up; movement for change
stalker, terrorizing Gretchen, 164
standing together, 200–202
standing up for yourself. *See also* badass
mentality; fighting back; movement for
change
being called *angry* and, 42
college women, 74–75
Gretchen's experiences and role models,
38–43
pushback for, 42
retribution for. *See* retaliation
STEM (science, technology, engineering,
math), women in, 60–62, 212

stereotypes
    blond-hair beauty example, 174–175
    "boys will be boys," harassment and, 182
    changing, 201. *See also* movement for
        change
    "good man," "real man" and, 136
    impact on young boys, 181–182
    impact on young girls, 174–177, 178–179
    Jameis Winston talk reinforcing, 177–178
    Jodi Norgaard changing, 174–176
    rejecting rigid gender roles, 185–186
    single-sex schools to counter, 179
    taking hold at young age, 178–179, 181
    "throw/run like a girl" and, 176–177
Sterling Jewelers, 86, 131–132
Stop Street Harassment, 210
Stoynoff, Natasha, 110–113, 160
Student Coalition Against Rape, 210
suits, legal. *See* legal action
support from other women
    Elizabeth's story (army lieutenant), 52
    Gretchen's experiences, 14
    Karla Amezola's story, 30
    value and importance of, 52–53

Tamra's story (assistant creative director),
    116–117
taping harassment interactions, 85
Tapper, Jake, 134, 137–138
Tarkenton, Fran, 147
Thomas, Clarence, 43–45
Thomas, Isaiah, 117–118
"throw like a girl," 176–177
Thurman, Bob, 152
Title VII, 16–17
Tomasello, Patricia, 155–156
training, sexual harassment
    for college students, 71–72, 74
    in companies, 101–102, 103–104
    helping boys become good men, 181–183
    mandatory, effectiveness of, 72, 103
    at naval academy, 147
    in the NFL, 148
    requesting, as remedy for harassment, 93
traps for complainants, avoiding, 33–34, 94–95
trauma of harassment
    Gretchen seeing in others, 8–11
    not reporting harassment and, 27–30
    persistent, insidious nature of, 9
    PTSD and, 8, 107–108, 112
Trump, Donald
    Access Hollywood tape of Billy Bush and,
        109, 112, 113, 137–138, 140, 144
    claims of harassment/assault by, 109–113
    evangelical reactions to claims against,
        120–121
    Giuliani defending, 138

    harassment-related comments by, 59, 160
    Jake Tapper challenging Giuliani on,
        137–138
    Larry Wilmore on, 144
    Melania defending, 112–113
    Natasha Stoynoff and, 110–113, 160
    perspective on his harassment view, 59–60
    rescinding forced arbitration ban, 132
Trump, Eric, 59
Trump, Ivanka, 59
Trump, Melania, 110, 111–112, 113
TSA, whistleblower taking on, 162–163
TV broadcasters
    Karla Amezola's story, 28–30
    Madeline's story, 18–19
tweets, mean, 1, 5, 83. *See also* bullying

Uber, 32–33

Values, sticking to, 199–200
veterans. *See* military
Vincent, Troy, 147–148
violin, Gretchen playing. *See* musician,
    Gretchen as
Visbal, Kristen, 196
visualizing power, 75–76

Wall Street, *Fearless Girl* sculpture, 196–197
Wall Street trader's story (Karen), 42, 159–160
Wang, Lihuan, 79
warrior, being, 203–205
West, Mary, 40–41
Willmore, Larry, 143–144
Winston, Jameis, 177–178
Women in the World Summit, 155–156
women's equality and rights. *See* gender
    equality
Women's March, 156–157, 203
Wright, Robin, 170

Zoe's story (teacher), 94

ABOUT THE AUTHOR

Named one of *Time* magazine's 100 Most Influential People in the World and a 2017 recipient of the prestigious Matrix Award, Gretchen Carlson is one of the nation's most successful and recognized news anchors and a tireless advocate for the equality and empowerment of women.

The former host of *The Real Story* on Fox News for three years, Carlson also cohosted the number-one-rated cable morning news show *Fox and Friends* for more than seven years.

Carlson started her television career in Richmond, Virginia, as a political reporter, and later served as an anchor and reporter in Cincinnati, Cleveland, and Dallas. She moved to the national scene as the cohost of *The Saturday Early Show* on CBS in 2000, where she also served as a CBS News correspondent, covering the 9/11 terrorist attack from the World Trade Center, the Bush-Gore election, and many other national and international stories. She also reported and produced a thirty-part series on domestic violence that earned her several national awards.

In 2015, Carlson's first book, *Getting Real*, became a national bestseller.

An honors graduate of Stanford University, Carlson was valedictorian of her high school class and studied at Oxford University in England. Carlson grew up a child prodigy on the violin, performing as a soloist with the Minnesota Orchestra at age thirteen, and, in 1989, became the first classical violinist ever to win the Miss America crown.

In 2016, Carlson became the face of sexual harassment in the workplace, gracing the covers of *Time* and *Good Housekeeping* magazines, standing strong in her determination to promote a safe working environment for all women. Carlson is active on Capitol Hill pursuing the issues surrounding forced arbitration clauses in employment contracts that often keep harassment claims shrouded in secrecy.

Carlson formed the Gift of Courage fund to financially support organizations empowering women and young girls, and believes that giving back is essential. She currently serves as a national trustee for the March of Dimes, as a member of the board of directors for the Catherine Violet Hubbard Animal Sanctuary in Newtown, Connecticut, and as a trustee of Greenwich Academy, an all-girls preparatory day school in Greenwich, Connecticut. She is an active volunteer and teacher at her church, and in 2016 hosted the Miss You Can Do It Pageant in Illinois to celebrate the achievements of courageous girls and young women with disabilities.